Modern Dramatists
Series Editors: *Bruce King and Adele*

Published titles

Reed Anderson, *Federico Garcia Lorca*
Susan Bassnett, *Luigi Pirandello*
Eugene Benson, *J. M. Synge*
Renate Benson, *German Expressionist Drama*
Normand Berlin, *Eugene O'Neill*
Michael Billington, *Alan Ayckbourn*
Roger Boxill, *Tennessee Williams*
John Bull, *New British Political Dramatists*
Dennis Carroll, *David Mamet*
Neil Carson, *Arthur Miller*
Maurice Charney, *Joe Orton*
Ruby Cohn, *New American Dramatists, 1960–1990*
Bernard F. Dukore, *American Dramatists, 1918–1945*
Bernard F. Dukore, *Harold Pinter*
Alan England, *Theatre for the Young*
Arthur Ganz, *George Bernard Shaw*
James Gibbs, *Wole Soyinka*
Frances Gray, *John Arden*
Frances Gray, *Noel Coward*
Charles Hayter, *W. S. Gilbert and Arthur Sullivan*
Julian Hilton, *Georg Büchner*
David Hirst, *Edward Bond*
Helene Keyssar, *Feminist Theatre*
Bettina L. Knapp, *French Theatre, 1918–1939*
Thomas Leabhart, *Modern and Post-Modern Mime*
Charles Lyons, *Samuel Beckett*
Gerry McCarthy, *Edward Albee*
Jan McDonald, *The New Drama, 1900–1914*
Margery Morgan, *August Strindberg*
Leonard C. Pronko, *Eugene Labiche and Georges Feydeau*
Carol Rosen, *Sam Shepard*
Jeanette L. Savona, *Jean Genet*
Claude Schumacher, *Alfred Jarry and Guillaume Apollinaire*
Laurence Senelick, *Anton Chekhov*

continued –

continued –

Theodore Shank, *American Alternative Theatre*
James Simmons, *Sean O'Casey*
Peter Skrine, *Hauptmann, Wedekind and Schnitzler*
Ronald Speirs, *Bertolt Brecht*
David Thomas, *Henrik Ibsen*
Dennis Walder, *Athol Fugard*
Thomas Whitaker, *Tom Stoppard*
Nick Worrall, *Nikolai Gogol and Ivan Turgenev*
Katharine Worth, *Oscar Wilde*

Further titles in preparation

MACMILLAN MODERN DRAMATISTS

ARTHUR WING PINERO AND HENRY ARTHUR JONES

Penny Griffin

M

MACMILLAN

First published 1991

Published by
MACMILLAN EDUCATION LTD
Houndmills, Basingstoke, Hampshire RG21 2XS
and London
Companies and representatives
throughout the world

Typeset by BP Integraphics Ltd, Bath, Avon

Printed in Hong Kong

British Library Cataloguing in Publication Data
Griffin, Penny
Arthur Wing Pinero and Henry Arthur Jones.
1. Drama in English, 1827–1900—Critical studies
I. Title
822.809
ISBN 0–333–37459–2 (hc)
ISBN 0–333–37460–6 (pbk)

Contents

List of Plates

To the memory of my dear friend
Roger Lancelyn Green

Editors' Preface

The *Macmillan Modern Dramatists* is an international series of introductions to major and significant nineteenth- and twentieth-century dramatists, movements and new forms of drama in Europe, Great Britain, America and new nations such as Nigeria and Trinidad. Besides new studies of great and influential dramatists of the past, the series includes volumes on contemporary authors, recent trends in the theatre and on many dramatists, such as writers of farce, who have created theatre 'classics' while being neglected by literary criticism. The volumes in the series devoted to individual dramatists include a biography, a survey of the plays, and detailed analysis of the most significant plays, along with discussion, where relevant, of the political, social, historical and theatrical context. The authors of the volumes, who are involved with theatre as playwrights, directors, actors, teachers and critics, are concerned with the plays as theatre and discuss such matters as performance, character interpretation and staging, along with themes and contexts.

BRUCE KING
ADELE KING

Acknowledgements and Author's Note

I should like to express my gratitude to Enid Forster, Reference Librarian of the British Theatre Association, for her unfailing assistance while I have been working on this book; also to my husband, Jack Waterman, who typed the greater part of the manuscript.

Where the theatre in which a play was first performed is not given in the text, details will be found in Appendix III.

1
Introduction

A farmer's son from Buckinghamshire, Henry Arthur Jones, and an Islington solicitor's son, Arthur Wing Pinero, both of whom were born in the 1850s, dedicated themselves to the reclamation of English drama from the doldrums into which it had sunk. They both saw as their aim not only to raise standards of acting and production in the theatre, but also the exploration on stage of issues which were of social and moral importance. They joined in a lifelong battle with the censor, and, owing to their early efforts, the climate of English opinion as to what was acceptable in a theatre changed. Perhaps, above all, they sought to establish an English drama which should be respected by other countries. In this they succeeded. Their plays were acted and read all over the British Empire, on the Continent, in the United States, in Russia. Both of them published their plays concurrently with stage productions, once new copyright laws enabled them to do so. Jones, particularly, was insistent on the necessity for English drama to be regarded as of worth by literary people: a good play must be fit to read as well as act. To this end he wrote many articles, and delivered countless lectures and speeches. Pinero wrote few articles and gave few speeches, but instead he worked continually for the theatre, sitting on many committees; on stage he was a martinet of a director, requiring and insisting on standards of acting, decor and stage-management far exceeding those of any of his contemporaries. Pinero was respected and honoured; Jones was respected, but made many enemies. Both men were cynical in their outlook on the world around them, although many of Jones's plays are characterised by a rigid moral earnestness; both offended audiences (and critics) by their outspokenness. Until Bernard Shaw, when he was a drama critic, began his mischievous, self-centred and destructive campaign against Pinero, there was little doubt in anybody's mind, both in England and abroad, that Pinero was a great dramatist, who had brought new life and respect to English drama.

Born in the reign of Queen Victoria, and living in two further reigns, Jones and Pinero experienced a time of extraordinary change. They lived through the aftermath of the Crimean War, the Boer War and the carnage of the First World War. They watched the expansion of the British Empire, and the formation of the Republic of Ireland. Against this background of expansion and fervent patriotism, there were also many events which changed the world irrevocably: the invention of electric light and power, of the telephone, of radio; the invention of the cinema, the motor-car, the powered aeroplane. Not only the relentless march of scientific invention was changing the face of the globe, but also ideas were being generated which have since thrown the world into a perpetual state of antagonism and fear. These were propounded by Marx and Engels, who met in 1844, and together wrote the

Communist Manifesto (1848); they took refuge in England, where Engels's family owned cotton mills, and working together wrote *Das Kapital*, the first volume of which was published in 1867. The British Socialist Party, based on their ideas, was founded in 1900, and the first minority Labour government, with Liberal support, was returned to power in 1924. Jones and Pinero opened their eyes on a world before the Matrimonial Causes Act; they lived to see the Bright Young Things of the 1920s, Amy Johnson fly solo to Australia, and the first woman Member of Parliament.

In such a period of vastly accelerating change, it is not surprising that for some years drama remained static. Drama is the most immediate of literary forms, reflecting the up-to-minute concerns of the year; even, in melodrama, of the week. However, because of the strictures of the censor, and the destructive rowdiness of disapproving cliques in the audience, and hostile critics, it was often extremely difficult to present any subjects of serious social concern, particularly those related in any way to the taboo subjects of religion, politics and sex. So, while the novel took great strides forward in realism and social concern, the theatre remained, in the 1850s, the domain of popular entertainment: Shakespearian revivals, historical romances, melodramas, burlesque, farce adapted from the French (and emasculated by censorship), low comedy, adaptations of French *drame*, translations from German, light opera, ballet and music hall. So it remained for many years. Of all these entertainments, the most worthy of attention is melodrama, a form of drama which survives today. It contains comedy, strong action, pathos, excitement, song and music, and, above all, clearly delineated characters. The basic formula is the battle of good and evil. Good usually wins, although there are some interesting melodramas where right is defeated. Evil, obviously represented by one of the rich variety of villains to be found in the genre, is frequently more subtly characterised than is popularly supposed. Good is divided between an active principle and a passive principle. The latter is represented by the heroine and members of her family, who symbolise innocence, purity, virtue; who are threatened by evil, and are quite helpless to protect themselves. The active principle is depicted by the hero and those characters who help him; and these symbolise manliness, courage, honour, ingenuity and any other quality that is required in the ensuing struggle. Coincidence (God's Hand) plays a part in the ensuing victory. Although there are many variations on this, it is, nevertheless, a useful guideline. The ethic is always clear-cut. There are few 'grey' moral issues in melodrama. The plot usually centres round something that is in the news: for example, a murder trial, a financial disaster, a massacre, miscegenation; the villain always represents the oppressing or threatening social factor: for instance, a factory-owner, a crooked financier, a slave-dealer. In hissing the villain, the audiences were releasing their own frustrations and anger at evils they were powerless to combat, and in cheering at his downfall they were rejoicing at the victory they wished they could see in real life. Many melodramas contained a scene centred round some astonishing spectacle. This came to be known as the 'sensation scene', and, as the century progressed, the sensation finally became more important than the play itself. Properly integrated within the play, it provided a marvellous addition to the enjoyment derived from the melodrama. Nothing seemed to be impossible. People went to the theatre to see a burning house, a railway engine, an avalanche, the Oxford and Cambridge boat race, the Derby presented for them on stage. But, also, the 'sensation scene' finally destroyed the melodrama as a form of theatre to be taken seriously. This is what made Jones's achievement with *The Silver King* so much the greater. He managed to write a melodrama, without a sensation scene, which people could take seriously as a play, rather than as a trivial entertainment. However, although it became a despised theatrical form, it passed happily into the early cinema, and for many years the melodramatic formula became the staple diet of cinema-goers. It is a vital, fascinating form of theatre; but, unfortunately, audiences grew so used to its strong flavour that it was difficult to present anything of a quieter, more serious nature with success.

The 1860s saw the brief glimmer of the hope of something better, with the plays of Tom Robertson, presented by the Bancrofts at the Prince of Wales theatre, in Tottenham Street. Light-hearted comedies, with naturalistic dialogue, they required a less exaggerated form of acting than did melodrama. They dealt lightly with themes of some social interest, particularly the class structure, and intermarriage between the classes. They proved to be immensely popular. Robertson, sadly, died when only forty-two, having written only six plays of worth. The Bancrofts kept these in repertory for many years, but this small flicker of hope was extinguished. Inveigh how they would at the state of English drama, the critics seemed to be powerless to goad any dramatist into serious, or worthwhile, work. Comedy was mere buffoonery, or pale imitation of French farce; there was no serious drama worth looking at apart from Irving's truncated, though magnificent, Shakespeare performances. There were no really great English performers – apart from Irving. English audiences saw Rejane, Bernhardt and Duse, the great Continental actresses; but there were no English actresses of that international stature.

Until the First World War, the London theatre was largely in the control of the actor–managers: Samuel Phelps, the Bancrofts, John Buckstone, J. L. Toole, Henry Irving, Charles Wyndham, John Hare, George Alexander, Edward Terry, Wilson Barrett, to name but a few. Parts had been written *for* them; plays were written at their request, with their needs in mind; obviously, this greatly limited a playwright. Frequently, they had a nucleus of a resident company, engaging a few performers for each production; therefore, parts had to be written for them also. Authors were often called upon to rewrite during rehearsals. Besides those controlled by the actor–managers, some theatres were leased out by managers, or productions engaged. Before Dion Boucicault, the great melodrama-writer, gave battle, and won a percentage of takings for the author, and for the impresario (very often the playwright), the manager would pay a sum outright for the play, and then pocket all the takings, paying no royalty on the play, or box-office percentage. None of these conditions was conducive to the creation of drama of high quality.

However, during these years, Pinero and Jones were consciously preparing themselves to be serious dramatists. In 1885, Pinero deliberately reformed English comedy with his comedy–farce *The Magistrate*. The praise heaped upon *The Magistrate* on its first appearance was boundless. It was seen as genuine *English* comedy of character, which had completely thrown off the mechanistic nature of French farce, along with its sexual innuendo, and the crude buffoonery of the English 'low' comic tradition. Because of Pinero's work, Oscar Wilde, Bernard Shaw, Brandon Thomas, Ben Travers, Noël Coward, and, more recently, Alan Ayckbourn and Alan Bennett were all able to write their comedy–farces – one of the most living of English traditions.

In 1889, Pinero changed the whole course of English drama with *The Profligate*. It is ironic that Pinero should present this play about six weeks before the first substantial Ibsen production in England: *A Doll's House*. It is therefore easy to take the credit away from Pinero, and say that serious drama owes it rebirth to Ibsen. This is nonsense. The theme of *The Profligate* was directly related to the most talked-about issues of the day, and, while it is true that it contained ideas similar to those in the Ibsen play, the themes are so specifically English that, even were the Pinero production not the prior one, it still could not be said to be influenced by Ibsen. Also, had Pinero not first staged *The Profligate*, the general public, rather than a small literary intelligentsia, would not have been prepared to accept a serious mode of drama on the West End stage.

Pinero, at this time, was greatly helped by Jones, and by the inception of the Independent Theatre. Created in 1891, in order to evade the strictures of the censor by providing private club performances of censored plays, it opened in March 1891 with the notorious performance of *Ghosts*. This performance was followed up in May of the same year by a public performance, which ran for a few weeks, of *Hedda Gabler*. Although the audiences for this were not very large, it was seen by the intelligentsia and the critics, who were, therefore, all the more prepared to give their support to *The Second Mrs Tanqueray* in May 1893. Although it had been written in 1891, it was two years before the popular actor–manager George Alexander dared to present *The Second Mrs Tanqueray*. Both he and Pinero expected it to be booed from the stage, because of its frankness and explicitness.

Despite the support given to the play by critics and the theatrical 'avant-garde', more important for the coming revolution in English drama was the amount of support and enthusiasm derived for this play from the theatre-going public. *The Second Mrs Tanqueray* is framed round the then vital issue: is it ever possible to reclaim a prostitute (no matter how high-class)? Can she ever, after her 'evil' life, have a virtuous heart? Is a man justified in installing at the centre of his home life, at its *spiritual* centre, a woman who is unchaste, and impure? Is the man's lack of purity as much to blame as hers? The issues, and the moral terms in which they were seen, may seem quaint to us today; but to late-nineteenth-century audiences such issues, regarded in their terms, threatened the very foundations of their home.

These questions all arise from a social issue with far-reaching political implications, which was of the greatest importance in Jones's and Pinero's lifetimes, and which is reflected in countless novels and plays. This was the emancipation of women, in relation to marriage and divorce, their children, and the right to vote. Prior to 1857, it was possible to obtain a divorce only by a private Act of Parliament. This was expensive, and was available only to men, anyway. The reason for this discrimination was that, once a woman married, she ceased legally to exist. She was considered as part of her husband – man and wife are one flesh. She could not use the processes of law, as she had no legal entity. On marriage, she became her husband's property, to do with as he wished (there were cases in working-class life of men selling their wives). Not only did she become his property, but the children were his also, as well as anything that she owned. Hence the importance of marriage settlements, by which the girl's family saw to it that the man was legally bound to allow her a certain amount of money for her own use during marriage, and a comfortable portion were she to be left a widow. A girl coming from an impoverished family, where she was taking little into marriage, was frequently in the humiliating situation of having to ask for every penny that she needed. On divorce, all her property, as well as the children, remained her husband's. Such seemed to be the vindictiveness of men divorcing wives who had left them, or gone off with another man, that the majority of them seem to have seen to it that their ex-wives were reduced to utter poverty. If the girl's family would not give her a home, she, untrained for any job, had nowhere to go. Many drifted to the world of the *demi-monde*, of prostitution at various levels, gradually descending through the scale of poverty, and declined to an unhappy death. It is not surprising that women would endure almost anything rather than face the cruelty of the world outside. A divorced woman was socially ostracised.

The situation changed little after 1857, when the Matrimonial Causes Act was passed. This meant that it was now possible to obtain a divorce in a special court set up for the purpose. Because the wife had no legal entity, if there was another man involved, divorce proceedings were filed against him, the husband suing for 'criminal conversation'. The Act did, however, enable a wife to divorce her husband in certain circumstances, but they had to be pretty extreme. Not only did she have to prove he had committed adultery; she had to show that he had deserted her as well, or was some kind of sexual pervert. Thus, many women shrunk from starting proceedings, because of the public shame and humiliation that would be involved in revealing her husband's sexual practices. Men only had to prove adultery. However, if a wife did take the plunge, and divorced her husband, he still kept most of her property, although she was given some rights. For instance, she was obviously in a position where he could no longer pocket her earnings. Nor did she have rights over her children.

The passing of the Married Women's Property Acts in 1870 and 1882 slightly improved the situation. A woman now retained control of her own property, be it monetary or real-estate, and what she earned became hers, but she did not gain control of her children. However, none of these advantages could offset the stigma attached to divorce. Although a woman was not now left penniless as a result of divorce, there was still no place for her to go in respectable society. The very wealthy went abroad. The moderately-off went to some other place, where they were not known, and tried to begin a new life, often by pretending to be a widow. Those who had no property anyway were as badly off as they had been before the Act.

Social historians writing of the Victorian and Edwardian periods emphasise that the ethic of female purity, and the social hypocrisy which accompanied it, were prevalent until after the First World War. Indeed, as late as 1939, a divorced woman, even if she were the 'innocent' party, was fortunate to be accepted into small town or country society. It was easy for a woman to compromise her reputation; the woman was seen as the spiritual centre of the family. She was to be her husband's helpmate, his haven from the sins and strife of the world, which he, the breadwinner, had to face every day. She was to bring up her children to be God-fearing and pure in word and deed. So that she might fulfil all this, she had to be protected from the world, from the evils of coarse language and behaviour, from promiscuity, and from the impurity of sex. There were many women who never saw their husbands naked in all their married lives. Sex was only for procreation; hence the large families. They must not be contaminated by women who had sinned in breaking their marriage vow, and who had put themselves before their husbands and families. Hence the outraged reaction at Nora leaving her husband and children at the end of *A Doll's House*.

Inevitably, the hypocrisy surrounding this set of shibboleths was enormous. Of course, respectable women were not ignorant of the more unpleasant aspects of life; they saw them in the streets whenever they went out, at the theatre, and frequently in their own homes. One of the greatest hypocrisies of all was what came to be known as the 'double standard' – one set of moral and sexual (very often the same thing) standards for men, and a completely different one for women. Men were not expected to be faithful to their wives. Many of them kept mistresses (if they could afford to) in bijou residences in such places as Chelsea and St John's Wood. There were hundreds of brothels catering for every taste, even a number of child brothels. Many men did not even go outside their own homes. Governesses and female servants were considered fair game, and many a girl was started on a life as a prostitute by being seduced by either the master of the house, or one of the sons. Many working-class men put their wives and daughters on the streets to supplement the family income. High-class prostitutes, the ones who were 'lucky' enough to be kept by some man, or a succession of men, were often girls from good homes who had been seduced away from home by a man who had then not married them; or divorcees; or women who had been turned out by their husbands; or women who fell easily into this kind of life because it attracted them more than the suffocating respectability of the social norm. The ideal of the family was exalted above all else, the example coming from the Royal

Family. The women who transgressed and offended against the ideal were seen as enemies of womenhood, of the family and of society. Hence the ostracism of divorcees, of 'unsuitable' wives, and the fear and hatred of the *demi-mondaine*. The reclamation and reform of 'fallen women' became a crusade for many people, Gladstone and Dickens among them; and a great argument raged as to whether it were ever possible to redeem them. Surely, said the bulk of respectable society, their hearts were irrevocably corrupted by their evil lives. Such a women could never be good. Debate raged in the newspapers and the periodicals, and in the lecture halls. The whole issue had been exacerbated between 1864 and 1869 by the notorious Contagious Diseases Acts, whereby all prostitutes in towns where there were troops were made liable to compulsory rounding-up and hospital examination for venereal disease. There was a great campaign, led by Mrs Josephine Butler, who herself worked among sick and dying prostitutes, for the abolition of these discriminatory measures. Why, said the female agitators, should not the men, who gave the women disease in the first place, also be examined and given compulsory treatment? Why should women be singled out? The Report of an 1870 Commission on Repeal of the Acts stated that the behaviour of men in sexual matters was 'the indulgence of a natural impulse'. This statement was quite naturally seen as outrageous by the female opposition. The Acts were eventually repealed between 1883 and 1886; but the issue was still alive in 1894, when *The Humanitarian* ran a long correspondence on 'Should the same Standard of Morality be required from Men as from Women?' A lively interchange of letters ensued.

But, despite the growing feeling among women of the need to change their social standing, many girls were still forced, or persuaded, into marriages for money, or for social advancement. This is not to say that many girls did not marry for love, but quite often they were disillusioned after marriage. Wealthy girls were particularly at risk from well-born wastrels and fortune-hunters on the look-out for a rich wife. With the widening of women's educational opportunities towards the end of the nineteenth century, both at school and university, many more girls received the education hitherto reserved for their brothers. Nevertheless, those girls fortunate enough to receive university education headed for the professions which had previously been closed to them: medicine, the law, science. However, working women were frequently seen as a threat to the family, and were stigmatised as unfulfilled spinsters, or held up as objects of ridicule. It was the First World War which finally freed women, bringing in its train the vote.

Another phenomenon of the times was the expanding number of the *nouveaux riches* – those who had made their money from trade, and through their great wealth endeavoured to buy their way into polite society, not only in London, but all over the country. They were resented by those whom they had left behind on the social ladder, and despised by those whom they wished to impress with their wealth, and whom they tried to emulate. Riches and ostentation became important for their own sake. Materialism became the new God, for rich and poor alike. However, materialism had its victims, and the rising poverty in industrialised England and the plight of the poor in the big cities became a matter for increased public concern. It was possible for the novelists to deal with their problems, but dramatists were subject to far more rigorous censorship, and also had hostile audiences to face, so they did not have much scope. Only at the beginning of the twentieth century were dramatists able to present problems engendered by poverty squarely on stage. There are two ways of portraying society in the theatre. One is to pose a social problem – for instance, prostitution, drunkenness, poverty – and move characters round the stage in relation to that problem to provide an exposition, exploration and possible resolution; in this instance, it is the problem which is of primary interest and the people are of secondary importance (examples of this type of play are *Strife* by John Galsworthy and *Major Barbara* by Shaw). The other method is to present a group of characters, and show the situations and problems that arise from the psychology of those people, just because they are *those* people, at that moment of their lives (examples of this are *Mrs Dane's Defence* by Jones and *The Notorious Mrs Ebbsmith* by Pinero). In the first type of play, an audience can all too often be irritated by an obvious political or didactic purpose. In the second, the audience can become too absorbed in the emotions and thought-processes of the characters, and fail to see the serious social criticism implicit in the story. While Shaw was trumpeting about marriage being 'legalised prostitution', Pinero, in plays such as *Iris* and *Mid-Channel*, was showing women trapped in situations which were just that. While Shaw was laughing at 'middle-class morality' in a play such as *Pygmalion*, Pinero and Jones were showing, in play after play, the crass materialism, hypocrisy, complacency and censoriousness of that same middle class. All through the late nineteenth century, English society was riven with conflict, controversy, and legislation about the status, education and legal rights of women. Shaw, in *Mrs Warren's Profession*, wrote *about* prostitution; in *The Second Mrs Tanqueray*, Pinero makes a prostitute his leading character. In *The Notorious Mrs Ebbsmith*, a play which Shaw hated, Pinero shows an 'emancipated' woman who fails, because her early conditioning and her own emotions prove too much for her. Shaw hated it *because* she failed; he thought Pinero was betraying his ideal. But Pinero was more realistic, and showed the agony inherent in betrayal. Pinero and Jones's way of presenting society is as significant and important as any other. They must be judged for what they do, rather than for what they do not do.

It is a common assumption that Ibsen was a great influence on late-nineteenth-century English drama. At the same time, it is important to realise that Ibsen never had a very wide audience when his plays were first produced in England. There were some nineteen Ibsen productions in the 1890s, but these had short runs and did not play to large houses. There is no doubt, however, that the publication of *The Quintessence of Ibsenism* by Shaw in 1891, and his constant glorification of Ibsen while he was a drama critic have done much to make Ibsen's influence appear far greater than it really was, *at the time*. This illusion has been handed down to later generations at the expense of the *real* influence of Pinero in gaining acceptance for serious drama among English audiences in those years. Shaw admitted in later years that he had championed Ibsen for his own ends, using him as a weapon in his campaign to lessen Pinero's influence. Shaw did not feel that Pinero used the theatre to present the right issues. He was interested in bringing socialist problems to the stage. He wanted to use the theatre for didactic and propagandist purposes. Pinero and Jones were dramatists of a different sort. They presented the society in which they lived as they saw it to be: in naturalistic not schematic terms. Their aim was to present the problems of society in a mode which their audiences would accept, and think about – and perhaps act upon. Interestingly, Shaw attacked

Jones far less than he did Pinero; probably because Jones's serious plays were far less successful that Pinero's. Pinero was all too aware of the constant attacks upon him. He wrote to the critic William Archer,

> A few years ago, the native authors were working with a distinct and sound aim and with every prospect of popularising a rational, observant, home-grown play. Then came the Scandinavian drama, held up by the New Critics as the Perfect drama and used by them as a means of discrediting native produce. Just for the present everything is knocked askew; the English dramatist has little influence and the public, urged to witness *A Doll's House*, patronises the Empire Theatre of Varieties.[1]

In the next year, *The Second Mrs Tanqueray* was staged, and the 'rational, observant, home-grown play' came into its own. No wonder Shaw was displeased. As a play, it ran counter to all his ideas and subsequent practice. Pinero's greatest strength lies in his minute observation of people, their motives and psychology. Shaw was not in the least interested in psychology, only in ideas.

It was not that Pinero was against change and experiment. He was a founder member of J. T. Grein's Independent Theatre; he was active on committees to abolish censorship, to build a national theatre, to negotiate for young playwrights better deals with management. Despite Shaw's continual criticism and carping, they became great friends, and it is amusing to see how Shaw's outrageous letters to Pinero provoke letters back in much the same vein.

Jones frequently had problems over finding a management, or casting, because of his bitter tongue, and his increasing animosity towards the actor–managers. Shaw, of course, after his early plays, *Widowers' Houses* and the successful *Arms and the Man*, did not find a West End management until 1908. Had it not been for the famous Vedrenne–Barker management at the Court Theatre (now the Royal Court) in Sloane Square, inaugurated in 1904, his plays might have been longer confined to matinees, the club theatres, the suburbs and the provinces. On the other hand, Pinero had no problem in this direction. Every Pinero first night, even to the end of his life, was an 'occasion'. He had no public quarrel with the actor–managers. Indeed, as an actor, he had grown up in the theatre under their aegis. His was an urbane, non-aggressive temperament; what is more, he was an 'insider', unlike Jones, whose humble origins made him defensive and belligerent, and Shaw, the Irishman, whose obviously hostile stance towards English society made him not only quarrelsome, but also a self-appointed, frequently irresponsible gadfly. Often Pinero had to soothe susceptibilities ruffled by Shaw on committees, and undo damage that he had done to careful negotiations. Jones and Shaw were unrelenting self-publicists. Never a week went by but they gave lectures, and wrote articles. Both were frequent correspondents to the newspapers. Pinero, by contrast, was an intensely private person, with a horror of, and contempt for, publicity. He hardly ever, in fact, took a curtain call at his own first nights.

Jones quarrelled irrevocably with Shaw over what he felt to be his anti-British writing during the First World War, and his subversive, Marxist-inspired activities. Despite Jones's public castigation of him in print, Shaw remained unrepentant, and unpunished; and lived on to become a British 'institution'. Jones died an embittered, disillusioned man – and now is all but forgotten.

Pinero remained aloof from all the public acrimony. He

was engaged in a great deal of committee work and production. He was also (as was Jones) actively involved in early British Cinema. A number of his plays were turned into films (see Appendix I); he was also asked to act in an advisory capacity over scripts. He turned to experiment in the theatre, particularly in relation to form and content. He tried his hand with Expressionist techniques. His interest in these late plays lay, as always, in psychology, in people and their interaction with each other. His plays reflect his concern with the increasing materialism he saw around him, and with suffering. The rising tide of socialism engulfed him, and has left him stranded – largely unread and unacted. Shaw, on the other hand, from the beginning the champion of the Marxist ideal, swam strongly with the current. Many of his plays, judged as theatre, are not good, unlike Pinero's. His characterisation is frequently rudimentary, his structure shaky, and his speeches far too long for the average audience; but his wit is such that it hides many glaring faults; and, for those that have the patience to sit them out, many of his debates are enthralling. He also lived to be nearly a hundred, a legend in his time. Over many years he continually told people that he was great; and, as he himself said, if you tell people something often enough, they will believe it. Thus his achievement has totally eclipsed that of Pinero, whose contribution to the mainstream of English drama is the greater. Shaw stands on his own – a dramatist of the mind. He is the dramatist of polemic and debate, who writes mainly from an objective, satiric viewpoint, frequently clumsy in his use of theatre. Pinero is a playwright of greater variety: of irony; of subtle psychology and emotion; of comedy; and whose knowledge of theatre is unsurpassed.

It is possible to read Shaw's plays completely divorced from the theatre. Most of them are intellectual exercises, where the ideas are represented by witty lay figures, most of whom speak like Shaw himself. Because of their coruscating wit, and the fascination of many of the debates, Shaw's plays have been included in Literature syllabuses, and he has come to be regarded as a great literary figure; it is on this set of criteria that his reputation rests, *not* on his practice of theatre. Pinero, on the other hand, wrote for the theatre, not for the study. His plays ironically, and sometimes despairingly, reflect the society around him; many of them are pleas for tolerance and compassion. His is no optimistic vision of a brave new world. He sees failure, despair, betrayal, greed and sorrow all around him. He writes with more sympathy and understanding of the plight of women than any other dramatist of his era; but he does not provide answers. He shows the reality of women who try to fight stifling social attitudes and fail; or women whose own characters defeat and destroy them. Even when, like Shaw, he laughs at the world he sees, it is laughter built on sadness, and the belief that the future is irrevocably determined by the past. It is time Pinero's plays were reconsidered; not just as period pieces, thought to be inferior as literature, overshadowed by Shaw. They should be reassessed, particularly those from 1900 to 1910, not only as major English plays, written by England's then leading dramatist, but also as plays which could quite easily be staged now, such is the skill and variety of their theatrical craft, and the interest of the issues they raise for today's audiences.

In their early experiments and struggles, Pinero and Jones were the leaders of the rebirth of worthwhile serious drama in England. They had powerful allies in William Archer and Clement Scott and other critics. They had an uncertain ally in Shaw himself, for Shaw was an enemy of the shoddy and second-rate in the theatre. Many of his best criticisms are directed against poor or exaggerated acting. He felt that both Jones and Pinero were badly served by the actor–managers for whom they wrote, requiring a more 'naturalistic' style of acting; a higher general standard of performance was needed. His strictures are confirmed by the fact that both Jones and Pinero comment on the damage done to their work by performers. A notorious instance is that of Mrs Patrick Campbell, who, after throwing tantrums all the way through *Michael and his Lost Angel* in rehearsal, walked out three days before the opening night; or Fay Davis, who had been brilliant as Fay Zuliani in *The Princess and the Butterfly*, but could not come to terms with the lead part in *Iris*, and so ruined the play.

As society changed, it was difficult for both dramatists to keep in the forefront of the reform they had initiated. Jones, in particular, did not alter, and was writing in the twentieth century much as he had written in the nineteenth. He grew old-fashioned. Pinero, however, changed with the times, although his fundamental deterministic view of human nature remained much the same. He did not grow old-fashioned. He simply became unpopular. Although he still retained a faithful following, the ideas he presented in his plays were not 'advanced' enough for one section of his audiences; he presented too pessimistic a view of society. On the other hand, he was too ironic and explicitly condemnatory of social values and behaviour to please many others. It is interesting that the great Russian director, Meyerhold, produced *Mid-Channel* at the Alexandrevsky Theatre in Moscow. It is one of the few English plays that he directed. *He* obviously felt that the play had something of interest to say.

With the deaths of Pinero and Jones, an important chapter in English drama ended. The impetus they provided for the consideration of serious ideas on the English stage, and the revolution in English drama that they brought about are now largely unknown, and unacknowledged. Many things that they fought for came to pass some years after; in fact, censorship was not abolished until the 1960s. If they could have seen some of the results of abolition, perhaps they might not have fought so hard. Even today, when the English theatre provides the setting for ceaseless experimentation inspired by international exemplars, the mainstream of English drama is still based on the reforms of nearly a hundred years ago: an interesting story, with believable and well-delineated characters, centring round some problem of human and social importance, presented in a more or less naturalistic style. English comedy and farce owes everything to Pinero: his rescue operation, a century ago, gave new life to a moribund form.

It is high time that Henry Arthur Jones and Arthur Wing Pinero, instigators and pioneers of the modern English drama, were acknowledged and admired for their life's work in a cause in which they both believed so much.

2
Henry Arthur Jones: His Life and Plays

The Life

Henry Arthur Jones was born in 1851, the eldest of five children. He was of Welsh descent, although both his father and his grandfather were farmers in Buckinghamshire. His upbringing was rigidly religious, as his family were dissenters. He first went to school when he was five, but was taken away when he was ten, and sent to his uncle in Ramsgate, where he was apprenticed to the draper's trade. He hated his uncle, a deacon of the Baptist Church, who was a hard, unloving man. The small boy was made to work for fourteen hours a day. He consoled himself by reading, and so began a long process of self-education, extending over a wide range of subjects. He went to London in 1869 to work, and that year attended a theatre for the first time, to see the revival of a melodrama, *Leah*. He was totally enthralled, and decided that he would be a dramatist rather than a novelist. He set about learning his craft by careful analysis of what was current and popular. 'I used to hurry from the City almost every evening at six to see the same successful play for perhaps a dozen times, till I could take its mechanism to bits.' However, he had to eat, so he became a commercial traveller in the drapery trade. He wrote several one-act plays during his first year in London. These he sent to managers without success. In 1869, while visiting a warehouse for making artificial flowers, he met Jane Seely, the owner's daughter, and they became engaged; but it was nine years before he was able to support her and they were able to get married. The marriage took place in 1878, at St Andrew's Church, Holborn. They went to Boulogne for their honeymoon; this was the first time Jones had been abroad.

During those nine years, Jones had been continually writing plays, but the first recorded performance in a public theatre is at the Theatre Royal, Exeter, on 29 May, 1879. Five months later he had his first London production, *A Clerical Error,* at the Court Theatre. He was helped and encouraged by the actor–manager, Wilson Barrett, and in 1881 was commissioned by Barrett to write a 'strong' play. He collaborated with Henry Herman, and they wrote *The Silver King,* a melodrama. Jones had by then left the drapery trade, so this commission was very welcome. Many years later, he said to his daughter, Doris, 'I had a wife and two children, and about £300 between me and the work-house, and night after night I used to think, "Good God! Will it come off?"' When his nurse asked him, in the year before he died, which was the greatest day of his life, he replied almost immediately, 'The first night of *The Silver King.*'[1] The play ran for 289 nights, and was revived by Wilson Barrett several times. It was produced at Wallack's Theatre in New York in 1883; chosen for a command Performance in aid of King George V's Pension Fund for Actors in 1914; revived by H. B. Irving in the same year. It was turned into a novel by Wilson Barrett, and into a serial. It has been filmed. The original but incomplete manuscript is in the Bodleian Library, Oxford. *The Silver King* was a runaway success, and made enough money to enable Jones to settle down to the life of a working (and acknowledged) playwright. In 1884, not yet feeling confident to 'go it alone', he contracted to Barrett to work as his house dramatist, while continuing to write freelance. Sadly, for the next four years, with the exception of *Saints and Sinners,* he produced hack work of little importance. However, in 1884 he embarked on a secondary career: that of writing articles, and giving speeches and lectures in the cause of a more literary and serious English drama, considered on a level with the other arts, untrammelled by foreign adaptations and 'popular' elements. He toiled indefatigably for the 'Renascence of the English Drama', not without considerable effect. His strong rhetorical style, conviction and dedication made him a powerful advocate, and this work was to continue when he was an old man and his plays had fallen from popularity.

By 1888, Jones had five children, so he needed to make more money than was possible by working for Barrett. Fortunately, in 1889 he had a great success, *The Middleman,* and from then never looked back. Success followed success until the turn of the century, when his plays ceased to have drawing-power in the theatre.

His health had never been good. Since adolescence he had been hampered by crippling fits of depression. It would seem that he was a manic-depressive, for these depressions alternated with 'highs' of hectic, exuberant activity. Occasionally he was on an even keel; but life was exhausting for himself and his family. Although in his personal relationships he was affectionate, kind and generous, he was also irascible and aggressive. He indulged in vitriolic abuse in print of those whom he disapproved, and who did not come up to his own high standards. He made many enemies; but was never really able to understand why.

His work was popular in the United States, and a number of his plays were studied in American universities on Literature courses. In 1907, he was given an honorary degree by Harvard, 'for twenty years leader in the revival of English drama and its re-union with English Literature'. After a visit to the United States in 1912, he collapsed, and was found to have cancer. He underwent a colotomy, which left him a semi-invalid. He was devotedly nursed by his wife and daughters. Nevertheless, he continued to write, and *Mary Goes First,* one of the most light-hearted of his comedies, was written in the aftermath of the painful operation.

In the last decade of his life Jones wrote no plays of substance. He was an ardent patriot, and in 1916, he had written a pamphlet, *Shakespeare and Germany,* which contains a long passage in praise of France. The pamphlet was translated into French and the original manuscript now belongs to the French people. The French wished (in 1928) to confer the Légion d'Honneur upon him, but, because of some ludicrous Foreign Office regulation, were prevented from doing so. In his earlier years he had been attracted to socialism, and he was an ardent admirer of William Morris; but he was appalled by the attitude expressed towards the English justification for fighting by those leading socialists Bernard Shaw and H. G. Wells during the 1914–18 war. He considered them both to be subversive, working for the overthrow of England, and by their writings actively helping the Germans. He spent the last ten years of his life attacking them in print, with the support and encouragement of many people. Although both, particularly Shaw, had been his friends, he never spoke to either again. To read the ferocity of his polemic against them, it is difficult to realise what an old and sick man he was. He did, however, write articles on many other subjects, and become involved in the early cinema in England. He was particularly involved in the battle to remove the censorship of plays.

All this while, he was in great pain, and became increasingly reliant on alcohol. His kidneys began to fail, and in 1926 he had a series of painful operations. One thing that cheered him was that Macmillan published a four-volume edition of his work that year. His working life was over, and in 1929 he died. In the last two years of his life he confessed that he wished he had not spent so much time and energy on his battles with Shaw and Wells, but had finished his book on Sir Henry Irving instead. He was bitter that he was not knighted, and it is difficult to understand why he was not. He, pathetically, thought that if he had had a name less plebeian than Jones it might have made a difference. It can only be assumed that his lack of tact, his irascibility and his powerful invective made him enemies who, despite his unremitting service to English drama, and his active patriotism, used their influence to see that this reward did not come his way. His disappointment was all the greater when *The Silver King* was requested for a Command Performance on 22 May 1914 in aid of King George's Pension Fund for actors.

He was a man of imagination, great courage, high principle and indefatigable energy. Sadly, although he had so many gifts as a dramatist, and did much to help to raise the status of English drama, his work has one great deficiency: he has no gift of style. His dialogue is uninspired. It is tragic that, while pointing the way for others, he himself failed to reach the high goals he set for English drama.

The Plays

Jones's first successful play, *The Silver King,* was called by William Archer 'quite the best of modern English melodrama'. Although it is no better than Tom Taylor's *Ticket-of-Leave Man* (1863), and lacks the humour and pace of Boucicault's melodramas at their best, there is some truth in Archer's dictat. Performed in 1882, *The Silver King* opened in the same season as three Boucicault revivals, including *The Corsican Brothers;* at least two adaptations of Sardou plays; three adaptations from novels *(Far from the Madding Crowd, Jane Eyre* and *Moths)*; a Tennyson play; Gilbert and Sullivan's *Iolanthe* at the Savoy; and a melodrama called *Pluck, a Story of £50,000,* by Henry Pettit and the great Victorian showman Augustus Harris, which was a fine exemplar of melodrama in decadence, where feasible character and story are weighed down by sensation and spectacle.

The critics fell with delight on *The Silver King* – it contains no sensation scene, or spectacle. The settings, it is true, are numerous. There were fifteen in the original production; some scenes were designed to be played downstage before the frontcloth on a bare forestage with no furniture and few props, while others were played in a completely furnished 'box set' which was set up while the apron stage was in use. This alternation led to great speed and fluency of performance. Much of the language is rhetorical, but this was expected by both actor and audience, as was the useful convention of the aside. The Lyceum is a big theatre, and rhetorical language and gesture was needed to keep an often restless and vociferous audience attentive. So, when the central character, Denver, shrieked, 'Fool! Fool! Fool!' or cried in anguish, 'Oh God! put back thy universe and give me yesterday', the theatricality was perfectly acceptable to audience and performer. In much of *The Silver King,* however, the language appears more naturalistic. Although, as in all melodrama, the plot dominates the characters (who are all labelled virtuous or vicious), there is some semblance of psychological insight. Denver, though in constant jeopardy, finally defeats Skinner, the villain, bringing about a suitably moral conclusion. The traditional materials are skilfully combined, and the play demonstrates no ordinary dramatic and theatrical talent on the part of the author.

After this success, Jones continued to write, in collaboration with H. A. Herman. They wrote a 'free adaptation' from Ibsen's *A Doll's House* entitled *Breaking a Butterfly,* which, although barely recognisable compared with the original, received some good notices (Prince's Theatre, 3 March, 1884); and a one-act drama, *Chatterton* (Prince's Theatre, 22 May, 1884). Wilson Barrett played the lead in the latter play and received 'magnificent notices' for his performance, while the criticisms of the play were, with few exceptions, 'very favourable'.

In September 1884, *Saints and Sinners,* a five-act drama entirely by Jones, was produced at the Vaudeville. The influence of melodrama is still very strong; the characters are either good or bad, and at nearly every point are dominated by the plot. The play is stuffed full of soliloquy and asides, and is constructed in the traditional manner, using the front and full stage. However, that said, the religious theme and the veracity of some of the character-drawing made it a remarkable play for 1884.

Even more remarkable is the uproar it caused, and also the characterisation, particularly of the dissenting classes. The characters were drawn from people Jones had known in his youth. When he was accused of copying Ibsen he replied, 'The setting in my play was mainly that of my own early life in a small English dissenting community, and the view that I took of English middle-class life was that of Matthew Arnold.'[2] His daughter states that Samuel Hoggard was drawn 'from his Uncle Thomas in whose shop he worked at Ramsgate and [her father] said, "He didn't know the use I made of him afterwards in *Saints and Sinners*."'[3]

Jones finally replied to the criticisms in a fine article printed in the *Nineteenth Century* (January 1885), entitled 'Religion and the Stage'. In spite of the hostility, the play ran for 182 nights, and did well in production in New York. It was the first of Jones's plays to be made available for reading by the general public. *Saints and Sinners* was published by Macmillan in 1891.

The Preface to *Saints and Sinners* contains an interesting discussion of the play, and an exposition of a viewpoint which Jones presents in many of his lectures and essays: namely, that drama must cease to be the poor sister of theatre, and must strive towards literary excellence. Only when the dramatic text can stand on its own, as literature, will drama be fit to take its place beside the other arts. He never denies the need that the text has, for its presentation on stage, of the arts of the theatre, but he says, 'there is but one way of advancing . . . and that is by making the theatre a national art with a definite intellectual and literary basis, disdainful of all theatrical effect that will not submit to take an auxiliary place'.

Saints and Sinners is also significant because it contains a number of the themes to which Jones returned in later plays: religion, and religious integrity; confession, retribution, suffering and salvation; the moral frailty and fallibility of women; the baleful influence of women on the life of a virtuous man; the frivolity and irresponsibility of women; the hypocrisy of the middle classes; the greedy pursuit of wealth. Above all, it contains strong characterisation, sometimes leading towards caricature, or recognisable social groups and types.

Jones did not realise the play was going to be a success, and this was why he contracted to Wilson Barrett to work with him. During his time with Barrett, Jones had no opinion of the plays he wrote himself! Of two of them, he wrote in 1886 to Barrett, with whom he had collaborated, 'I cannot help feeling that *Hoodman Blind* and *The Lord Harry* are not good plays, that they are really not such good work as I could have done, and have done on my own account.'[4] With *A Noble Vagabond* (Princess's Theatre, 22 December, 1886), Jones's partnership with Wilson Barrett came to an end. In January 1887, *Hard Hit* was produced at the Theatre Royal, Haymarket, and so began his long association with Beerbohm Tree. The play was a reworking of old material, as was *Heart of Hearts,* also in 1887.

In 1889, Tree starred in a play of Jones's call *Wealth,* also at the Haymarket. It was not successful, though the principal character, Matthew Ruddock, a wealthy ironmaster, played by Tree, was praised as a fine psychological study. The play did, however, do much better in New York, where it was a success, and it was later translated and produced in Germany, Austria, Holland, Denmark and Belgium. One play, *Welcome Little Stranger,* which Jones wrote between 1885 and 1889, was refused a licence, because a baby is being born off-stage.

After this essentially unproductive artistic period in the theatre, Jones then had a great success: *The Middleman* (1889). In technique, it is still melodramatic, and, in places, over-rhetorical. It does, however, possess a satirical depiction of an election, written in the humorous vein developed to good effect in Jones's later plays. Furthermore, the playwright is exploring, albeit tentatively, important social themes – the relationship between capital and labour; the differences between the landed aristocracy and the new industrial rich. Although these are themes treated previously in *The Factory Lad* (1832) and *New Men and Old Acres* (1869), the importance of *The Middleman* lies in the fact that Jones is introducing serious themes to the stage, and trying to present them in ways that are theatrically viable. He is also presenting a figure as hero who is a prototype of many of his heroes to come: a man of principle endeavouring to maintain his integrity in the face of almost insuperable odds.

Russell Jackson, in the Introduction to his edition of *Plays of Henry Arthur Jones,* says, 'The sense of personal spiritual responsibility and guilt (a sense fostered by his own religious upbringing), anger at the stupidity and narrowness of provincial life, sympathy for the prophet who is ignored and persecuted in his own country – these themes dominate many of Jones's plays.' This is an excellent analysis, but what it does not say is that Jones's man of principle is frequently tempted from the path of virtue by a woman. Jones's attitude to women, though typical of a certain type of Victorianism, is, a century later, largely unacceptable. In his plays, women may be frivolous and unthinking, or cynical, or weak, or depraved. Jones often shows women to be worthless objects, victims of the double standard of sexual behaviour prevalent in his day, standards which he appears to condone. This is the least attractive characteristic of his plays, and one which now makes him uncongenial to many readers. His women always pay: either by being humiliated, or punished in some other way; banished from any hope of happiness. 'Duty' is the word which drives them, and their masculine 'superiors'. Jones seems to assume that most women are morally inferior to men;

if they are not, they have to endure the promiscuity and hypocrisy of their husbands with patience and passivity. His daughter, interestingly, says that there were very few women that her father cared for deeply.

Nowhere is Jones's attitude to women more telling than in his next play, *Judah* (1890). Vashti Dethic, the worldly girl who threatens the integrity and purity of the hero, Judah Llewellyn, is one of the most interesting characters that the author ever created (see Chapter 3). *Judah* was followed closely by *The Dancing Girl* (Haymarket Theatre, 1891), another study in female psychology. Drusilla Ives is a Quaker girl who has deliberately 'gone to the bad'.

As with Vashti, the portrait of Drusilla is believable. The strict puritanical environment of Drusilla's home and the moral rigidity of he father make her escape and deliberate repudiation of it all quite understandable. She is not led astray. She chooses her path in life willingly, without shame or remorse. Perhaps, here, Jones is showing the conflict which arises between the religious rigidity of a childhood and environment such as his, and the blandishments of a pleasure-loving, irresponsible way of life once escape comes. However, Drusilla, in her heartless and flippant way, is evil – a moral emblem shown to the audience. Unlike *Judah,* which is a drama growing from character rather than situation, *The Dancing Girl* returns to the melodramatic tradition, despite the psychological insight into the characters; but moral earnestness, so much a trademark of Henry Arthur Jones, colours the whole play.

Soon after the immensely successful production of *The Dancing Girl* (310 nights), Jones engaged in a virulent battle in the papers with the actor–managers. Like George Bernard Shaw after him, he felt that the grip the actor–managers had on the theatre was pernicious; that people such as Beerbohm Tree, E. S. Willard, Henry Irving and

Wilson Barrett had authors completely at the mercy of their whims. Jones argued that authors were often obliged to alter their plays to suit the leading actor, who would not produce them otherwise. Also, the billing-system was such that the author's name, in small letters, often went unnoticed. Jones naturally aroused a great deal of hostility, but was reconciled with E. S. Willard, and presumably Tree. Over the years, he did modify his opinions slightly, however.

During the run of *The Dancing Girl,* he had been writing the first of his satirical comedies. It is called *The Crusaders,* and such was his faith in it that he mounted the production himself, and gave William Morris carte-blanche as designer. On the first night, beautifully printed programmes on hand-made paper were distributed free. This led to a typical legal fracas with the man who owned the programme and refreshment monopoly at the theatre. Despite all the thought and care spent on it, the play was booed on its first night (2 November 1891), and was severely criticised in the press. Jones's venture cost him more than £4000.

The play is not the story of an individual, but, rather, the picture of a social group. It is a satire on a band of upper-class dilettantes who decide to reform London. The sum of all their endeavours is to spark off a revolution in South America and add twopence to income-tax! The characters divide into two groups; the leading ones recognisable as naturalistic characters, but the minor ones appearing as one-dimensional caricatures. In utilising this technique, Jones was adhering to the traditions of English comedy. The play was, perhaps, too experimental to succeed. William Archer felt that, because it was 'patently fantastic', it did not provoke the necessary 'provisional credence'. It set forth events which purported to be, but were not, matters of history. They might be more or less possible and probable, but their 'factual' unreality was obvious from the outset.

After burning his fingers with *The Crusaders,* Jones went to the United States on a visit, where he met Brander Matthews, the leading American theatre historian and critic, who was Professor of English at Columbria University. Matthews was to become a lifelong friend and correspondent. On his return, Jones recouped his finances by 'collecting his public' around him again with a play called *The Bauble Shop,* starring Charles Wyndham. It was a play centred round the House of Commons, and was a modest success. Jones straightway plunged into another experiment, *The Tempter.* This was staged at the Haymarket, with Tree in the main role of the Tempter, i.e. the Devil. It is a verse tragedy, with passages in prose. It does not in anyway slavishly imitate Elizabethan verse, but glows freely in surprisingly powerful and varied lines. Where the play is extra-ordinary is in the technique that Jones uses with the Devil, who exists outside the action yet is also a part of it. He serves to put into concrete terms the subconscious motives and desires of the characters themselves. The author tries to show that all human misery, from domestic quarrelling, drunkenness and gluttony to deceit, hate, jealousy and murder, is caused by the prompting of the Devil, who may appear in many guises and whose sole delight is to cause as much misery and chaos as he can. The play presents a double vision: the evil that men do, and the Devil causing that evil to be done. The atmosphere is strongly reminiscent of Marlowe's *Dr Faustus,* and of certain parts of *Paradise Lost.* The result is a dramatic anachronism. The play has all the fervour of the 'hell-fire' preacher, combined with an earthy vitality. As Shaw put it, 'Altogether a rum business.' Needless to say, it failed, and Tree lost a great deal of money.

Undeterred, Jones moved on to the next experiment. It is interesting to see him seeking for a form in which to express himself. The play, produced in 1894 by George Alexander at the St James's Theatre, was *The Masqueraders*. This combines two earlier forms: the impassioned love affair of *Judah* with the 'group' satirisation of *The Crusaders*. It also presents for the first time one of Jones's favourite themes: the unhappily married young wife, deeply in love with another man, who through 'duty' is unable to find happiness with her true love. The first three acts are excellent, full of well-observed characters and interesting situations; but the tone of fervent morality, and talk of a wife's duty, in the last act, though outwardly acceptable to audiences of the time (being the standard by which so many of their number were forced to live), now seem hypocritical cant. Were the curtain to come down at the end of the third act, it would be an actable and entertaining play. Shaw summed it up when he said, 'Every one of that woman's illusions to duty elicited a howl of rage from me. She morally outrages my tenderest sensibilities.'[5] In condemning Jones, it is necessary to remember the power of the Lord Chamberlain's Office to censure scripts, and the power of the public to shut a show, both by hissing and booing, and by writing to the papers.

The Masqueraders shows very clearly another characteristic of Jones's writing: his dislike of the landed gentry and 'society'. His characterisation is savage and ruthless. With an outsider's eye, he picks on all the worst characteristics apparent to him, and exposes them. The heroine, Dulcie, is superficial, without a thought in her head; her husband, Sir Brice, is a caricature who would not be out of place in Restoration comedy, a brother to Sir John Brute in *The Provok'd Wife*. The other men and women are gossipy, malicious, trivial, deceitful, or spinsters! Jones, of course, had to break into the theatre, and also win his way in society. To the end of his life he retained a slight rural accent, dropping his aitches occasionally, and had to acquire the outward marks of a man of the world; had to learn how to behave in polite society, without making a fool of himself. He hated the society from which he had come, the world of dissenters and small tradesmen, and in many of his plays his satire sprays over *them* also.

In his next play, *The Case of Rebellious Susan* (1894), the satirical eye and hand are at work again, but this is a much more successful play. It is the first in a long line of society comedies which were to be so popular with the public. Rebellious Susan is a young lady who, finding that her husband is having an affair, goes off on holiday and does the same herself – or does she? The play is deliberately ambiguous. She is nearly exposed, but keeps her head, and we, the audience, are not quite sure at the end whether she has been unfaithful or not.

There is also an underplot, in which Jones tilts at a favourite target, a 'New Woman', using her marriage as a counterpoint to Lady Susan's. The play is more light-hearted than its predecessors. The characters, though satirical portraits, are drawn with amusement rather than dislike, and are less one-dimensional than the author's previous comic characters. They also dominate the action, so little seems over-contrived. The Criterion, where the play was staged, was a very 'upper-class' playhouse, so Jones was holding up a mirror to the very people whom he was portraying.

The play is not only good, and eminently performable, but interesting in that it is a perfect image of the standards and mores of upper- and middle-class society of the 1890s. The play is the first in which Jones employs the *raisonneur*, a stock figure derived from French drama, who acts as the author's mouthpiece and provides a link between author and audience. Usually the character is a charming, worldly, middle-aged bachelor (in this case, Sir Richard Cato, Lady Susan's uncle), a kindly man of the world, who tries to set things right, and dispenses good advice.

Sir Richard urges conformity upon Lady Susan; but, then, Jones would never have got the play past the censor if he had not done so! For the most part, however, and from the evidence of other plays, it is obvious that Sir Richard is urging what Jones really thinks. In later years, he went to great lengths to effect reconciliations within his own family, and to prevent divorce. He is, it would seem, a believer in the *status quo* for the sake of stability.

Jones had the greatest difficulty with Charles Wyndham, who was presenting the play and taking the part of Sir Richard. He wrote to Jones,

> I stand as bewildered today as ever at finding an author, a clean-living, clear-minded man, hoping to extract laughter from an audience on the score of a woman's impurity .... I am equally astounded at a long-experienced dramatic author believing that he will induce married men to bring their wives to the theatre to learn the lesson that their wives can descend to such nastiness, as giving themselves up for one evening of adulterous pleasure and then return safely to their husband's arms, provided they are clever enough, low enough, and dishonest enough to avoid being found out.[6]

Despite this broadside, Jones, according to his daughter, would not alter his play, and, although the critics were unenthusiastic after the first night (3 October, 1894), the play was a great success. It was revived several times, and was also a success in New York in December 1894, where the notices were favourable.

When Jones published the play, he prefaced it with a dedication to 'Mrs Grundy', that 'august and austere effigy of our national taste and respectability', to whom he says, 'if you must have a moral in my comedy, suppose it to be this – "That as women cannot retaliate openly, they *may* retaliate secretly – and lie"'. He then adds, rather more significantly, 'My comedy isn't a comedy at all. It's a tragedy dressed up as a comedy . . . .'

In his next play he returned to the style of *The Crusaders* and that of satirising the smugness and obtuseness of middle-class tradespeople. Called for brevity *The Triumph of the Philistines,* the play's full title is *The Triumph of the Philistines, and how Mr Jorgan Preserved the Morals of Market Pewbury under Very Trying Circumstances.* On its first night (11 May 1895) it met a very hostile reception, and adverse criticism. However, the critic of the *Saturday Review* (Shaw) saw it favourably:

> The attack is not the usual sham attack of the stage moralist: it is courageous, uncompromising, made with sharp weapons, and left without the slightest attempt to run away at the end . . . . When Mr Jones appeared before the curtain several persons howled piteously, like dogs who had been purposely run over. Every play which is a criticism of contemporary life, must, if it is an honest play, involve a certain struggle with the public . . . .

William Archer was in favour also, but somewhat more portentously: 'A profoundly melancholy, infinitively suggestive drama, filling us with an awe-stricken sense of the mystery that enwraps the moral government of the universe.' The play ran for only forty-four nights, though it was more successful on tour.

Jones's first book, *The Renascence of the English Drama,* had been published in 1895. It was a selection from the articles, lectures and speeches that he had been producing over the previous ten years, and was a great success. Perhaps this helped to mitigate his sorrow at the failure of his next play, *Michael and his Lost Angel* (1896). Of all his plays, this was the one he liked best. Even at the end of his life he still felt it to be his finest work. It was dogged with disaster. He first offered it to Irving and Ellen Terry, but Irving turned it down. Johnston Forbes-Robertson then decided to do it, and engaged Mrs Patrick Campbell. Forbes-Roberston wanted Jones to change the title ('Lost Angel' was a euphemism for 'fallen women' or prostitute), but Jones refused, because much of the point lay in the double meaning of the title. Then Mrs Campbell, playing Audrie, the Lost Angel, wanted him to change lines, because she said they were profane. Jones is said to have thundered at her, 'It is not profanity at all, it is in the part.' Mrs Campbell continued to make scenes, quarrelling with Forbes-Robertson and complaining about the play, and finally withdrew three days before the opening. Miss Marion Terry stepped into the part, but, although a good actress, was quite unsuited to it, being far too sweet and gentle. The play opened on 15 January, 1896 at the Lyceum. Doris Jones reports,

> The play aroused a storm of criticism and discussion, and it is possible, in spite of Miss Terry's unsuitability for the part of Audrie, that it might have been a financial success. However, my father told me that Forbes-Robertson took it off without informing him of his intention to do so.[7]

Jones also told his friend Clayton Hamilton that Mrs Campbell had persuaded the management to withdraw it 'because of her enmity against him at the time'. Once again, Shaw went into battle for Jones in the *Saturday Review:*

> When I respond to the appeal of Mr Jones' art by throwing myself sympathetically into his characteristic attitude of mind, I am conscious of no shortcoming in *Michael and his Lost Angel.* It then seems to me to be a genuinely sincere and moving play, feelingly imagined, written with knowledge as to the man and insight as to the woman . . .[8]

Shaw went on to say that the acting was bad, and in no way did justice to the piece. Jones was in no position to take an active part in rescuing the production, as his eldest son, Philip, now seventeen, was desperately ill with double pneumonia and pleurisy, and died during the short run of the play.

To appreciate the play, it is necessary, as Shaw says, to be able to identify sympathetically with Jones's 'characteristic attitude of mind'. Parts of the play are fine, but it is so difficult to be sympathetic to Jones's viewpoint: that of the noble man who must be brought low by the wiles of a temptress, and learns through suffering and repentance. Also, alas, he does not have the essential genius to make Michael's exaltation of soul, his spiritual agonies, acceptable. Jones just does not have the supreme gift of language. Audrie Lesden, the 'Lost Angel', is a far more believable character than Michael Feversham, the idealistic priest, and the dialogue of her death scene is touchingly written. But nowhere is Jones's rigid morality more clearly portrayed, or the deeply puritanical roots of his religious upbringing more clearly evidenced. It needed a greater writer than he to succeed with this play.

After the shattering failure of *Michael and his Lost Angel,* both in London and New York, Jones wrote two 'pot-boilers': *The Rogue's Comedy* (1896) and *The Physician* (1897). On the opening night of *The Rogue's Comedy* (21 April, 1896) at the Garrick Theatre, Jones was booed for twenty-five minutes. It is amazing he stayed on stage that long. He vowed that he would never take a first-night call again, and kept his vow for twenty-one years, until the production of *The Pacifists,* a satire on conscientious objectors, in 1917.

The Rogue's Comedy goes back to a theme in *Judah,* that of impostors in the world of psychic phenomena – in this case, fortune-telling. The Rogue, a fortune-teller, Bailey Prothero, is unmasked by his son, who does not know his parentage. Shaw was not over-impressed, calling the play melodramatic farce rather than comedy. *The Physician* was presented by Wyndham at the Garrick Theatre. It opened on 25 March, 1897, and had only a moderate success. It is interesting in that the bare bones of the story obviously provided a blueprint for Shaw when he came to write *The Doctor's Dilemma.* A famous physician tries over several months to save the fiancé of the girl he loves. The fiancé is a temperance leader, who is secretly an alcoholic. Despite the doctor's efforts, the fiancé dies, and the doctor marries the girl.

Wyndham followed up *The Physician* with another comedy of manners, *The Liars,* which is generally considered to be Jones's finest play (see Chapter 3). The critic of *Punch* thought it the best comedy that had been seen on the London stage for some time. Produced at the Criterion on 6 October, 1897, it was a great success. Shaw wrote, 'In *The Liars,* the "smart" group which carries on the action of the piece is hit off to the life.'[9]

With *The Liars* Jones finally established himself securely in public opinion as one of the leading dramatists of the day, but this did not mean that he was proof against failure. *The Manoeuvres of Jane* (1898), the story of a young girl's efforts to upset her chaperones and guardians was slated by the press (yet ran for 281 nights). *Carnac Sahib* (1899), the story of a rebellion in India, was a total disaster. *The Lackey's Carnival* (1900) was another failure. This play is of interest in that it shows Jones tempting to display class distinctions and class attitudes from the servants' point of view in a tale of an aristocratic family and the servant's hall (a theme presented much more amusingly by J. M. Barrie in *The Admirable Crichton,* 1902). Jones was to return to this theme in *The Heroic Stubbs* six years later.

But during the run of *The Lackey's Carnival* Jones had another great success, *Mrs Dane's Defence* (see Chapter 3). This was the last of his smash hits. Slowly Jones was becoming old-fashioned. His values were representative of an age which had passed. The tastes of audiences were changing. Pinero, J. M. Barrie, John Galsworthy and Harley Granville-Barker were much nearer the public pulse. In 1900, Jones was all but fifty years of age: too old to change; too young to stop writing. Nothing he wrote from then on widened his horizons as a dramatist, or detracted from his reputation.

Jones continued to write society comedy in the early years of the twentieth century. Of the plays of this period, *Whitewashing Julia* (1903), *Dolly Reforming Herself* (1908) and *Mary Goes First* (1913) are the best. Jones, typically, got involved in an acrimonious correspondence at the time of *Whitewashing Julia* because he had the critic A. B. Walkeley barred from the theatre because of previous 'unfair' criticisms. Needless to say, this created a number of 'shock-waves' in an already none-too-friendly press. With the exception of Max Beerbohm, few critics were now friendly to Jones. Nevertheless, a loyal following of the public continued to support his plays; but in diminishing numbers.

Whitewashing Julia concerns itself with a now-familiar Jones theme: a woman's 'reputation'. *Dolly Reforming Herself* pokes fun at New Year Resolutions. Dolly is a trivial lady, and her reformation is to consist of keeping within the dress allowance granted her by her husband. It is a play with little substance, but to the upper- and middle-class audiences of the time, whose women only ever handled pin-money, as all the bills were paid by their husbands, it seemed amusing. It was Jones's first success for several years. Easily the best of the three is *Mary Goes First.* In this play, Jones is not acidly revealing the habits of the upper classes, but is concerned with would-be social climbers and people involved in politics. It is an amusing play, with splendidly comic characters and situations. It revolves entirely around how charming, popular Mary Whichello, who has been first in precedence in the country neighbourhood where she lives, is expected to give way to *nouveau-riche* Lady Bodsworth, a lady of little charm and less self-control. The play centres round the battle between them; and around the methods by which knighthoods can be obtained, and parliamentary seats won. Of all Jones's plays, this one would probably appeal to a modern audience best. It is well-constructed; the action springs believably from the characters, who are convincingly delineated; and unlike Jones's 'Society' comedies, it is not acid. Cynical it may be, but it is good-humoured, and genuinely funny.

One of the 'strongest' of Jones's plays of this time was first produced in America. *The Hypocrites* (Hudson

Theatre, New York, 1906) ran with great success for an entire season. Jones visited America in 1906, 1907 and 1908. He greatly enjoyed his visits, and was, interestingly, more highly thought of there at this time than in England. Indeed, an American, Clayton Hamilton, produced the first edited collection of Jones's plays in 1926. *The Hypocrites* reworks a number of old ideas, but quite skilfully. The passionate, idealistic clergyman, Edgar Linnell (Judah, Michael), is involved in the task of sorting out a tangle of seduction, illegitimacy and hypocrisy. Linnell acts more in the role of the *raisonneur,* controlling the actions of the characters. Jones uses him as a mouthpiece to castigate the 'respectability' of society as little more than organised hypocrisy. It is a curious play, in that it combines familiar themes from Jones's serious plays, with a satiric technique. The characters are well-drawn, although Linnell seems to operate on a different plane from the rest of them. He is shown as the reforming idealist, pursuing his beliefs in the face of seemingly insuperable obstacles placed in his way by the hypocritical materialists who surround him. The fact that the play ends happily is incongruous, and at odds with the intrinsic material.

The Hypocrites was not well-received by the critics when it was performed in London in August 1907, and was a failure. Max Beerbohm in the *Saturday Review* put it down to the fact that Englishmen took their national hypocrisy for granted, but 'Mr Henry Arthur Jones is exceptional in that he has never got used to the national feeling.' The *Daily Mail,* however, said that *The Hypocrites* was 'a crude and wholly silly play'. A far cry from its reception in New York, where the enthusiasm of the house, on the first night, was so great that Jones was compelled to make a speech from his box.

His next play, *The Lie,* is a sombre piece, concerning two sisters, Eleanour and Lucy Shale. Lucy, the younger, has an illegitimate baby, and Eleanour shields her from the consequences of her folly, and herself suffers as a result. The play was produced in New York in 1914 and was well-received. It was not performed in London until 1923; but, with Sybil Thorndike in the lead as Eleanour, it was a hit. It was the last important play of Henry Arthur Jones to appear on stage and, significantly, despite its success, was taken off to make room for Shaw's *St Joan.* The despairing, tragic moral – that truth and unselfishness can be successfully outmanoeuvred and defeated by unscrupulousness and treachery – is somehow a fitting end to Jones's dramatic career. Through his writing life, he had always firmly upheld the moral standards in which he believed. This play, written in the aftermath of pain and sickness, shows his final defeat. Jones's tragedy lay in the fact that he was a good, workman-like dramatist – but had no genius. He outlived his reputation, and died an embittered and disappointed man. Looking at the criticisms of his nineteenth-century plays, the enthusiasm with which many of them were received when they were first performed is startling to anyone reading them now, Some are very good, and would revive well in the theatre; but his values are rigid. His ideas on the role and duties of women, and his apparent identification with all that is most offensive (to present-day minds) in a certain kind of 'Victorianism', obscure the considerable interest and actability of many of his plays. As social documents, also, mirroring a particular brand of victorian middle-class life and outlook, they are invaluable. His work has always been more appreciated in the United States and Germany than it has in his native country.

3
Three Plays by Henry Arthur Jones: 'Judah', 'The Liars', 'Mrs Dane's Defence'

The three plays examined in this chapter represent different phases of Jones's career, and different aspects of his art. *Judah*, an early play (1890), finds him experimenting with form, characterisation and the presentation of serious ideas. *The Liars* (1897) is a satirical society comedy, the most successful (though not the funniest) of the comedies which made him such a popular dramatist. *Mrs Dane's Defence* (1900) is his most successful foray into that type of play which so fascinated nineteenth-century audiences: the woman with a past struggling to achieve respectability in the face of society's 'double standard'.

Judah must first be considered against the great interest at the time in paranormal and psychic phenomena. At the time Jones was writing, the Society for Psychical Research (founded in 1882) was making it its business to investigate such phenomena, and to unmask fraudulent mediums. Madame Blavatsky, one of the founders of the Theosophical Society, and a noted medium, was writing a number of books concerned with magic and the paranormal in the late 1880s. Her claims were largely discredited by the Society for Psychical Research. The Order of the Golden Dawn, of which Yeats was a committed member, initiated people into the mysteries of the Cabbala, and into other magical practices. Small wonder, then, that so puritanical a person as Jones should express scepticism in such a climate. Therefore, the focus of *Judah* is on the possibility of faith-healing, and on those people who attempt it. Jones is not prepared completely to deny the existence in some practitioners of healing-power. He merely strongly condemns its misuse, and the credulousness and gullibility of the public.

In *Judah*, Jones has largely discarded the influence of melodrama. Although the plot is important, it does not dictate to the characters, by improbable coincidences or well-worn devices, such as mislaid letters or dropped handkerchieves; rather the story derives entirely from the characters which Jones has created. The play gains, also, by being constructed in three acts, rather than in the popular four-act format; and so the action does not fall away into anti-climax and obvious plot-resolutions. Indeed, up until the last few minutes of the play, it is not possible to predict what the end will be.

Judah presents characters and ideas which Jones returned to in different guises through his subsequent career. There is Judah Llewellyn, the noble-minded, ardent young man, who is nearly destroyed by his love for a young woman who has a chequered past, Vashti Dethic. Unlike her counterpart in later plays, the young woman in this instance is intrinsically virtuous, but made to pursue her ignoble course by the threats of her dishonest father. Another character who foreshadows others is

Sophie Jopp, a satiric portrait of a 'New Woman – Eton-cropped, bemonocled, dogmatic and supercilious. She is presented as having no sentiment, compassion or sense of humour.

Jones's hatred of hypocrisy and deception gives rise to a strongly moral atmosphere; the plot turns on his particular abhorrence – lying. Judah lies to save Vashti from exposure as a fraud, and is tormented by guilt and despair. Other characters lie, out of compassion, or out of self-interest. When, then, if ever, is it justifiable to lie? A central paradox of the play rests in the fact that a main character, the scientist Jopp, is forced by his daughter Sophie, and her obnoxious 'young man', Juxon Prall, to try to unmask Vashti, in the interests of science. Vashti allegedly fasts for days before she effects her cures. However, Jopp himself lies to a young girl, Lady Eve, about the state of her precarious health, thus perpetrating a different kind of 'scientific' deception. Another paradox lies in that Vashti herself, though in some senses a fraud, in that she does not genuinely fast (her father surreptitiously feeds her), can really cure people. Jopp cannot deny this; but to accept that she has a 'power' is to negate all he believes in as a rational scientist who has made it his life's work to unmask fraudulent mediums, healers, and any other person claiming more than human capabilities. The play, therefore, turns on axes of 'What is truth?' What is scientific truth, and can it explain all phenomena, as Jopp claims it can? Does there exist some psychic power? Judah, who is a Nonconformist preacher, hears voices, like St Joan. To him, they are as 'real' as Vashti's 'powers' are to her, although no one, not even Vashti, believes in the voices. Jones seems to be voicing some of his own religious queries. Despite, or perhaps because of, his rigid Christian upbringing, he was at this time of his life not a practising

Christian. His daughter, Doris, said that for many years he was a 'pronounced agnostic'. Nevertheless, his plays are shot through with the puritanical values of his early years, and the metaphysical questions of good and evil trouble him constantly.

Judah opens in the Tapestry Room of Asgarby Castle – a magnificent room hung with tapestry copies of Raphael's cartoons. Over the rear wall is, symbolically, a cartoon of the healing of the paralytic at the gate of the Temple. It provides an immediate recognisably aristocratic setting for Lord Asgarby: '*a very distinguished man about sixty*'. This is the only direction given about his appearance, though other characters are described in detail. Lord Asgarby is writing, and is interrupted, almost as soon as the curtain goes up, by Mr Papworthy, mayor of the neighbouring town of Beachampton, who has come to complain about the young minister, Judah Llewellyn. Judah has espoused, too ardently, the cause of a faith-healer, Vashti Dethic, and Mr Papworthy does not approve. Although there is no physical description of Papworthy, his dialogue vividly creates the man: pompous, self-satisfied, hypocritical.

The interview has been attended by Professor Jopp, a friend of Lord Asgarby's for many years. He is '*keen, alert, intellectual; bald, very high forehead, bright deep-set eyes, genial Voltaire type of face*'. Jopp immediately, by implication, states his disbelief in Vashti: 'I never believe in miracles that do not happen either in a remote century or a remote country'; but he approves of Judah, thinking him a fine natural orator and impressive preacher. Papworthy leaves, to fetch Judah for Lord Asgarby, and, as he is going, he meets Lady Eve, Lord Asgarby's daughter. As he exits, he uses that favourite device of melodrama – the aside. This aside furthers the story by a great leap.

He says to the audience, 'Fifty thousand a year, and one dying child.' Immediately, an audience realises the ingredients of the play to follow: a dying daughter of a wealthy aristocrat, a faith-healer; a preacher who is showing a great interest in this faith-healer; a 'professional' sceptic, who does not believe in miraculous cures. The curtain has been up for about five minutes, and an audience is already aware and involved.

Lady Eve is described as '*a girl of fifteen, with beautiful, hectic complexion, feverish, fidgety, with sudden fits of languor and restless energy*'. It is never stated precisely what is wrong with her, but, by the description of the complexion and manner, it is presumably tuberculosis of the lungs – consumption, the great killer disease of the nineteenth century. Lady Eve is the least successfully written character in the play. Jones does not appear to understand adolescent girls, and puts words into her mouth more suitable to a hysterical and self-dramatising middle-aged woman. Her actions, even for a sick girl, are not entirely convincing. It would require a very accomplished actress to create a believable character from Jones's writing. It does, however, appear from the critics at the time that Bessie Hatton, the original Lady Eve, succeeded very well. It is interesting that Doris Jones says that her father was not understanding with his children, four of whom were girls.

Lady Eve (somewhat precociously) has read an article of Jopp's entitled 'The Scientific Conception of Truth', and she says to him 'Do you always tell the truth yourself?'

JOPP (*a little taken aback*; *after a short pause*). Almost invariably.

LADY EVE. Will you tell me the truth now?

JOPP. Certainly.

LADY EVE. How long shall I live?

Here Jopp evades the issue. He says, 'Well, I'm not in practice now, you know.' Thus, knowing that she is almost certain to die soon, he, the great seeker after 'truth', for compassion's sake, does not tell her the truth about her health, as he sees it, but neither will he tell her a direct lie. He shows his scepticism when Lady Eve says that she wants to see Vashti and ask her to cure her; but one feels that his affection for Lady Eve and her father are such that he will hold his peace in the affair, if it is for Lady Eve's good. Jopp is an attractive character, and in many ways is more important than Judah.

However, whatever Jopp's intentions regarding Vashti, matters are taken out of his hands by his unattractive daughter, Sophie, and her friend, Juxon Prall. Sophie's first words, heard off-stage, are 'Decidedly – put the girl to a scientific test.' Juxon's father is a convinced believer in Vashti's powers, and has written a number of books and articles about her; and Juxon, a know-all, of parasitical tendencies and unattractive appearance ('*a thin, wizened, old young man, spectacles, sharp features . . . Holds his head on one side, as if he hadn't muscular strength enough to hold it upright*'), is determined to humiliate his father if he can. To this end, he is determined to help Sophie prove Vashti a fraud. Despite an initial unwillingness to be involved, Jopp is drawn into the plan. Judah makes his entrance, an attractive figure '*about twenty-five, dark complexion, shaggy, clustering curls. Quick nervous step, a glowing enthusiastic manner, Welsh accent.*' It now only remains for the audience to see Vashti; but Jones skilfully delays her entrance. Close on the heels of reports of yet another miraculous cure comes Vashti's father, Dethic, '*a suave, furtive, sallow, oily man of about fifty, with a touch of the manner of the second-rate platform orator . . . uneasy, underbred*' (by the use of the last word, Jones shows his innate snobbery). It is obvious from Dethic's whole manner that he is dishonest. This immediately casts a doubt on Vashti's authenticity in the audience's mind. Then, at last, she makes her entry; and Jones's sense of theatre is well demonstrated: Judah carries her on, in a dead faint. He carries her with the '*utmost tenderness*'. She has a '*pale, saintly, beautiful face*'. The question which immediately arises in the mind is whether her faint is genuine, or whether she is acting. Her pallor, and her trembling as she recovers, would point to a real faint. There is no doubt at all that Vashti has many cures to her credit. Even Jopp is puzzled: 'Father – genus, cheat; species, religious; variety, bogus-miracle business. Daughter – hum!'

Once left alone on stage together, Vashti and Dethic reveal their whole racket. Vashti does not fast; Dethic feeds her. She does not want to go on with it, but, by threatening her with the certainty of jail if she does not continue, Dethic forces her compliance. He justifies himself by saying that it is the gullibility and craving for marvels of the public that force such a course of action on her; a point made by Browning twenty-six years earlier in his brilliant poem 'Mr Sludge, the Medium'. The critic of *The Times* and *The Star*, A. B. Walkley, picks up the resemblance, and refers to Dethic as Sludge.

Judah returns to see Vashti and, left alone with her declares his admiration: 'Your goodness, your purity take my breath away.' Vashti desperately tries to disillusion him: 'But oh! Mr Llewellyn, you must not think so well of me. I am not an angel. I am a *woman*.' Judah will not listen, so besotted is he with her. The act ends with Vashti undertaking to try to make Lady Eve better; in the face of Jopp's incredulity, she submits to his terms. These are that she shall fast for three weeks, and be locked up in the old keep of Asgarby, which has just been fitted with a new 'safety' lock and is therefore impregnable. The only key to the keep is to be given into the safe-keeping of the unsympathetic Sophie Jopp.

The sympathy of the audience has been skilfully won for Vashti, particularly as she asks for no reward for herself, rather for a new church for Judah. Terrified of her father, afraid of Jopp, whose reputation she knows, she has been manoeuvred into an impossible position. She knows that she can help Lady Eve, but unless her father can get food to her, she will die in the attempt. Judah's admiration for her and belief in her add to her sense of guilt and shame. The curtain falls on Judah's impassioned cry of belief: 'The power she serves stands ready to vouch for her, and your own lips shall be the witness of her truth, and goodness to all the world.'

The middle act is set spectacularly on a terrace outside the old keep, joined to the castle by a conservatory. This was not, apparently, an entirely successful set. William Archer, critic of the *Manchester Guardian*, refers to 'a certain maladroitness of scenic construction'. However, the faults of the scenery did not detract from the success of the act, which was received with undiluted praise, despite the fears of author and cast that the sight of a clergyman lying might evoke a storm of disapproval. The act concerns itself largely with Dethic's attempts to get food to Vashti. She has only three days to go. But Jopp has found the loose window-pane through which Dethic has been smuggling food to Vashti, and has sealed it up. Vashti is starving. Jopp realises this, and tries to get her to give in, out of concern for her. 'You've set yourself a task beyond your strength. Give it up.' Vashti will not yield. 'I want no victory, Miss Dethic', Jopp says; 'Come, let's both give up.' When she still refuses, he delivers one of the key lines of the play: 'you're trifling with the truth, you're playing upon sacred feelings'; but she will not surrender, so once again she is locked in. The forces stacked against her seem too great, and the tension which builds in the act is remarkable. Judah, having climbed up from the moat (he used to be a mountain shepherd), has declared his love for her, and despite her pleas, refuses to believe that she is anything other than the angel she resembles.

Jones needs to relieve the tension before he builds to the climax of the act, and the main climax of the play. He provides a satiric parallel to Judah's ardent wooing of Vashti, by showing Juxon Prall propose to Sophie Jopp. It is cold-blooded and mundane. Both of them are shown to be selfish, complacent people, without warmth or emotion. (A similar couple appear in *The Case of Rebellious Susan*.) In many ways this episode is out of place, because the characters are one-dimensional and their 'proposal' scene is written in comic vein, quite out of key with the rest of the act. Apparently, however, it worked well in performance, and critics comment on the skilful admixture of comedy and drama. Jones also indulges in a passage of obvious symbolism, when an over-excited Lady Eve recounts a dream she has had, where she and Vashti are drowning; she is pulling Vashti down to death. The prose in this passage is not at all believable, although to a nineteenth-century audience it may have been less of a problem. It is difficult to accept that any adolescent girl would talk like this, even in 1890! It is understandable *why* Jones includes this scene. It is necessary for him to emphasise that Vashti is starving, and how her determination to cure Lady Eve will kill her. Nevertheless, like the comic wooing, it strikes a false note in a play which heretofore has flowed logically and absorbingly.

The end of the act is magnificent theatre. Judah returns to watch over Vashti, and witnesses Dethic providing her with food, which she falls on wolfishly. Dethic has managed to get another key made for the keep. This he gives her. Appalled, Judah watches. When Dethic leaves to fetch more food, Judah confronts Vashti. She implores his forgiveness:

> You don't know what my childhood and girlhood were like – how often we were pressed for money. Sometimes we had scarcely bread enough to eat. We went to Spain. I found I was able to cure many of the foolish country people if only they believed in me; and my father persuaded me that if I could only show them that I could live without food, it would be a sign of my possessing supernatural power. I began, and it was as he said. I found everybody believed in me. When I had once begun, I was obliged to go on. We came to England, and then I met you; and at first I was pleased to see what power I had over you. But when I saw that you believed in me and loved me, I gradually felt how wicked I had been. I tried again and again to give it up; I tried to tell you. I wanted you to know the truth about me, and yet I couldn't bear you to think that I was not worthy of your love. You know it now. Oh tell me you forgive me.

She implores him not to betray her – and he responds by saying that he loves her, how can he betray her? He calls her his wife, and Vashti says something which provides Jones with the theme for a number of his plays: 'I won't drag you down to me.' Quite a few of his heroes, both in comedy and in straight drama, are 'dragged down', and, through sacrificing their love, or suffering and expiation, regain their honour and their souls.

Jopp and Sophie nearly catch the returning Dethic, but Judah saves both Dethic and Vashti. He hustles Dethic back into the conservatory, and makes Vashti hurry back to the keep, and lock herself in. Jopp and Sophie, baffled because the search does not reveal Dethic near the keep, discover Judah, who has retreated to the warder's seat in the keep wall. Faced with an inquisition from Jopp, Judah lies to save Vashti.

JOPP. Give your oath – you have not brought Miss Dethic any food.

VASHTI *looks at* JUDAH.

JUDAH. My oath – I have not brought Miss Dethic any food.

JOPP. Your oath – you have not seen her take any.

VASHTI *looks at him.*

JUDAH (*after a pause*). My oath – I have not seen her take any.

VASHTI *shows relief.*

JOPP. Your oath – she has not been outside that door to your knowledge.

Longer pause.

JUDAH. My oath – she has not been outside that door to my knowledge.

JOPP (*looks at him*). Enough! I take your word. I was mistaken.

CURTAIN

Judah's lies to save Vashti form the climax of the play, and are the third variety of lie so far encountered. The first was Jopp's lie by omission to Lady Eve, through compassion; the second, Vashti's claim to fast, through fear of her father, and the desire not to be poor. Now Judah lies to save Vashti, whom, like Milton's Adam with Eve, he puts before his God.

In the manner of the nineteenth century, the end-of-act tableau will have been held, and then the curtain brought down. The last moments of the act are gripping, because of the struggle taking place within Judah, which is theatrically demonstrated by the use of the pause. Notice Jones's stage-directions. The timing of the second-act curtain is crucial.

A year passes, and in Act III we are back again the Tapestry Room. Lady Eve (apparently much better) and her father are discussing the new church. Lady Eve is pettish because she feels that Vashti's part in her cure has not been sufficiently acknowledged. This mood of hers gives the excuse for her exit, and opportunity for Lord Asgarby to deliver a key speech to the audience: 'She's better, she's stronger than she has ever been. What does it matter what the cause is.' He is here stating the diametrically opposite opinion to that of Jopp, who demands scientific proof for all phenomena. Asgarby speaks for the great majority, who will gladly accept a 'miracle' if it does some good. He is prepared to let it rest at that, although he knows that Dethic is a fraud, and that Vashti has deceived him. When Jopp comes to him later in the act, and says that he can prove Dethic to be an impostor, that he has the 'whole history of these people', Asgarby replies, 'Of course he an impostor; but Eve loves the girl, and has made me promise to make her a settlement on her marriage, and – blame me if you like, Jopp – I know I'm being duped – I know I'm a coward, and a fool perhaps – but I can't deny Eve anything.' And later he says, 'I know it's only superstition: I know there's no reason for it, but I feel that somehow Eve's life does depend on Miss

Dethic' – and he implores Jopp not to expose Dethic and Vashti's fraudulent practices. Notice once again the ambiguity. Although Vashti is known to act dishonestly, nevertheless she does make Eve better. How?

Jopp is also pressurised by Juxon Prall not to reveal all Dethic's past history: Juxon wishes to blackmail his father into paying an allowance large enough for him to marry Sophie Jopp, and to live in comfort! His father, a committed advocate (in print) of Vashti's powers, is sure to be made to look ridiculous, and totally discredited, if Jopp publicly reveals his damaging knowledge. Juxon threatens to reveal everything about the Dethics' career, starting with a letter to *The Times*, if his father does not pay up. As in Act II, the placing of the Sophie – Juxon scene is important. It lies between an impassioned scene of remorse and despair between Judah and Vashti, and the finale – a scene of confession and expiation. Thus, it lowers the emotional climate by its satiric, quasi-humorous nature, and also provides a further reason for the rationalist 'seeker-after-truth' Jopp to 'lie' by omission. Jopp is persuaded by two means to keep quiet: in both instances, his revelations would damage his closest friends, Prall and Asgarby. Essentially a compassionate man, he does not reveal the 'truth' because to do so would be to damage those he cares about. He will lie by silence. 'After all, why not believe in fairy tales? Why not pretend there is a dryad in every tree, and a nymph in every brook? Dryads may be as good names for the great secret as any other. Perhaps there is not a great secret after all!'

It is left to Judah himself to force the issue; and the third-act climax is built round Vashti's confession of fraud, followed by Judah's own confession of telling a lie to save her. In this confession scene, and in the build-up to it, all Jones's horror of lying is revealed. Judah's love for

Vashti is absolute, but he will not found his marriage to her, and their subsequent life together, on untruth. He has defied Jopp, at the point where Jopp intends to expose Vashti: 'Prove your worst against her. Write down "Liar" on her forehead, make her name a byword all over England, hunt her to shame, to prison, to another country: I'm her partner. I love her!'; but he says to Vashti, 'The oath I took that night has burnt into me. Every fibre of me is a lie.'

In response to this, Vashti cries,' Oh I have ruined you for ever. You were the best, the most honourable man on earth. You were truth itself, and I have dragged you down to me. How can you love me?' – and in this impassioned cry lies the moral heart of Jones's play. Those who touch pitch are defiled; the pure in heart are tainted by the corrupt, no matter how great the love that lies between them. Love cannot cancel out sin. In play after play, Jones shows love to be an emotion which can defile and destroy, no matter how virtuous the man and woman concerned; and, in order to regain their integrity, they must suffer, and be separated. *Judah* is exceptional in that Vashti does not have to renounce Judah so that he can lead the life to which he has been called. They are not parted, but they have to go through the fire of public confession and penitence before they can start a new life on a true foundation.

Judah refuses both the money and the church which Lord Asgarby was to have given them as a wedding-present; but, unlike Michael in *Michael and his Lost Angel*, Judah does not go into exile. Nor does he lose the woman he loves. Vashti and he decide to stay in the community which knows them, and work together for their joint salvation. Dethic has been sent away, in the hope that he will never return, by Jopp. The religious moral is again pointed in the last lines of the play:

Lady Eve runs on.

LADY EVE (*coming down to* VASHTI). Why didn't you tell me you were ready? Where are the deeds? Are they signed?.

JUDAH. No, Lady Eve, there was a mistake in the title deeds. The building stones were not sound. There is to be no new church. (LADY EVE *shows great disappointment.*) Yes, we will build out new church with our lives, and its foundation will be the truth.

CURTAIN

Judah is Jones's most successful attempt to present openly religious ideas on the stage. The characters, especially those of Vashti and Jopp, are subtle and well-delineated; the overall examination of aspects of truth and morality is thought-provoking; the central examination of paranormal phenomena and their implications is as relevant now as it was when Jones was writing. A. B. Walkley declared in *The Star*, 'The true Ibsen spirit seems to me to pervade the play: it breathes in the discussion of the *pros* and *cons* of spiritualism v. materialism in the first act; one detects it again in the final oath-breaking situation of the second; it is the very essence of the remorse and sacrifice of the third.'[1] Although Jones categorically denied any influence from Ibsen, there is no doubt that in *Judah* his own vision of drama, and its duty to present real life and real moral issues on stage, succeeded brilliantly. *Judah* was seen as a very important play by the audiences and critics of 1890.

In *The Liars*, Jones again takes as his central idea the

subject of truth and falsehood. In this stance, the lies are told by a group of characters trying to protect an indiscreet wife from the sullen vengefulness of her unpleasant husband. The play, a highly successful comedy in its time, creates a cynical and contemptuous picture of matrimony and sexual relationships in 'society'. It reveals the social and moral values of a group of people, representative of a wide section of English life at the time, which to modern eyes are distateful and, to a woman, deeply enraging. The values of the society, the conventions, the cruelties are mercilessly shown. It is difficult, however, to gauge where Jones's own moral values lie. I think it is wrong to assume that they lie with Sir Christopher Deering, the *raisonneur*, or mouthpiece of society. Although it is usual to criticise Jones for subscribing to the prevalent hypocrisy of his day, it is obvious that he thought that women had a very raw deal, and that the attitude of men towards them was intrinsically unjustifiable. Nevertheless, he earned his living by writing plays; and, unlike Pinero, he seems to have found censorship, both by the Lord Chamberlain and by the press and general public, too powerful a force to fight head-on. Therefore his plays, with the possible exception of *The Case of Rebellious Susan*, always appear to subscribe to the current social mores: the marriage bond should be indissoluble; men can behave in any way they please, and society will accept it, but an 'erring' woman will not be forgiven; wives, because they appear to have no alternative, must put up with whatever treatment their husbands mete out to them; honour and duty must always come before love. Most women, having no occupations, are of necessity trivial, shallow and vain – creatures to be petted and humoured, but not taken seriously. All these, and more, opinions are stated in the play. But where Jones stands in relation to the values that he so caustically represents it is difficult to discern. It was inevitable that a man with his religious convictions would regard marriage as sacred; and in *The Liars* he argues forcibly, through Sir Christopher, for the permanence of the marriage tie. Sir Christopher's reasons, however, are all pragmatic and cynical, and, although he says that 'marriages are made in Heaven', he obviously does not believe it of the marriages which he sees round him. He does, however, arrogantly assume that his own marriage will be different, because Beatrice, the woman he intends to marry, is so unlike the usual society woman. Jones also seems to believe sincerely that men can be deflected from the paths of duty and honour by love. Falkner, the man 'at risk' in *The Liars*, is prepared to give up everything for Lady Jessica, another man's wife; but she 'saves' him from himself. In the end, it is the woman who must make the sacrifice of her 'happiness', to enable the man to move on to 'nobler' things.

All the male characters in *The Liars*, with the possible exception of Falkner, are contemptible, an opinion shared by the critic of the *Illustrated Sporting and Dramatic News*: 'From first to last there is little but priggery, frivolity and selfishness. One does not care a great deal for anybody in the play; no single person invites sympathy or inspires emotion. They are not nice people, any of them.'[2] Sir Christopher (played by Charles Wyndham, the most charming and sophisticated actor–manager of his time) would be totally unacceptable: the attitudes he assumes and the moral platitudes he mouths appear cynical, hypocritical and offensive. However, to Clement Scott, the critic of the *Daily Telegraph*, Sir Christopher appeared to be 'laughing, chaffing, persuading, warning the wanderers, until at last his cheery voice points out the right road and the correct turning, and the comedy – or shall we say tragedy – of life is happily ended in uprightness and honour'.[3] The suppositions which lie behind these comments are typical of the day. Scott sees the sadness underlying the play, but appears to accept it, albeit with understanding. Elsewhere he remarks that the play is unbalanced by the actor playing Falkner, who was 'too weak, too yielding, too sentimental'. This comment shows that he has a very good understanding of the play, but does not question the values displayed. Now, no 'thinking' person would dare to mouth some of Sir Christopher's opinions in public! Some people might secretly agree with them, for there are many who still subscribe to the 'double standard' of behaviour (one for men and another for women), even though the late twentieth century pays lip-service to the equality of women.

The play is divided into four acts, each of which has a different setting. It centres round a closed circle of socialites, who, as the play opens, are gathered at a house-party for the Henley Regatta. The action runs over a week, the longest gap in time being five days, between Acts I and II. This close time scale adds to the feeling of social claustrophobia which the play engenders. Each act follows a different structure. Jones is a good 'man of the theatre', and in this comedy he uses the traditional techniques of comedy to good effect.

Act I is set in an elaborate Eastern-style tent on the banks of the River Thames. The act is mainly concerned with exposition and with introducing the main characters. These he moves on and off stage to provide different combinations of relationship, and so reveal different aspects of the story to come. The act begins with two irritated and ineffectual husbands: the weak fool Freddie Tatton, and the pompous bore Archie Coke. They are discussing the difficulties of managing their wives. They are also gossiping about a dangerous flirtation in which Freddie's sister-in-law, Lady Jessica, is indulging with Edward Falkner, who has 'behaved gallantly in Africa' and is at present the idol of society. These two subjects are the core round which the action of the play revolves. Very quickly, we are introduced to Sir Christopher Deering, soldier and man of the world; to Mrs Crespin, a '*sharp, good-looking widow*', who obviously dislikes Jess and is bent on making trouble if she can. Sir Christopher unsuccessfully tries to control her malice. We meet Dolly, Coke's wife. She is frivolous, empty-headed, good-hearted, but defiant to her husband. Rosamund (otherwise known as Rosy), Freddie's wife and Jess's sister, is pretty, vivacious and flippant; yet she is full of common sense and has a strong idea of propriety, even though she treats Freddie as if he were an amiable nitwit. Lady Jessica appears to be spoiled, wilful and frivolous, yet underneath is capable of sincerity and feeling. Sir Gilbert Nepean, Jess's husband, is oafish, vindictive and sullen; his brother George is shown to dislike Jess, and is determined to bring her into disrepute. Falkner, the 'hero', is head-over-heels in love with Jess, but is far too earnest and humourless to play the game of flirtation according to the accepted rules. The last character to be introduced is Beatrice Ebernoe, a 'good woman'. She is a widow whose husband has recently died in Africa. She was rescued from danger at the hands of natives by Falkner. It is implied that she is 'different' from the other women. She has led a useful life in Africa, and was devoted to her husband. She is heard playing the piano before she is seen, and her music is used as a symbol of her 'spiritual' quality. Sir Christopher aspires to her hand in marriage, but as yet she is unwilling to wed him. After showing very clearly the potential trouble ahead for Jess if she continues to flirt with Falkner, the act ends with

Sir Christopher trying to persuade Falkner to give up all thought of Jess and to return to his duty in Africa. Falkner has been reminded of his duty (and his honour) by a letter which he has received telling him that he alone can negotiate the required treaty in Africa. (Letters fulfil the same function in drama of the nineteenth century as telephone calls do in plays of the twentieth.) At the crucial moment, when Falkner is still trying to decide what to do, Jess appears. Falkner's choice is visually presented to the audience: on one side of the stage, Jess – and dishonour; on the other, Sir Christopher, Beatrice – and duty. The curtain falls on this carefully arranged tableau.

The intermingling of the characters and the orchestration of the dialogue are skilful. Through the men's talk, we get their view of women, marriage, and the relationship between Jess and Falkner. Through the women's chatter we get the feminine point of view. There is a close rapport between Jess, Rosy and Dolly, although it is obvious that the dislike of Mrs Crespin for Jess is reciprocated. Jess is seen on stage with the other women, with her husband, with Falkner. The act is full of movement and bustle. We learn that Jess's husband, Gilbert, is furiously jealous. As the act begins, she is on the river with Falkner, and Gilbert has to go away, to attend to some family business. George, his brother, who is as unpleasant as he himself is, refuses to accept the assurances of all the others that Jess's activities are quite harmless, although outrageous. We realise that George is going to make trouble for Jess if he can. We see Gilbert's abominable manners: keeping his cap on, and smoking in a lady's presence without asking permission; we observe his vile temple. We sympathise with Jess, and watch with some amusement as she runs rings round him. As he flings off stage, followed by his ill-wishing brother, we are given a contrasting scene with the emotional Falkner, who does not understand that she is playing a game, largely to punish her boorish husband, and mitigate her own boredom and unhappiness. He behaves with a passion and sincerity which both amuse and move her. She finds it almost impossible to contain his ardour; and he is only brought under control by the arrival of Sir Christopher. Jones shows us, with some humour, the situation of the girl to whom life's surface and laughter are all-important (she can't stand Gilbert because he cannot see a joke). She becomes the focus for violent emotions: first, her husband's jealous rage frightens her; then the fierceness of her would-be lover's passion for her becomes almost too much for her to keep within proper limits. She avoids deep feelings if possible. She wants life to be a game, because the reality of her unhappy marriage is too much for her to face. But she makes the game a perilous one: deliberately she courts danger. Her trip on the river with Falkner has already inflamed him. In fact, she manoeuvred him to dive into the river to retrieve a brooch, to damp down his ardour! Her husband has been maddened by the incident. Wilfully, although she knows her husband's mood, her brother-in-law's watchful malice, and Falkner's inability to conduct a harmless flirtation, she sets up an assignation with Falkner. If she is found out, her very survival as a member of society will be in danger. It is possible that Falkner's sincerity and glamorous reputation fascinate her. Falkner is so enamoured of her that he pays no heed to the danger to him, or to her. He does not feel his love for her to be wrong. He says to Sir Christopher, who tries to get him to see 'sense',

> I love a woman with the deepest love of my heart, with the purest worship of my soul. If that isn't moral, if that isn't sacred, if that isn't righteous, tell me, in

Heaven's name, what is? And you come to lecture me with your cut-and-dried worldly-wise philosophy, your mean little maxims . . ..

It would seem to me that Jones himself speaks here, with great sincerity; but he has Sir Christopher put the accepted view of society: 'you're a fool if you think that anything can come of this passion of yours for Lady Jessica, except misery and ruin for her, embarrassment and disgrace for you, and kicking out of decent society for you both'. The confrontation scene, towards the end of the act, between Falkner and Sir Christopher quite mercilessly puts the case for society. Sir Christopher asks Falkner to tell him 'what the devil you mean by making love to a married woman, and what good or happiness you expect to get for yourself or her? Where does it lead? What's to be the end of it?' Falkner cries, 'I don't know – I don't care! I love her.' The dialogue which follows establishes clearly the two viewpoints: that of care for the individual, and the individual's right to make a life of his or her own choosing; and that of society, hypocritical and cynical.

SIR CHRISTOPHER. But my good Ned, she's another man's wife.

FALKNER. She's married to a man who doesn't value her, doesn't understand her, is utterly unworthy of her.

SIR CHRISTOPHER. All women are married to men who are utterly unworthy of them – bless 'em! All women are undervalued by their husbands – bless 'em! All women are misunderstood – bless 'em again!

FALKNER. Oh, don't laugh it off like that. Look at that thick clown of a husband. They haven't a single idea, or thought, or taste in common.

SIR CHRISTOPHER. That's her look-out before she married

him.

FALKNER. But suppose she didn't know, didn't understand? Suppose experience comes too late?

SIR CHRISTOPHER. It generally does – in other things beside marriage.

FALKNER. But doesn't it make your blood boil to see a woman sacrificed for life?

SIR CHRISTOPHER. It does – my blood boils a hundred times a day. But marriages are made in Heaven, and if once we set to work to repair celestial mistakes and indiscretions, we shall have our hands full. Come down to brass tacks. What's going to be the end of this?

FALKNER. I don't know – I don't care! I love her.

In this exchange, Sir Christopher states his basic case. Despite the fact that Jess is obviously unhappily married to a 'thick clown', she *is* married to him, and that's that. His basic contempt for women is shown in the reiterated, would-be humorous and patronising 'Bless 'em!', and he has no sympathy for an unhappy wife. She should have chosen her husband more carefully. If she makes a mistake, it's her fault, and she will have to put up with it. This position was the predominant one until well after the Second World War, when attitudes towards divorce became less rigid, and it was possible for a woman to get at least care and control of her children, instead of having them taken away from her by the courts, upholding the rights of the husband.

Sir Christopher then analyses for Falkner the alternative lines of action open to him: he can leave off loving Jess; one or both of them might die, through natural causes; they could die together, committing suicide; he can keep on 'dangling after' Jess, getting nowhere; he can attempt a liaison with her, either with her husband's compliance or in secret; they can create an open scandal, which will ruin Falkner's career; or he can give the whole thing up, and return to Africa. It is significant that nowhere does Sir Christopher suggest that it might be possible to make something worthwhile of the relationship.

To a late-nineteenth-century audience, Sir Christopher's sentiments would not have seemed as objectionable as they do today; what to us seems to be patronising and cynical, to them would have been sound common sense, voiced by an experienced man of the world.

After this leisurely, expository opening act, the tempo changes in Act II to that of farce, with continual exits and entrances through the door and two pairs of French windows of the set, which represents a private sitting-room at the Star and Garter Inn, Shepperford-on-Thames. This has been mentioned in Act I and is the place where Falkner is staying. Most of the entrances are through the door, but George and Rosy both make their entrances through the windows. The action is swift. Jess arrives to keep her assignation with Falkner. She is armed with a cover story about having missed her way, a tale which deceives nobody, least of all the French waiter, who, agog to know for whom Falkner has ordered a sumptuous dinner, quickly realises that Jess is the guest, despite Falkner's denials. While waiting for dinner to be served, Falkner makes passionate advances to Jess. She keeps him at bay with the menu, and with flippant badinage. Although she is well in control of the situation, she shows herself to be not without sensitivity. She is sincerely moved by his love for her, and deeply admires his achievements, honesty and sincerity. The *tête-á-tête* is interrupted to good comic effect by the waiter, and then by a barrel-organ playing outside. Jess, to cool off Falkner's overheated emotions, sends him outside to get the music to stop – and is at that moment confronted by George.

George immediately thinks the worst, and rushes off to communicate with his brother. Panic-stricken, Jess sends the returning Falkner, to see if he can catch George. She is then faced with her sister, Rosy, who, like George, enters through the windows. Faced with her desperate sister, Rosy shows some sense and resolution. She says that she and Freddie will provide Jess with an alibi; she writes a note to George saying that, if George will call on her at home in Cadogan Square, in the morning, she will undertake to explain everything. To write this letter, she borrows Jess's stylograph, which she leaves on the table when she has finished the letter. She cannot persuade Jess to leave with her and Freddie. Jess says that she is hungry. Falkner, unable to catch up with George, returns. He does not want to conceal their assignation, but rather wants to 'reveal all', and take Jess away. However, Jess is afraid of Gilbert, her husband; afraid of social ruin: 'Save me from it. I can't face it. I can't give up my world, my friends.' Earlier, Falkner has made the opposite point to her: 'It's better to feel, it's better to suffer than to be meanly happy. I love you, but I'd rather smother you in tears and blood than you should go on living this poor little heartless withered life, choked up with all this dry society dust.' In stating this, he shows himself to be quite oblivious of what social 'ruin' will mean for Jess; he can think only of his passion for her. He wishes it had been possible to tell the 'truth'; but Jess tells him not to be disagreeable. He almost persuades her to stay despite a promise to Rosy that she'd not have dinner with him, but would leave. She is saved from further compromise by her maid Ferris, who arrives with a telegram from Gilbert, announcing his return to London that evening. Ferris has had the foresight to conceal Jess's whereabouts from the other servants; she has also brought a cab, so that her mistress can catch the express to London, which is due to leave almost immediately. Ferris whisks Jess away, leaving a baulked and sulky Falkner to eat a solitary dinner, sympathetically attended by the fascinated waiter. He is not alone for very long. Enter Sir Christopher, introduced somewhat mischievously by the waiter as 'the friend of the dinner'. Falkner is monosyllabic and sullen. Sir Christopher gives him more 'good advice' about women, ironic in view of what has just happened. 'Love 'em, worship 'em, make the most of 'em! Go down on your knees every day and thank God for having sent them into this dreary world for our good and comfort. But, don't break your heart over 'em! Don't ruin your career for 'em! Don't lose a night's rest for 'em! They aren't worth it . . . .' He adds, 'except one!', further emphasising his sense of his own superiority, for he considers that Beatrice, on whom his interest is fixed, must be the exception to the rule.

Humour is derived from the circumstance that Sir Christopher thinks that Falkner has ordered the gourmet dinner for himself alone; and he is eager to share such a splendid meal. Falkner, however, bolts from the room, and it transpires that he has rushed off to catch the train for London. Sir Christopher, in the meantime, picks up Jess's pen, which he identifies from the monogram. Enlightenment dawns. He pockets the pen, and then sits down to the table. He rushes through the meal, obviously having made up his mind to go to London like everyone else; but he cannot bear to leave so much delicious food. Good meals have a particular importance for Sir Christopher, as we find later in the play. The act ends with him '*throwing spoonful after spoonful of soup down his throat*', accompanied by the barrel-organ, which starts up very loudly, playing '*a rowdy street tune*'. The act is short, rapid, farcical and genuinely comic. The waiter is a particularly happily conceived character, although nowadays a familiar comic stereotype. His exists, entrances and comments punctuate the act, and add to the breathless staccato rhythm. No new ideas are introduced – the dizzy pace precludes that; but the act is the mainspring of the rest of the action of the play, which is concerned with the big 'cover-up' for Jess, and its results.

Act III keeps up the pace generated by Act II, and it is constructed in accordance with the 'snowball' technique described by Bergson in his essay '*Laughter*'. The action accelerates, as more and more people are persuaded to support Jess in the lies with which she hopes to deceive Gilbert. The act in fact, 'snowballs', building up incrementally until the entrance of Gilbert, followed finally by Falkner, who blows the deception and the liars sky-high. He proclaims his love for Jess to her husband, and everyone else. The act is punctuated by the constant entrances of the footman announcing successive visitors. It is divided in half by the entrance, and short visit, of Mrs Crispin, who has come to see Rosy, ostensibly to obtain an address. She makes it impossible for Rosy to provide the promised alibi for Jess. Freddie and she had dined with Mrs Crispin the evening before, and, as they did not want to take her into their confidence, they dare not try to protect Jess with a story which can so easily be proved false.

Humour in this act is generated by the reactions of the husbands, Freddie and Archie, as they are unwillingly drawn into the scheming. Even Sir Christopher is persuaded to lend his countenance. Rosy tells him that his presence will be an immense moral support, 'because everyone knows that you are such an honourable man'. No one, she says, would suspect him of telling a lie.

Dolly is induced to say that she dined with Jess the night before. There is not, unfortunately, time enough to brief her properly before Gilbert arrives: 'After George went away, you were so upset at his suspicions that you came back to town without any dinner. Did I stay and have dinner? . . . Where did I dine? Do tell me, I know I shall get into an awful muddle if I don't know.' Nobody has time to tell her! When confronted by an angry and disbelieving Gilbert, primed and backed up by brother George, this proves to be the weakness in her story, which Gilbert seizes upon. Her husband, Archie, who has said he will keep his mouth shut and not give them away, but will not lie himself, becomes embroiled as well, and is not able to lie convincingly to back poor Dolly's story. Gilbert's rage explodes at Falkner's entrance, and he makes to attack him. At this point, Jess unexpectedly and dramatically takes the stage:

> JESS (*rises very quietly*). Mr Falkner, tell my husband the truth.
>
> FALKNER. But, Lady Jessica –
>
> JESS. Yes, if you please – the truth, the whole truth, and nothing but the truth. Tell him all. I wish it.

This is a theatrical moment, and a surprise. Although Jess has been presented sympathetically in the play, and has shown genuine feeling and emotion, we hardly expect her to possess the courage to do this, for her fear of Gilbert and her dread of social disgrace has been amply demonstrated. Her intervention provides Falkner with the opportunity to declare publicly this passion for Jess, and the act storms to a splendid climax.

> FALKNER. I love Lady Jessica with all my heart and soul.

I asked her to come to me at Shepperford last evening. She came. Your brother saw us and left. The next moment Lady Rosamund came, and she had scarcely gone when the maid came with your telegram and took Lady Jessica back to town. If you think there was anything more on your wife's side than a passing folly and amusement at my expense, you will wrong her. If you think that there is anything less on my side than the deepest, deepest love and worship, you will wrong me. Understand this. She is guiltless. Be sure of that. And now you've got the truth, and be damned to you. (*Goes to door and turns.*) If you want me, you know where to find me. (*To* LADY JESSICA) Lady Jessica, I am at your service always. (*Exit.*)

Stunned, the characters look at each other, and the curtain falls.

Speed of playing is essential in this act. It must not be allowed to falter, as the act builds up with the entrance of each character, culminating in Falkner's declaration. The comedy resides in the speed, and in the muddle in which the characters find themselves with each new entrance. Another source of comedy lies in the exploitation of the men and their distinctive modes of speech. Freddie's line 'I may be an ass, but I'm not a silly ass' is very funny in context, as is Archie's 'I should have thought my character was too well known for me to be asked to – a – a – It is too disgraceful! I will not lend my countenance to anything of a kind.' The exchanges between Freddie and Rosy, and Dolly and Archie, are also amusing, building on the foundation already laid in Act I, and revealing much more about the relationships. It transpires that Rosy is really rather fond of Freddie. Sir Christopher also has a number of amusing lines in the scene.

Sir Christopher, although manipulated into an awkward situation, continues to dispense 'good advice' and disseminate his contempt for women. To Freddie, anxious to know what Rosy and Jess are 'hobnobbing and whispering about', he says, 'Oh, my dear fellow, when two women get together, do you think it can ever be worth a man's while to ask what nonsense or mischief they're chattering?' To Archie, who says, 'I am an honourable man', he replies, 'So are we all, all honourable men. The curious thing is that ever since the days of the Garden of Eden, women have had a knack of impaling us honourable men on dilemmas of this kind, where the only alternative is to be false to the truth or false to them.' His key speech in the scene is to Gilbert, a speech paralleled in other plays which contain similar situations:

> Now, if I may offer you a little advice, if I were you I should gently take Lady Jessica by the hand, I should gently lead her home, I should gently use all those endearing little arts of persuasion and entreaty which a husband may legitimately use to his wife, and I should gently beguile her into telling me the whole truth. I should believe everything she told me. I shouldn't listen to what anybody else said, and I should never mention the matter again. Now, do as I tell you, and you'll be a happy man tomorrow, and for the rest of your life.

Gilbert, not unnaturally, refuses to follow his counsel.

There is a singular inappropriateness in this speech of Sir Christopher's and it is a measure of his complacency that he does not realise it. To expect a man who has been built up as vindictive, jealous and vile-tempered to act with such self-control, balance and trust is ludicrous. This is another sidelight on Sir Christopher's good opinion of himself. This is how he likes to think that *he* would behave in similar circumstances.

An intrinsic weakness of the four-act structure is that, after the required 'strong' third-act curtain, the fourth act is anti-climactic. One of the great strengths of *Judah* lies in the fact it is written in three acts. To complete *The Liars*, Jones has to develop two threads: Sir Christopher's relationship with the 'exceptional' woman, Beatrice, and the resolution of Jess and Falkner's relationship. Act IV begins with Sir Christopher packing to go to Africa, and at the same time wooing Beatrice, in masterful fashion. This 'masterfulness' is apparently what she requires to make her change her mind about marrying him: 'I've given you some trouble to win me, Kit . . . I'll give you none now you have won me.' There is humour in the curious love scene, in the total self-centredness and complacency of Sir Christopher, and in the improbable speed with which Beatrice yields to his bullying, and decides not only to marry him, but to do so immediately, and to go with him at once to Africa. The courtship is presumably there as a counterpoint to the other, 'illicit' relationship, between Jess and Falkner: it is a proper courtship, between two mature, unattached people. Sir Christopher, although admitting to a past, has declared earlier in the play, 'I owe no woman a sign or sixpence. I've never wronged any friend's sister, or daughter, or wife.' Beatrice is a widow, who has declared that she must enjoy 'the luxury of self-sacrifice'. Sir Christopher somewhat aptly replied, 'Marry me. I'll give you the most splendid opportunities.' Sir Christopher, the man of the world, with his eyes wide open, is contrasted with idealistic Falkner, whose love has blinded him to all sense of self-preservation and propriety; Jess is contrasted with Beatrice. She is in Sir Christopher's opinion so useless that she would be very much 'in the way' were Falkner to take her to Africa. His basic contempt for Jess (and women) is shown clearly in this act, for, when confronted with Gilbert trying to collect more evidence against Jess, he first suggests to Gilbert that he should take her out to dinner (Sir Christopher's mind rather runs on dinner) and then says, 'My dear fellow, she's only a woman. I never met but one woman that was worth taking seriously. What are they? A kind of children, you know. Humour them, play with them, buy them the toys they cry for, but don't get angry with them. They aren't worth it.' Beatrice, whom Mrs Crespin has called 'a little stiff and unsociable', does not belong to the 'set' of frivolous wives, and, because he loves her, she is obviously, in his eyes, superior and different.

The worst hypocrisy of which Sir Christopher is guilty in his refusal to accept the genuineness of Falkner's love for Jess. Even despite his avowed friendship for Falkner, he announces his intention of behaving as he tells them the rest of society will – he will have nothing to do with Jess if she leaves her husband: 'Lady Deering will not recognize Lady Jessica.' This is a crushing blow to Falkner, because Jess has recognised his worth, and has declared her love for him. Sir Christopher, having played the card 'ostracism' comes out with another trump card: DUTY, closely followed by CONTEMPT. Falkner is the only person who could successfully negotiate with the fractious African chieftains:

> You know that your going out may save hundreds, perhaps thousands of lives .... You know that you have a splendid chance of putting the crown on your life's work, and you know that if you don't seize it, it will be because you stay skulking here after her .... if you

> turn tail now there's only one word will fit you to the end of your days, and that word is 'Coward' . . .. there's only one epitaph to be written on you by and by – 'Sold his honour, his frame, his country, his duty, his conscience, his all for a petticoat.'

Falkner, however stands up to this barrage:

> Very well, then, when I die write that over me. I tell you this, Kit, if I can only win her – and I shall, I shall, I feel it – she'll leave that man and come to me; then I don't care one snap of the fingers if Africa is swept bare of humanity from Cairo to Cape Town, and from Tenerife to Zanzibar!

Sir Christopher (still trying to pack his trunks to go away) is then confronted by Jess and Rosy. Jess has made up her mind, despite Rosy's pleadings, that the only way out of 'the glorious muddle' that her affairs are in is to run away with Falkner, who has 'behaved splendidly'. Falkner is just about to take Jess away when Sir Christopher intervenes, and delivers the most important speech in the play:

> Now! I've nothing to say in the abstract against running away with another man's wife! There may be planets where it is not only the highest ideal morality, but where it has the further advantage of being a practical way of carrying on society! But it has this one fatal defect in our country today – it won't work. You know what we English are, Ned. We're not a bit better than our neighbours, but, thank God! we do pretend we are, and we do make it hot for anybody who disturbs that holy pretence. And take my word for it, my dear Lady Jessica

and my dear Ned, it won't work. You know it's not an original experiment you're making. It's been tried before. Have you ever known it to be successful? Lady Jessica, think of the brave pioneers who have gone before you in this enterprise. They're all perished, and their bones whiten the anti-matrimonial shore. Think of them! Charley Gray and Lady Rideout – flitting shabbily about the continent at cheap *table d'hôtes* and gambling clubs, rubbing shoulders with all the blackguards and demi-mondaines of Europe. Poor old Fitz and his beauty – moping down at Farnhurst, cut by the county, with no single occupation except to nag each other to pieces from morning to night. Billy Dover and Polly Atchinson – cut in for fresh partners in three weeks. That old idiot, Sir Bonham Dancer – paid five thousand pounds damages for being saddled with the professional strong man's wife. George Nuneham and Mrs Sandys – George is conducting a tram-car in New York, and Mrs Sandys – Lady Jessica, you knew Mrs Sandys, a delicate, sweet, little creature, I've met her at your receptions – she drank herself to death and died in hospital. (LADY JESSICA *moves a little away from* FALKNER, *who pursues her.*) Not encouraging is it? Marriage may be disagreeable, it may be unprofitable, it may be ridiculous; but it isn't as bad as that! And do you think that the experiment is going to be successful in your case? (FALKNER *is going to speak.*) No, Ned, hear me out. (*Turns to* LADY JESSICA.) First of all there is the shabby scandal and dirty business of the divorce court. You won't like that. It isn't nice! You won't like it. After the divorce court, what is Ned to do with you? Take you to Africa? I do implore you, if you hope for any happiness in that state to which it is pleasing Falkner and Providence to call you, don't go to Africa with him.

You'd never stand the climate and the hardships, and you'd bore each other to death in a week. But if you don't go out to Africa, what are you to do? Stay in England, in Society? Everybody will cut you. Take a place in the country? Think of poor old Fitz down at Farnhurst! Go abroad? Think of Charley Gray and Lady Rideout. Take any of the other dozen alternatives and find yourself stranded in some shady hole or corner, with the one solitary hope and ambition of somehow wriggling back into respectability. That's your side of it, Lady Jessica. As for Ned here, what is to become of him? (*Angry gesture from* FALKNER.) Yes, Ned, I know you don't want to hear, but I'm going to finish. Turn away your head. This is for Lady Jessica. He's at the height of his career, with a great and honourable task in front of him. If you turn him aside, you'll not only wreck and ruin your own life and reputation, but you'll wreck and ruin his. You won't! You won't! His interests, his duty, his honour all lie out there. If you care for him, don't keep him shuffling and malingering here. Send him out with me to finish his work like the good, splendid fellow he is. Set him free, Lady Jessica, and go back to your home. Your husband has been here. He's sorry for what is past, and he has promised to treat you more kindly in the future. He's waiting at home to take you out. You missed a very good dinner last night. Don't miss another tonight. I never saw a man in a better temper than your husband. Go to him, and do, once for all, have done with this other folly. Do believe me, my dear Ned, my dear Lady Jessica, before it is too late, do believe me, it won't work, it won't work, it won't work!

It's all there: the hypocritical pretence of respectability;

the ruthless punishment exacted society on those who deviate: the importance of men, their duty and honour, before the general welfare and happiness of women. No wonder the women are frivolous and pleasure-seeking; trapped in this social prison, what else is there for them to do?

As Jones shows in other plays, and also Pinero, it is the women who keep the jaws of the trap shut even more than the men. They have no mercy on those who try to escape the prison that they themselves inhabit. In the face of the truth of the picture Sir Christopher has painted, Jessica's common sense reasserts itself: 'We've got to part .... Yes, my friend, I won't ruin your career .... You can always cherish your fancy portrait of me, and you'll never find out how very unlike me it is. And I shall read about you in the newspapers and be very proud – and – come along, Rosy!'

It is ambiguous whether her motive for giving up Falkner is self-preservation, or a genuine concern for him. In the light of Jones's stage-directions as to her misery when she says 'Goodbye' to Falkner, presumably Jones means it to be thought that she genuinely cares for Falkner. This, then, reinforces Jones's central concern for honour and duty, which touches Jessica as nearly as Falkner. It is *her* duty to sacrifice the love of a man who adores her, and for whom she cares, in return retaining her own honour as a married woman, to return him to his duty to his country, with *his* honour unblemished. Her future is uncertain; Falkner's is assured. Sir Christopher asks Gilbert whether he may tell Jess that 'for the future you will treat her with every kindness and consideration', Gilbert says, 'Tell her what you please. Say I know I've behaved like a bear. Tell her I'm sorry, and if she'll come home, I'll do my best to make her happy in future.' It is difficult to believe that this humility will last. He has been presented as unattractive: '*stout, heavy figure, dark complexion, uninteresting features, large coarse hands, a habit of biting his nails*', and his disposition has been shown to be intrinsically unpleasant. One has little faith in Jess's future happiness, once the shock of her possible desertion has worn off. Rosy's final words to Gilbert, 'Take good care of her, or you'll lose her', have a prophetic ring. Even Sir Christopher says to him, 'Try and keep her. She's worth the keeping!' Presumably she has worth to him now because she has given up Falkner.

The play ends with Beatrice telling Falkner that he'll get over it. Symbolic this, for Beatrice (even the name is significant, with its overtones of Dante's Lady) shows the way ahead. At the final curtain Sir Christopher stands triumphant, his chosen wife at his side and his arm round his friend, now set on the right path. Looking towards the future, he says, 'Tomorrow! My wife! My friend! My two comrades.'

Values and the boundaries of accepted social behaviour have changed so much over the last century that it is difficult now to appreciate *The Liars* as the brilliant comedy of manners that it was originally judged to be. Shaw called it a 'Keen and accurate picture of smart society . . . chronically bored with itself'.[4] He sums up the play fairly and shrewdly, saying that Jones writes with 'affectionate contempt for women and friendly contempt for men, applied to their affairs with shrewd worldly common sense and much mollifying humour; whilst its essentially pious theology and its absolute conceptions of duty belong to a passionately anti-comedic conception'. Herein lies the crux of the matter for a modern audience. Beautifully crafted though the play is, and funny though the second and third acts are, the central character, Sir Christopher, obviously urbane and witty to the audience of 1897, is declaring sentiments and taking attitudes quite alien and distasteful a hundred years on. Therefore, the play does not, in the end, succeed now as a comedy. We can laugh at Restoration comedy – the society is sufficiently distanced by time; but the late Victorians are still too close to us; their values have too recently been rejected. A play which declares them, albeit satirically, as this play does, can not be wholly acceptable. We do not feel that 'the way of the world' in *The Liars* has led to a happy 'comic' conclusion. This opinion was shared by the critic of the *Illustrated Sporting and Dramatic News*, who wrote, 'I hope that Mr. Jones will never have to live in such a world as he pictures, where all the men are dogmatic, or silly, or dishonourable, and all the women pert, spiteful, vain and foolish.'[5]

Nevertheless, the importance of *The Liars* is incalculable. The satire is so strong. It presents to us with clarity the double standards and cruelty of a rigid society, observing the forms of a dual morality, serving the interests of men, and degrading the women.

Mrs Dane's Defence takes up the same themes of the double standard and of social duplicity, but not in satiric vein. It is a play which, like the *Second Mrs Tanqueray*, centres on the figure of a young women with a dubious past which is concealed, who is defeated by 'society' in her attempt to attain security, respectability and happiness. The characters are, with one exception, similar but not identical to those in *Judah* or *The Liars*; one of Jones's great strengths as a dramatist lies in his ability to depict a galaxy of well-observed social types, which are all drawn with great vitality. The exception is the part which, once again, was played by Charles Wyndham, Sir Daniel Cartaret (a judge this time, not a soldier). Sir Daniel is, if anything, even less likable than Sir Christopher, possibly because unlike Jessica, Mrs Dane is anything but frivolous. She is courageous and dignified, and Sir Daniel's deliberate destruction of her, which forms the climax of the play, is ultimately tragic; she has all our sympathy. Sir Daniel is counterbalanced by Lady Eastney, a widow whom he wishes to marry. She is compassionate and honest, and tries to save Mrs Dane: first, unsuccessfully, from Sir Daniel; and, secondly, from public exposure and disgrace. In this latter she succeeds. Sir Daniel speaks for society at its most rigid and hypocritical; she, I think, speaks for Jones.

Like *The Liars*, the play is constructed in four acts; but the fourth act here is much more satisfactory, because 'society', represented by Sir Daniel, Mrs Bulsom-Porter and the Duchess (who is never seen), is not allowed to win an unqualified victory. Mrs Dane is defeated personally, but not ruined socially. The play has two sets only. There was obviously nothing remarkable about these, as the critics do not comment on them. They do, however, comment on the ladies' dresses, which appear to have been sensational. The *Daily Telegraph* even went as far as to describe, in great detail, each dress worn by each female character in each act. Acts I and II are set in Lady Eastney's Blue Drawing Room. The fact that it is the Blue Drawing Room immediately gives one her social status: she is wealthy enough to possess a house with more than one drawing-room. Acts III and IV take place in Sir Daniel Carteret's Library. The change in locale is significant. In the feminine atmosphere of Lady Eastney's home, Mrs Dane is safe; once in Sir Daniel's ambience, with his values in the ascendant, she is defeated. Both establishments are in Sunningwater, about twenty-five miles from London. The action takes place within about three weeks, the longest interval being between Acts I and II, a period of about two and a half weeks.

The play opens with vigour, in the middle of a row between Mr and Mrs Bulsom-Porter. She is forty-five, moralistic, overbearing, intolerant, uncontrollably jealous, and, above all, a dedicated trouble-maker. He, a little older, is described by Jones as '*Flabby*, *affable*, *easy-going*'. He speaks in '*a quiet*, *drawling*, *good-humoured voice*'. Immediately the audience is introduced to the mainspring of the play.

> MRS BULSOM-PORTER. I warn you that, if you continue to pay such marked attention to that woman, I shall tell the whole neighbourhood her history.
>
> MR BULSOM-PORTER. You will please hold your tongue about Mrs Dane. Jim says that he is mistaken, and that she is not the lady he knew in Vienna.
>
> MRS BULSOM-PORTER. He is only saying that to shelter her. The fact is, she is leading Jim by the nose, the same as she is leading you and young Cartaret.

In these few lines of dialogue, we are given the salient points of the play: Mrs Bulsom-Porter, jealous of Mrs Dane, intends to publish abroad the fact that Jim (as yet unidentified) has said that he thought Mrs Dane was a girl he'd known in Vienna. The implications here are that there is something a bit disgraceful attached to the 'lady' from Vienna. Bulsom-Porter, by taking Mrs Dane's part, only inflames his jealous wife further – and in her claim that he, along with two other men, is being 'led by the nose' we see the depth of her jealousy of the attractive, younger woman. She names 'young Cartaret' as one of the victims.

Both these characters are familiar social types in Jones's

plays. Mrs Bulsom-Porter (and her counterparts in other plays) is one of 'society's' staunchest supporters. Unhappy herself, trapped in a loveless marriage, she cannot bear to think of anyone escaping from the chains of respectability which she has worn all her life. It is probable that she has had a married life (twenty-five years we learn later in the play) punctuated by her husband's infidelities. He is tolerant, lax, unable to control her, but makes no effort now to humour her. Behind them, one can see the kind of marriage which the younger characters of *The Liars* may well face in the future: a marriage which is the better alternative to social disgrace. Mrs Bulsom-Porter senses 'immorality' in Mrs Dane's past; she will do all in her power to take her revenge through the rules of the society which has condemned her to a life of unhappiness.

We are then shown Jim (Risby), who turns out to be Mrs Bulsom-Porter's nephew, once again denying that he had recognised Mrs Dane as one Felicia Hindmarsh. He had been mistaken. She will not believe him – because he refers to Mrs Dane as a 'very charming woman'. Bulsom-Porter makes matters worse by asking, 'What does it matter whether you're mistaken or no? Suppose Mrs Dane is Miss Hindmarsh, what then?' Mrs Bulsom-Porter snarls back, 'Do you consider her fit to mix in the society of your wife?' This is the crucial point. Compare this with Sir Christopher's remark in *The Liars* 'Lady Deering will not recognize Lady Jessica.' A woman may be unpleasant, hypocritical, cruel, complacent, but, if she is 'respectable' (or never found out to be otherwise), she may draw her skirts aside from someone less fortunate than herself, who has made some moral 'error' in the past. Bulsom-Porter, in fact, puts the matter in a nutshell when he then says, 'I dare say she's as fit as nine out of ten of the women you meet, if the truth were only known.' Thus, immediately, the moral issue of 'who is to cast the first stone' is raised. The whole situation of Mrs Dane's possible past is then revealed to the audience by Risby, who tells the story of the unfortunate Felicia Hindmarsh. She had been a governess to the children of a middle-aged couple, the Trents. She had also been Mrs Trent's companion. The entourage had been in Vienna when Risby had been attaché there. Mrs Trent discovered that her husband was having an affair with Miss Hindmarsh, and committed suicide. The husband, shattered by his wife's death, 'refrains from doing the sensible thing – in fact, goes out of his mind, and is at present in an asylum in the North of England'. Felicia Hindmarsh disappeared. Risby reiterates that Mrs Dane is not she, although there is a resemblance. Mrs Bulsom-Porter, not to be baulked of her prey, announces, 'I shall fully inquire into Mrs Dane's antecedents.'

Everything is now set in train for the action. The audience has been flung *in media res*. Is Mrs Dane Felicia Hindmarsh? What kind of a person is she anyway? We know immediately. Mrs Dane enters, '*a pretty, soft-voiced, dark little woman of about twenty-eight*'. Mrs Bulsom-Porter sweeps out, cutting her; Bulsom-Porter follows, and Mrs Dane is left with Risby, who has unwittingly stirred up this hornets' nest around her. He confesses the fact, and she denies that she has ever been in Vienna. He is obviously uneasy, for he says,

> I am obliged to leave for Paris tomorrow morning on my way to Switzerland. If you find yourself in any difficulty, write to me and I will reply in such a way that there can be no doubt .... I can't tell you how vexed I am to have made such a horrible mistake. But having made it, I thought I'd better put you on your guard.

This is ambiguous. Although Mrs Dane has not reacted to his disclosure in any guilty way, this last sentence has a double meaning. It can be taken at its face value; or it can mean that he's sorry he didn't keep quiet, because he knows that she *is* Felicia Hindmarsh, but he doesn't want to betray her – and so thinks he'd better warn her to prepare herself. This latter interpretation is reinforced by his next lines: 'Mrs Dane, if you think of passing the winter away from Sunningwater, I have the most delightful little villa near Mentone – untenanted – I should be pleased to place it at your disposal.' This, also, is ambiguous. It implies, first that she is going to need a bolt-hole, and, secondly, that he is prepared to act as her 'protector'. She very properly refuses his offer: 'Why should I leave Sunningwater?' He does not answer her directly, but leaves, saying that she may rely on him. Left to herself, she shows no signs of guilt, merely signs of a quite natural anxiety: '*She watches him off*; *then in anxious deliberation walks up and down the room for a few moments*.' So we, the audience, like Mrs Bulsom-Porter, do not know, and also, like her, are by now anxious to find out.

The scene continues with the entry of a character who has already been mentioned in connection with her – Lionel ('Lal') Carteret, '*a fresh*, *bright*, *enthusiastic*, *clear-complexioned English lad of twenty-four*'. It is obvious that he is head-over-heels in love with her, and just as obvious that she cares for him. She behaves, however, with great propriety, pointing out to him that she is older than he is (by three years), and that he knows nothing about her. We learn the last important fact for the future course of the play: Sir Daniel, Lal's guardian, does not approve of the relationship.

MRS DANE. Did you notice Sir Daniel looking at us down

the table? He was thinking, 'I must get Lal away from Mrs Dane.' And he has made up his mind to do it.

LIONEL. He won't wish to part us when he knows how much I love you.

MRS DANE. You haven't told him?

LIONEL. No. The truth is, a year ago I thought I was in love with Miss Colquhoun. But Lady Eastney and my father said she was too young.

MRS DANE. So it was broken off?

LIONEL. We were to wait a year, and then, if we were both of the same mind, we were to be formally engaged.

So other facts are dropped into the exposition: Lal falls in and out of love easily; he already has an 'understanding' with a 'suitable' young girl, obviously approved by his guardian. This does not augur well for the future. How reliable is Lal going to be should any crisis with Mrs Dane break? He says that he will disobey his guardian, whom he regards as his father, and marry her anyway, but she says, 'I won't come between you and your father.' We then learn that Sir Daniel is a judge ('the pleasantest judge that ever hanged a man'), and that Mrs Dane is afraid of him. Lal, however, is certain that there is nothing to fear, and that Sir Daniel will not withhold his consent. Sir Daniel's entrance has been cleverly anticipated. Our curiosity has been whetted in the same way as it was over Mrs Dane. When he enters, Mrs Dane leaves, and there follows an interview between Lal and Sir Daniel, the latter wishing to stop Lal 'making an unhappy fool' of himself! He immediately establishes himself as self-opinionated, domineering, cynical. He wishes Lal to leave England at once to 'take this post under Sir Robert Jennings'. This attitude is not as far-fetched as it may seem. It was quite customary to send young men abroad in order to part them from what were considered to be unsuitable women. Sir Daniel feels Mrs Dane to be unsuitable – in fact, distinctly shady. Where was her husband? Where has she been? How old is she? He quickly shows himself to be as contemptuous of women as Sir Christopher Deering. When Lal says that Mrs Dane would not lie about her age, Sir Daniel jeers,

> My dear Lal, fifty women out of a hundred have no notion of what truth means, and don't bother about it. The other fifty have the rudiments of a truth-sense in various stages of development, and will generally tell the truth where their own interests don't clash. But in matters of love, there isn't one woman in a hundred – there isn't one woman in a thousand, that, when she's put to it, won't lie right and left, up and down, backwards and forwards, *to* the man she loves, *for* the man she loves, *with* the man she loves, *about* the man she loves, to gain her ends, and *keep* the man she loves.

But, nevertheless, he says he won't stand in Lal's way if he truly loves Mrs Dane, 'unless there is some good reason why you shouldn't marry her'. The matter of Lal's 'understanding' with Janet Colquhoun is brought up, but Lal says there had been no engagement. Pat upon cue, Janet enters, accompanied by Lady Eastney, and in the ensuing scene, as the news is broken to her of Lal's defection, it is obvious that she is hard-hit. However, she behaves impeccably, giving Lal his freedom with grace and dignity, saying that *she* has changed her mind.

There follows an important scene between Lady Eastney and Sir Daniel. Lady Eastney, a widow, '*thirty*, *bright*, *fashionable*', quickly shows herself to be lively, sympathetic and sensible. Sir Daniel confides to her the story of the great love of his life. 'I was thrown very much into the company of the wife of one of my clients. We grew to love each other deeply, passionately . . .'. They parted, were reconciled

> and after a few mad weeks we determined to make our own happiness in our own world. She arranged to leave her home and to meet me at Liverpool by a certain train. I had our passages taken, and I remember waiting for her, waiting, waiting, waiting. She never came. I went back to town and found a letter from her. Her boy, her only child, was dangerously ill and she had stayed to nurse him. She was a deeply religious woman, although she loved me, and she had vowed to God that if her child's life was spared she would never see me again. I was heart-broken, but I send her a message that she had done right. The boy's life was spared. I never saw her again. In a few months she was dead.

The boy, of course, is Lal. At his father's death, 'fifteen years ago, Sir Daniel took Lal, and gave him his own name of Carteret, 'and I love him – I've never allowed Lal to see how much I love him – I don't think I quite know myself'.

So now we see how the cards are stacked against Mrs Dane, even though we do not know whether she is Felicia Hindmarsh or not. Not only is Mrs Bulsom-Porter baying at her heels, but a more formidable enemy has emerged in Sir Daniel. Behind the charming but weak figure of Lal there stands the image of a 'virtuous' woman, who sacrificed Sir Daniel's illicit happiness for Lal's life. Lal is the symbol of Sir Daniel's frustrated love and lost hopes. He represents the cost, in pain, of rectitude. If he can prevent it, Sir Daniel will not let Lal go to any woman other than one whom he, personally, can approve, and, preferably, mould, despite his avowed love for his adopted son.

It transpires that Sir Daniel wants Lady Eastney to marry him, despite the fact that he cannot offer her the same love as he felt for Lal's mother, only a 'very genuine attachment and perfect fidelity'. Like Beatrice in *The Liars*, she cannot make up her mind, but asks him 'to keep the offer open', and promises to assist him to help Lal make a happy marriage. The act ends with the final phase of the exposition by introducing Canon Bonsey, '*a rather jovial, good-natured clergyman about sixty, shrewd, plausible, worldly*'. He enters on the line 'Do you know, I'm rather afraid we are going to have another scandal.' Mrs Bulsom-Porter has begun her campaign by spreading Risby's story about Mrs Dane. Lady Eastney quickly shows her colours: 'How is it that everything horrid in this neighbourhood radiates to and from that woman?' It transpires that the Canon himself has been responsible for introducing Mrs Dane into Sunningwater society: 'when a delightful lady comes to church, and subscribes regularly to all the parish charities, and has a perfect mastery of the piano, and is evidently a very dear sweet creature in every way, and a gentlewoman, I don't think it's the duty of a clergyman to ask her for her references as if she were a housemaid, eh?' But, despite this, he wants 'this little matter cleared up', as Mrs Dane is to take a stall at the bazaar, and the Duchess is to open it: 'Our dear duchess is not a latitudinarian in these matters'. What are they to do? Now, Church (albeit tolerant), Law and Society are poised to investigate Mrs Dane. She goes into the conservatory, apparently much interested in the plants. Lal bursts in, indignant at Mrs Bulsom-Porter's 'malicious story', but is hustled off by Sir Daniel. The Canon quickly disappears, leaving Lady Eastney and Mrs Dane alone together. There is a short exchange between them:

LADY EASTNEY. Is there anything the matter?
MRS DANE. No! No! What should there be?
LADY EASTNEY (*with meaning*). Can I be of any service to you?
MRS DANE. In what way? (*Pause – the two women look at each other.*) I'm only a little faint. Please don't wait.
LADY EASTNEY. I'll send my maid to you. Let me know if there is anything I can do.

It is obvious from this dialogue that Lady Eastney will help Mrs Dane *even if she is Felicia Hindmarsh*, although nothing specific is said. She goes, leaving Mrs Dane alone on stage – and then we know the truth. Mrs Dane's actions betray her to the audience.

MRS DANE *watches her off* furtively, *then after a second or two*, *rises*, creeps *round at back to behind the curtain hanging over door*, *peeps through*, *watching*, *listening*, *with* drawn, frightened *face*. *Laughter*, *buzz and hum of conversation*; *strains of distant dance music*.

QUICK CURTAIN

So – she *is* Felicia Hindmarsh. The act, beautifully, tautly constructed, has given us all the relevant facts, and shown us the psychology and motivations of the characters, the formidable forces stacked against her. She has allies, but can she possibly hold out, and not betray herself? The rest of the play shows us her desperate fight for her future happiness and security.

In the next act, events move more quickly. It is two

and a half weeks later; Mrs Dane has refused to comment on the accusation; refused to prove her innocence. Mrs Bulsom-Porter has hired a private detective, Fendick, to prove that Mrs Dane is Felicia Hindmarsh. This he has done, assisted by a photograph he has had taken without Mrs Dane's knowledge. But he is sorry for her, and, with the added inducement of a large sum of money from her, denies that she is Felicia Hindmarsh. Sir Daniel, Lady Eastney, the Bulsom-Porters, the Canon and Lal all hear a letter from Risby affirming that he was mistaken. Sir Daniel, against his inclinations, for he would have preferred Mrs Dane to be guilty, agrees, at Lal and Lady Eastney's instigation, to help Mrs Dane prove her innocence. He insists, in the light of the present evidence, that Mrs Bulsom-Porter sign a formal withdrawal of her accusation. Mr Bulsom-Porter, who has already had to pay legal costs for slander suits for her past forays into the guardianship of public morality, is likewise anxious to apologise, and offers Mrs Dane his 'sincere regrets'. Unthinkingly Mrs Dane replies, 'Thank you. I was so sorry I was not at home the other day when you called. You will forgive me for not answering your note.' After that, there is no chance that Mrs Bulsom-Porter will sign anything: 'But this is a public apology!... No. I'm quite sure from my nephew's manner that he was concealing something. I shall not apologise or withdraw anything until I have made further inquiries.' As the act ends, she sweeps off, defeated temporarily but unbowed, the apology still unsigned.

Our sympathies lie with Mrs Dane; we breathe again. Perhaps she's safe? In the face of Fendick's and Risby's denials, how can she be exposed? But, like Mrs Dane, we fear Sir Daniel – and rightly so.

Act III, set in Sir Daniel's library, is the finest scene Jones ever wrote; indeed, it is one of the finest dramatic scenes of its period. William Archer declares in the *Manchester Guardian*, 'the third act is as strong a piece of dramatic writing as has been seen in our time'. In it, Mrs Dane pits her wits against Sir Daniel's, fighting for her future with Lal. She has already told Sir Daniel that she only wishes for Lal's happiness, not her own. We believe her, because she so obviously loves him. We are also aware that in the previous act Sir Daniel said to Lal, 'if I take this story to pieces and find it false, you shall marry Mrs Dane as soon as you please .... But – don't be angry with me – if I find it true, of course there's an end to everything between you and her?; Lal replied, 'Of course, Sir – presumably because he believes implicitly in her innocence; but it is a promise, and we know Sir Daniel will somehow keep him to it.

Mrs Dane has made a detailed history of her whole life, accounting for every moment since her childhood. Mr Fendick has sent 'satisfactory' written evidence. Mr Risby is returning to London to give his evidence. Lady Eastney is firmly on Mrs Dane's side. 'I shan't rest until I've worked the whole neighbourhood into a frenzy of virtuous sympathy for Mrs Dane, and a frenzy of virtuous indignation against Mrs Bulsom-Porter. Give my love to Mrs Dane, and tell her that, will you?' Sir Daniel appears to be reconciled to Mrs Dane. 'I find I'm beginning to like her very much. I think the boy will be happy with her.' Everything augurs well for Mrs Dane. We wait for her entry, but it is delayed by a further proposal of marriage from Sir Daniel to Lady Eastney. Her views on marriage are a little offbeat.

> My first essay in marriage was not a conspicuous success. On the other hand, it was not a disastrous failure. Altogether, I'm quite willing to make a fresh experiment.

But, on the other hand, I'm quite happy in my present state. It has very great advantages. I shall need a very great deal of wooing before I am induced to change it. Indeed, on second thoughts, why should I change it at all? . . . I like you very much, but, honestly I don't love you. At least (*looking him up and down critically*) I don't think I do. But there again, I'm open to persuasion . . ..

This little scene, where she again refuses him, may seem a diversion, but it performs two important functions. One is to point up the vulnerability of Mrs Dane's 'widowhood' compared with hers. Lady Eastney is wealthy, socially secure, virtuous, with an 'open' past. Mrs Dane's reticence up to this point has left her open to a great deal of attack. She has no protection, except innocence, which we know she doesn't possess. The other important point is that Lady Eastney's independence of mind is exhibited clearly. Having made herself a partisan for Mrs Dane, we feel that she will not desert her.

The hopeful mood of the act changes with the arrival of Risby. Although he steadfastly protects Mrs Dane to Sir Daniel, he shows he is unwilling to go to court if it should come to that. Left alone with Mrs Dane, he reiterates this: 'You must keep Sir Daniel from bringing it into court.' He is afraid everything will come out. We then become aware of how much he knows about her:

RISBY. . . . This history of your life that you've given to Sir Daniel?

MRS DANE. Yes?

RISBY. He has read it?

MRS DANE. Yes, and he is quite satisfied. He says it is perfectly plain and straightforward. Naturally it would be, as I knew Lucy's life almost as well as I know my own.

RISBY. And she really was Mrs Dane?

MRS DANE. Yes; when she died I took her name and became her.

When Risby leaves her, she is faced with Fendick, priming her as to pitfalls to be avoided. Through this, we learn more facts of her past, and of her cousin, Lucy Dane. Together, they face Sir Daniel, who cross-examines Fendick, to his satisfaction. Fendick leaves, and Sir Daniel professes himself convinced. He kisses her forehead, and says, 'it gives me the greatest pleasure, my dear Lucy, to welcome you into my family as my daughter'. She bursts into tears – and then makes a great mistake. She continues to cry for too long. Sir Daniel leaves her to send a note to Bulsom-Porter. She is still crying when he returns. Not in itself suspicious, but curious. Then he begins to question her about her written statement, in great detail. Gallantly, she holds her own, as he fires question after question. Then he asks her, 'Who taught you? Did you go to school?' and she blunders. With horror we hear her say, 'No. We had governesses.' He's on it like a terrier chasing a rat. '"We"? You say you were an only child. Who's we?'

From then on she's lost. All the force of the 'hanging judge' is brought to bear on her, and, struggle as she may, she cannot fend him off. Remorselessly he closes in on her. As he senses her fear, he becomes more insistent, more probing. Then, suddenly, he thunders, 'Woman, you're lying! [note the impersonality, the contempt of the term "woman"] . . . I say you're lying! You are Felicia Hindmarsh!' She can fight no more. She confesses her pitiable story to him, and tells him that she has a child by her seducer, her late employer. The boy is ten, living in

North Devon with an old servant. She implores him not to tell Lionel, not to part her from him; she loves him so much. But Sir Daniel is adamant: Lal must be told. It is unbearable as she humbles herself to plead for mercy that we know he will not give. The existence of the child is obviously the deciding factor. How can he let Lal, the son of his 'pure' love, the symbol of his own lost happiness, marry this 'fallen' woman, who has also a son, the badge of her disgrace?

Broken, in defeat, her future in ruins, she seeks Lady Eastney's help. 'I want a friend. Don't be hard on me! Don't be hard on me!'

The curtain falls, on Sir Daniel restraining Lal from following her, as she leaves with Lady Eastney.

After the great theatrical tension and power in this act, anything is bound to be an anti-climax. Yet we still do not know what Mrs Dane's fate is to be. We know that she has no future with Lal, but what about Mrs Bulsom-Porter? Having served his own ends in separating Lal from Mrs Dane, is Sir Daniel going to ruin her as well? It is with this question that Act IV opens, still at Sir Daniel's house, three days later. It is here that the importance of Lady Eastney is confirmed. She will have no truck with Sir Daniel's attitude. She is determined that Mrs Bulsom-Porter shall apologise. She calls them all humbugs.

> Isn't it all a sham? Don't we all have one code on our lips and another in our hearts; one set of rules to admonish our neighbours and another to guide our own conduct? Why should I lecture the poor woman on her duty to Society? Why should I take her name off my visiting list and pretend I can't know her?

Sir Daniel retorts, 'Because you're a virtuous woman, and

she isn't.' The outside of the 'platter' must be clean.

Lady Eastney will have none of it:

> Oh aren't you the Pharisees and tyrants, all of you. And don't you make cowards and hypocrites of us all? Don't you lead us into sin and then condemn us for it? Aren't you first our partners and then our judges?

Sir Daniel justifies the double standard:

> The rules of the game are severe. If you don't like them, leave the sport alone. They will never be altered.
>
> LADY EASTNEY. But where's the justice of this whole business? Here is this poor woman whom Lionel loves, and who loves Lionel with all her heart. Why shouldn't he marry her?
>
> SIR DANIEL. If he were your son, would you wish him to marry her? Would you wish all his after-life to be poisoned by the thought that she had deceived him, that she had belonged to another man, and that man and his child still living? Do for heaven's sake, let us get rid of all this sentimental cant and sophistry about this woman business (*unconsciously getting very heated*). A man demands the treasure of a woman's purest love. It's what he buys and pays for with the strength of his arm and the sweat of his brow. It's the conditions on which he makes her his wife and fights the world for her and his children. It's his fiercest instinct, and he does well to guard it; for it's the very mainspring of a nation's health and soundness. And whatever I've done, whatever I've been myself, I'm quite resolved my son shan't marry another man's mistress. There's the plain sense of the whole matter,

so let us have no more talk about patching up things that ought not to be patched up, that can't be patched up, and that shan't be patched up if I can stop them from being patched up!

LADY EASTNEY (*looks at him very much amused*). I wouldn't get in a temper about it if I were you!

She is quite unimpressed by his hypocritical diatribe, and asks him flippantly, 'Couldn't you manage to put a little of the fervour you waste on social ethics into your love-making?'; but she is quite determined that Mrs Dane 'shall leave the place, if she does leave it, without a stain on her character. And I intend that Mrs Bulsom-Porter shall stay in it, if she does stay in it, as a self-confessed scandal-monger.' She holds good to her word, and makes certain that Mrs Bulsom-Porter signs the apology. Sir Daniel leaves it to her, and keeps quiet, presumably because he wants to win her favour, and so her hand. But Sir Daniel still has to deal with Lal, who is being recalcitrant. This he does, quite unscrupulously, by telling Lal about his own relationship with Lal's mother, and how 'I gave her up: we gave each other up; it broke our hearts, but we did it', and asking him to renounce his 'unworthy love'. Lal, shown to be over-emotional and weak throughout the play, is momentarily persuaded, and goes out leaving Sir Daniel to tell Mrs Dane. Sir Daniel turns his attention to Mrs Dane. He knows that he has not really finally persuaded Lal. Mrs Dane could still take him away. He must force her to renounce Lal.

He is on the threshold of a fine career; devoted to his work, with a large circle of friends. If you become his wife, will you tell them your history? They will all fall away from you. Will you hide it? That's impossible. He loves you now, but in a few years time – dare you put his love to such a test? Dare you marry him, knowing that day by day he must help you deceive, till disclosure comes; and then, day by day, he must endure social isolation with you, disorder and failure in his career for you – dare you marry him? Will it be for your own happiness?

'My happiness!' she says; 'What does that matter? Tell me what is best for him.' So, outmanoeuvred, she leaves, to go to Devonshire, to her son. To Lady Eastney, who gives her Mrs Bulsom-Porter's apology, saying that it will save her reputation, she says bitterly, 'Reputation? Reputation isn't much, is it, when love has gone?' She says to Sir Daniel, 'Don't you think the world is very hard on a woman?'

SIR DANIEL. It isn't the world that's hard. It isn't men and women – Am I hard? Call on me any time and you shall find me a true friend to you and yours. Is Lady Eastney hard? She has been fighting all the week to save you.

MRS DANE. Then who is it, what is it, drives me out?

SIR DANIEL. The law, the hard law that we didn't make, that we would break if we could, for we are all sinners at heart – the law that is above us all, made for us all, that we can't escape from, that we must keep or perish.

MRS DANE. Won't it do if we pretend to keep it and force our neighbours to keep it instead.

SIR DANIEL. Even that shows we own the law.

MRS DANE. Only we mustn't get found out. I'm afraid I've broken that part of the law.

She says 'goodbye' to Sir Daniel and Lady Eastney. Lady Eastney tells her to keep in touch with her; and Mrs Dane says, 'If ever I come here again, will you receive me?' Firm to her principles to the end, Lady Eastney replies, 'If you call, I shall be at home.'

Mrs Dane leaves, to go to her son. Lal comes in, sleepy from a draught that Lady Eastney has given him. 'Well?' he inquires, meaning, has Sir Daniel got rid of Mrs Dane? 'I shall get over this, you know', he says. Left alone on stage, he falls asleep. Janet enters and, seeing Lal asleep on the sofa in the moonlight, kisses him as the curtain falls. His future, safe and conventional, is assured.

Unsatisfactory as the ending is to a present-day audience, it is interesting to reflect that it would not have been accepted entirely in its time – but for different reasons. Society had many Mrs Bulsom-Porters, and many members of the audience would have felt that Mrs Dane had got off lightly. Clement Scott, the critic of the *Daily Telegraph*, however, clearly states a different view. He condemns Sir Daniel more than Mrs Dane, and shows his full awareness of the implications underlying the play:

> When Mr. Justice Carteret utters his beautiful, moral sentiments, we feel him to be a more or less oleaginous impostor, whose desperate attempts to make the morality of his later years atone for his early want of moral tone in no wise excuse the hypocritical bias of his airy philosphisings . . . . The moral of Mr. Jones's play is that the law is harder for a woman than for a man; but it is nevertheless a trifle hard to have this enforced from the lips of such a plausible fraud as Mr. Justice Carteret.[6]

Without doubt, Jones's own heart was with Lady Eastney's views; and he shows the mitigating force that such views could have in a hypocritical social ethic. A number of critics agree with him – Lady Eastney is seen as an attractive, sympathetic figure. In *The Liars*, he shows his disapproval of society by strong satire; in *Mrs Dane's Defence* he makes an eloquent plea for tolerance and humanity. Set against the social values of its day, it is a fine and courageous play.

4
Henry Arthur Jones: Prophet of the Modern Drama

Henry Arthur Jones used his considerable powers of rhetoric and persuasion, both written and spoken, in the cause of English drama, encouraging and accelerating change and experimentation, preparing the ground in which others, including his friends Pinero and Shaw, could develop and grow. He wrote, between 1882 and 1929, a constant flow of speeches, articles and letters on all aspects of theatre, advocating, among other things, a national theatre and municipal theatres, and attacking censorship of plays. He also wrote a number of articles and letters about the cinema (a medium which attracted him) and its relation to the stage. Before his own version of *A Doll's House (Breaking a Butterfly,* written in conjunction with H. A. Herman in 1884) and long before the efforts of J. T. Grein and the Independent Theatre to bring Ibsen to public attention, Jones was pleading for a serious English drama, and inveighing against popular taste. He declared that drama should be a national art, definitely related to the great intellectual movements of the time, dealing with large themes and questions of moment; it should be brought into relation with literature to make it strike its roots into every corner of national life, to make it representative of the age. He summed up his main beliefs in a letter to a friend, M. H. Spielmann, in January 1918:

> (1) The modern drama must be recognised as a branch of English literature, and English men of letters must know and study and love it, not only in books but in the *theatre,* and must make their influence felt there.
>
> (2) The *drama* must be seen to be in many ways opposed to the *theatre,* and must no longer be considered by play-goers as a negligible appurtenance to the theatre.
>
> (3) Actors and actor–managers can never reform the *drama.* It is not their business, nor is it their interest to do so. But they can render the drama some useful service at times. They can also do the drama an immense injury if they are allowed, as they have been during the last 15 years or so, to get the upper hand of the drama, and pursue their own aims.
>
> (4) The drama will only flourish when the author has authority and vogue with the great play-going public, and when he is in supreme command of his own work.
>
> (5) The drama must be recognised as something different from popular entertainment, although it must always supply popular entertainment. On the actual stage there will never be a clear line between them. But it must be judged from a different standpoint from popular entertainment and with a different measure – it must be judged and criticised as a fine art.

(6) The drama should be encouraged and supported by Government and the municipalities, but care must be taken to endow only very charily and with the utmost circumspection, and only according to the growing knowledge and taste of the general public. It will, I think, be hopeless to endow a national theatre for many years to come.

(7) Plays must be read by playgoers – a habit of play-reading must be cultivated, as in France.[1]

Heading this list of criteria is the need for a change of attitude among literary critics. Jones constantly endeavoured to make them view drama as a serious art form, and to treat it as such; not to dismiss it as mere 'popular amusement'.

The modern English drama needs to be established on a sound intellectual basis first, and then we may begin to ask ourselves what literary adornment may be employed upon it. But in the meantime, eminent literary men must not be contemptuous of those who are fighting a tough fight against all the giant forces of theatricality, conventionality, indifference, jealousy, folly and ignorance, that they may gain a little secure foothold where the art of portraying our national English life can be practised without the terrible necessity of immediately pleasing the first, big ignorant crowd . . ..[2]

When Jones talked about the literary aspect of a play, he meant the quality of the ideas and language. The test of a popular play was 'How will it act?' but the test of a good play was 'Can it be read as well as acted?'[3] Jones felt that the passing of the American Copyright Bill in

1891, giving protection in the United States to English dramatists, was a fact 'of the highest importance of English playwrights, and the future of the English Drama. . . . It will, indeed, afford an accurate gauge of any individual playwright's pretensions, and of the general health and condition of the national drama.'[4] If an author did not publish quickly after the first performance of his play, 'it will be an open confession that his work was a thing of the theatre merely'. If the publication did not draw an interested reading public, as in France, 'then it will be a sign that our stage remains in the same state of intellectual paralysis that has afflicted it all the century'.[5]

Jones felt, however, that it would be urged that many successful plays did not 'read at all', while in many others the passages that pleased most in the study were those that bored audiences most on the stage. This led him to remark that 'there is a certain very strong antagonism between the literary and theatrical elements of a play . . . the intellectual and art values of any drama, its permanent influence and renown, are in exact proportion to its literary qualities'.[6] There had been a definite literary standard below which it was impossible for any French dramatist of standing to sink. In England, there had been no literary standard, and so no ready means of marking the literary and intellectual position of the modern drama. Jones referred also to the desirability of 'vigour and felicity of language'.[7] The language of drama must be true to emotion and action, and appropriate to character 'no matter how great the idea of a play is. If the language is inadequate it is ruined.'[8]

The second of Jones's criteria shows that, although he saw drama and 'theatre' as 'in many ways opposed', he did not envisage a divorce. By 'theatre' he meant the physical presentation of a play on stage: the arts of performer, designer, stage carpenter and scene-painter working hand in hand to enhance the text.

For a play to be 'well put on the stage' it should be so mounted that the scenery and accessories illustrated and sustained the author's meaning, and did not disturb the spectator by their inadequacy, poverty and unsuitability on the one hand, or by their over-elaboration, ostentation and irrelevance on the other. Nor should the effects created by technical theatre in any way pass for 'realism' or 'truth'. Jones considered that there was a great difference between the 'realism' created by the stage carpenter when he presented a picture of a 'real lamp-post' in a 'real London Street' and the 'truth' created by Shakespeare in his representation of life. The lamp-post and the street were 'illusions of the stage'. Scenery was necessary only to provide a background for the actors. Neither did 'truth' in drama depend on naturalistic dialogue or the 'real-life' nature of the scenes enacted. Jones considered Shakespeare to be 'a splendid rebuke to modern realism' in that Shakespeare's plays are realistic enough in all conscience, yet not mere realism. He said that Shakespeare could paint the sheer, hard, bare facts of life as truthfully as Zola, and did so paint them, with infinitely more suggestion and relation. But he never rested in them, or thought them of value in themselves.

Jones felt that one of the biggest difficulties faced by 'realism' in the theatre was the time factor:

> but never in this world was there anything approaching to a dramatic *three-quarters of an hour* in the lives of half-a-dozen people, passing in such a way and with such a volume and variety of incident and emotion as to be satisfactory or even endurable in representation to a modern audience. . . . Therefore the realist has to accept

> this astounding convention to start with, and having accepted it, why should he hesitate to accept a host of minor conventions, provided that they advance the dramatist's main business, the exposition of human life and character?[9]

Because of these conventions, Jones felt that dramatic moments in life could not be put on stage exactly as they occurred. No real life occurrence could be exactly staged; it became a question of arguing out what details should be selected, and what left out, and what proportion one should bear to the other. The type of details selected was of great importance to him:

> Lately a school has arisen amongst us which proclaims that the details of ugliness and disease are of the chief importance for us to study, and that curious and distorted forms of vice and selfishness and human degradation are the essential elements to be preserved and treasured in our plays. I protest against this with all my might. . . . I think that in this respect art should strictly follow nature by preserving a balance as nature always does – a balance of health, of beauty, and pleasure in life.[10]

In holding this opinion, Jones represents that large body of people, as evident today as in the nineteenth century, who believe that the purpose of any art should be present an ideal, which will encourage people to strive towards a higher goal, rather than to present that which, morally ugly, violent and perverted, deprives mankind of the vision or hope of anything better.

Nevertheless, Jones himself was adamant that a dramatist must have the inalienable right to use whatever matter he chooses for the subject of a play: 'The only restriction that should be placed upon him is that he shall not offend against the recognized code of social decency, and here we have a sufficient safeguard in the censorship and the 'common-sense' of most.'[11] The crux of the matter, of course, lies in the words 'recognized code of social decency'; and it is on this ground that he joined issue with the 'school which has risen amongst us', by whom he meant, presumably, J. T. Grein and the Independent Theatre, and the admirers and followers of Ibsen's 'social dramas'.

However, although at odds with the avant-garde over the proper subjects for drama, Jones was very much at one with them over the issue of actor–managers, and what he considered to be their undue influence on the theatre – despite, or perhaps, because of, the fact that he was not contemptuous of theatrical success, nor, he said, did he have any disrespect for those 'whose devotion to their own art naturally inclines them to rank it in the highest place. . . . But I hope I shall not be misjudged or censured if I continue to insist upon the comparative worthlessness of all mere theatrical success.'[12]

He felt that the demise of serious drama had occurred because of the exaggerated importance of the actor and company, and the desire for theatrical and histrionic effect, which led to the subordination of the purely literary elements in a play. He considered that the custom of writing plays as a vehicle for some star actor had largely contributed to the decline of the drama, leading to a lack of spontaneity and conviction. While the playwright was 'the actor's servant' how could anybody be seriously concerned about the drama? Because audiences tolerated almost anything, it was impossible for an actor who saw nightly audiences deeply impressed and stirred by theatrical devices not to suppose that these were more important than the text. Nevertheless, he acknowledged his inability to work without the performers, and hence, their influence on his work. An actor's personality sometimes immensely aided and vivified an author's sketch, while at other times it deadened and destroyed it. It was almost impossible to see an author's meaning except through the interpretation given on stage. An actor's interpretation could destroy the fine equilibrium of a play, and make it impossible for the author's intention to be seen; or, it could save a worthless part (and play). Jones said that any given representation of any play was only one of a possible thousand, all varying, all of them more or less embodying the author's ideas, so that he could hardly say of any one of them that it was not what he intended. But the very slightest difference of balance, of relation, of proportion, of casting, could make all the difference with the public. 'But a new play is always judged as if the author's share of it were there definitely imaged once for all, graven in the rocks.'[13]

Again, different performances of the same play by the same company could show wide variations, just as in rehearsal a play changes from morning to morning. And very often it seemed that the failure or success of a piece was due to the same causes that made it go heavily or brightly at rehearsal. Jones felt that, if very great forbearance should be asked for the *play* on the first night, much more should be asked for the actors and actresses. An author could keep out of the way and, if he were fortunate enough to have a healthy, sanguine temperament, could appraise a first night's failure at its due value; but the actors and actresses not only had to face that dreary ordeal, but had to perform a very delicate artistic operation at the same time. While the house was with them, they were buoyed up in their task; but, the moment they felt that even a small portion of the audience was antagonistic, it was quite impossible for them to keep their self-control and do justice to themselves and the author.[14]

In Jones's opinion, most members of an audience looked upon going to the play 'as an alternative to going to see a new giantess, a new conjuring trick, a new feat of horsemanship, or a new murderer at Madame Tussauds'[15] The standard of drama was lowered by the need for popular success, and by the smug complacency, the petty conventional morality of British philistinism. The main reason why there was (in 1883) no great national modern drama was deeply rooted in the social condition of the English people. There was a reluctance to face important issues in the theatre, particularly those of religion or politics. Jones felt very strongly about this taboo:

> The whole of the nature of man is sacred to the dramatist. . . . Those who would deny to the dramatist the right to depict religious life upon the stage would show, either that religion has become a quite unessential and useless portion of human life . . . or they should show why religion should not occupy the same part in the dramatist's scheme and view of human life that it is supposed to occupy in the outer world around him.[16]

Politics too could raise deep moral issues, but Jones's opinion of politicians was such that he thought politics 'a very worthless theme for any dramatic work except a farce'.[17]

Not only were audiences generally unreceptive to serious ideas on stage, but first-night audiences were also actively destructive. There appeared to be two main criteria in the judgement of a play: 'The public is the judge' and 'The public must not be bored.' In relation to the first, Jones commented that public taste was modifiable within wide limits. The public could be led almost anywhere – easily but temporarily to any kind of new sensation or falsity, strenuously but permanently to the appreciation of what was of lasting worth. Although it was believed that the public could not be educated, it *had* been educated to appreciate burlesque, and other forms of popular theatre; therefore 'shall we say that it cannot be trained to delight in the wise picturing of what is real, essential, enduring, and of perennial influence and far-reaching result in our national life?'[18]

In response to the criterion 'The public must not be bored', Jones observed tartly that the English public laughs at anything that is meant to be funny, whether it is or not. 'It is all optional, it is all relative: and when one reflects upon the huge sempiternal dullness that pervades two thirds of English life . . . one is puzzled to know what a people . . . may or may not find humorous or dull.'[19] Nevertheless, a first-night audience could kill a play, especially one of serious intention, which very rarely recovered from the hisses and jeers of a first night. Once things had gone wrong, and hissing had set in, all judgement became impossible to the majority of the audience. At the same time, 'Very often the enthusiasm of a first night is as ill-judged and uncalled for as the hissing . . . the noise that mechanically thunders over the safe advent of some outrageous masterpiece of bunkum is far more noxious than any amount of hissing.'[20] Jones considered that it was better to be blamed for work either good or bad than to be praised for work that was transparently bad; and to hiss a man who had spent perhaps some five or six months 'in the stupendous task of trying to please two thousand people, each of them with different tastes, notions, ideals, prejudices, whims, and standards, simply because he has failed to satisfy them all at all points, seems a little uncharitable and discourteous, as well as illogical'.[21]

The taste of audiences, Jones pointed out, varied, and, the more heterogeneous the spectators, the more difficult it was to please them; but it was absolutely vital for the growth of a serious English dramatic movement that the public should be educated as to the difference between popular entertainment and serious drama. Unfortunately a drama was not only an art, but also a popular amusement:

> It is a hybrid, an unwieldy Siamese Twin, with two bodies, two heads, two minds, two dispositions, all of them for the present, vitally connected. And one of these two bodies, dramatic art, is raw and pinched and starving, and has to drag about with it, wherever it goes, its fat, puffy, unwholesome, dropsical brother, popular amusement.[22]

Jones, however, was not as prejudiced against popular entertainment as his forceful style might lead one to suppose. He declared that 'of course' it was necessary for there to be 'escapist' drama 'in this over-anxious, over-wearied age . . . there is a public large enough in London, to support the widest variety of theatrical entertainments, and that will be the healthiest state of the drama when they shall be all flourishing'.[23] He also admitted that the instinct to go to the theatre to be 'amused' was a right one. By 'amuse' he meant interest and entertain.

> If a work of art bores us to begin with, there is an end of the matter. . . . To avoid ambiguity, we will put the matter thus: 'The *first* end of a play is to amuse: the chief end of a play is to amuse rightly'. . . . There is a right way and a wrong way to be amused. . . . I used

> the word 'amusement' to cover the different kinds of pleasurable excitement that a theatrical audience can obtain from a play, whether of laughter, or tears, sympathy with virtue or detestation of vice, delight in the author's work, the actor's, the scene-painters' or the carpenters'.[24]

He was tolerant of the music hall, and, contrary to a number of his fellow dramatists, saw no reason why dramatic sketches should not be allowed on the music-hall stage, thinking that the real difference lay between some half-dozen leading West End theatres, and all the other places of entertainment, be they theatres or music halls.

However, by 1893, Jones was seeing an improvement in the condition of serious drama: 'We have travelled far this last ten years. . . . We have almost ceased to translate and adapt from the French . . . the dramatic intelligence of our audience has been awakened during the last ten years; and today we appeal to a slightly more intellectual public than did the dramatists of the last generation.'[25] He observed that there had been an emancipation from puns, Puritan prejudices, timidity, and lack of criteria, and from the tendency to view the theatre merely as a pastime. He saw hope for the future:

> Not only have the ordinary subjects been treated in a more serious and daring manner, but many matters that ten or twenty years ago were considered to lie outside the sphere of the theatre altogether have been dealt with during the last few years. . . . Religion, politics, science, education, philosophy, are all likely to be dealt with on the English stage during the next generation. . . . But one cannot help asking whether it will not be a still greater and wider influence in our national life in the

> generations to come . . . if the Pulpit loses it power, will the Drama take its place?[26]

In drawing this parallel between the pulpit and the stage, Jones was stating a thesis which he developed further, on the educative power of drama. He said all drama was capable of teaching:[27] even the silliest farce or the most outrageous melodrama called forth some criticism of life and raised issues; and so drama had very strong claims to be considered a teacher. It had many advantages over the pulpit. The pulpit was a direct and absolute teacher, the drama was not:

> The drama does teach, must teach, is a potent influence and also a great art in direct proportion as it does teach; yet the moment it sets out to teach . . . it stultifies itself; it usurps a function and an authority that it has no right or business with, and it becomes a meddler and a bungler. The drama cannot directly and explicitly affirm or teach or solve or prove anything.[28]

The doctrinaire dramatist was in a dilemma: 'He must either solve his problem or leave it unsolved.'[29] If he chose to solve it he had to 'set up' both characters and story in such a way that he could provide a solution. Because of this manipulation, the solution could be accused of non-validity. On the other hand, if he set up the problem and did not resolve it, he could then be accused of not proving anything. Life does not teach directly: it is 'profounder than any copy-book', We learn from life in an indirect way, interpreting our experience. It was the same, Jones felt, with great drama. Drama follows life. It should teach, but indirectly. It should never be didactic. When it is didactic, it is 'meddlesome, one-sided, intolerant, irritating, and tiresome. Briefly, we may say, it should teach, but it should never preach.'[30]

Towards the end of his life, Jones was diverted from his role of prophet of the modern English theatre. He became embroiled from 1920 in an increasingly public political quarrel with H. G. Wells and George Bernard Shaw, both of whom he saw as traitors to England and its cause during and after the First World War (see Appendix II). He ceased to involve himself with his accustomed fervour in the affairs of the drama, although he never quite neglected it. In 1923 he made an important addition to his writings on the drama in a detailed reply to a questionnaire from Professor Henderson of the University of North Carolina: 'Dramatic Technique Revealed by Dramatists'. In this he answered very fully and scrupulously seventeen questions, among which were 'What mental process occurs when you write a play?', 'Do you always first draw up a scenario?', 'Does a specific incident constitute the starting-point of a drama?', 'Is it possible to train anybody to be a dramatist?', 'Do you visualise your characters?', 'Do you draw your characters from real life?' and 'Have you at any period altered your dramatic technique?' Jones's answers are interesting and informative. For example, in answer to question 9, 'Do you visualise your characters?', he answered,

> In most cases, not very clearly. The outside of Hamlet may be different in a dozen different impersonations, and not one of them can claim to be the Hamlet that Shakespeare *visualised.* But every one of them may claim to be the Hamlet that Shakespeare *conceived.* When I set out to draw a character, I have some general idea of his appearance, dress, cast of features, etc. But it is clear that many characters can be played with equal

> truth and effect in various guises and make-ups, and sometimes with widely differing personalities. I try very hard to *conceive* and realise every character, before I bring him on the scene; to know exactly his spiritual make-up, his mental habits and ways of expressing himself, so that, if I were compelled, I could give reasons for his acting and speaking as he does at any moment of the play. I take great pains with my dialogue, and, so far as the necessary conventions of the theatre will allow, I try to make it the exact utterance of the character in that situation. When I write a scene, I hear every word of it spoken. Here, again, the best work is automatic, and the best and truest dialogue is not that which is taken from real life, but that which registers itself upon the inner ear as the veritable utterance of that particular character.

In reply to question 16, 'Do you take your plots from real life?', he replied,

> I have indicated in my former answers how my plots grow. Any incident in real life, any paragraph in a paper, any scene of history, or even some small scrap of talk, may be the starting-point of a plot. I have never been without a good supply of plots. God sends them without my asking. I have a large drawer full of incomplete plots, jottings, suggestions, characters, and themes waiting for stories to be fitted to them.[31]

Writing of his involvement with Wells and Shaw, his daughter, Doris, said,

> All his family deplored the amount of time we felt he was wasting in unprofitable work, especially when it

1a. Henry Arthur Jones (1851–1929)

1b. Arthur Wing Pinero (1855–1934)

2. *The Silver King.* First performed at the Princess's Theatre, 16 November 1882.

3. *Judah*. First performed at the Shaftesbury Theatre, 21 May 1890.

4. *Trelawny of the 'Wells'*. First performed at the Court Theatre, 20 January 1898.

5. *Iris*; scene from the end of the play. Laurence leaves Iris: 'You could trust me now, dear, if you would but take me back with you'. First performed at the Garrick Theatre, 21 September 1901.

6. *The Thunderbolt*; scenes from the first performance at the St James's Theatre, 9 May 1908. George Alexander played Thaddens.

7. *The Second Mrs Tanqueray.* Felicity Kendal as Paula Tanqueray, in the National Theatre production, in December 1981.

8. *The Magistrate.* Colonel Lukyn (John Clements) tries to warn Mr Posket (Alistair Sim) that his wife Agatha has been arrested, and is to appear in court. From the production at Chichester, May 1969.

9. *The Liars*. Lady Jessica attempts to restrain Falkner's ardour: 'Mr Falkner! If you please. Do you hear? Mr Falkner!' Scene from Act II in the production at the Mercury Theatre, Colchester, February 1973.

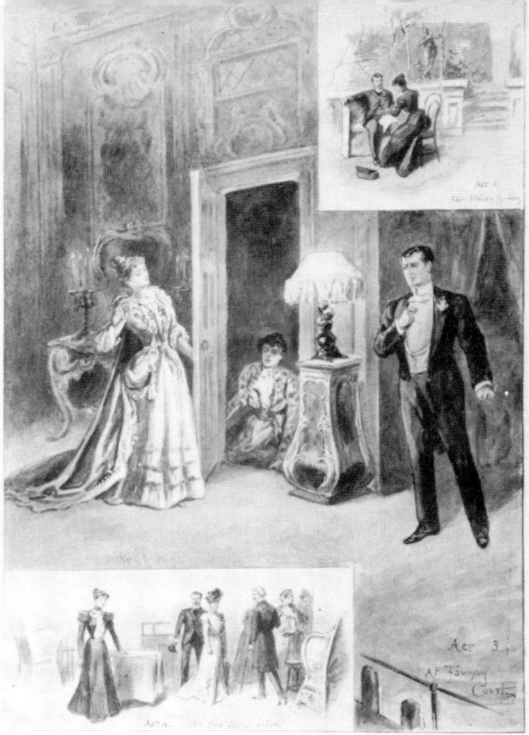

10. *The Gay Lord Quex*. First performed at the Globe Theatre, 8 April 1899.

11. *The Notorious Mrs Ebbsmith*. First performed at the Garrick Theatre, 13 March 1895. Agnes Ebbsmith was played by Mrs Patrick Campbell.

12. *Mrs Dane's Defence*. First performed at Wyndham's Theatre, 9 October 1900.

began to tell very severely on his health. But he would listen to neither reason nor persuasion, even from his doctor. Several of his more intimate friends also attempted to dissuade him from continuing his campaigns, but alas! – their efforts did not weigh in the scales against the very much larger number of people who encouraged him and told him he was doing work of national importance.[32]

When he died in 1929, he left a last message to the English people in his will. This was largely misinterpreted by an unsympathetic press in articles entitled 'Disappointed Dramatist', 'Henry Arthur Jones in his Will Scolds the Public', and the like, but the message was a summing-up of his life's work:

> I have attained great and continued success on the English stage, and my efforts have been abundantly recognised and rewarded. I acknowledge this with deep and hearty gratitude, but, on several occasions when I have felt encouraged to offer to the Public my best work, regardless of popular success, I have been so unfortunate as to meet with the condemnation alike of the Press and the Public. I say this in no spirit of bitterness or disappointment, but as an excuse for sometimes offering to the Public plays that have been below the level of my aspirations, and of their expectations. I have done this in the hope of capturing that wide and popular approbation without which no dramatist can hope for influence and authority. I am convinced that England cannot have a modern Drama worthy of he place among the nations, a modern Drama in which she can take a just and lasting pride, and for which she can claim the esteem of other nations, until our Theatre is brought

> into relation with our literature and until the great body of English men of letters take a diligent and understanding interest in the Theatre. In this conviction I have endeavoured, through the greater part of my life, to draw English men of letters to the Theatre. I have also tried to persuade English playgoers to read and study modern plays, that they may take a more intelligent interest in what is set before them in the Theatre, and may get a more refined and enduring pleasure from plays when they see them acted. I am conscious that I have largely failed in both these aims. It is with some hope that the causes I have advocated may yet succeed that I ask English men of letters and English playgoers to accept from me, in a spirit of forbearance and friendliness, this legacy of a last few words.[33]

Sadly, despite the great influence that Jones exerted in his own time through his writings and lectures on the drama, and, indeed, through his plays, very few people now realise that he existed. His theoretical writings on the drama have passed into near-oblivion; his plays are hardly ever performed, largely because the 'Victorian' sentiments expressed are distasteful to the modern mind. Nor have his plays passed into the body of dramatic literature, because his style lacks grace and, when read, his dialogue seems mannered, even unrealistic.

Unlike Pinero, some of whose work survives (though not his reputation), and many of whose plays contain issues of relevance today, Jones seems, in all but a few plays, old-fashioned and out of touch. Nevertheless, he succeeded better than he knew in his *aims* for the drama. It is tragic that he himself has failed.

5
Arthur Wing Pinero: His Life and Plays

The Life

Arthur Wing Pinero was born on 24 May 1855, four years after Henry Arthur Jones, and a year before George Bernard Shaw. His early childhood was spent at 21, Dalby Terrace, Islington, in north London, a respectable middle-class area. His parents were quite well-off when he was born, as his father and grandfather before him were solicitors. The family, originally of Portuguese Jewish extraction, by name Pinheiro, had migrated to England in the eighteenth century and, anglicising their name to Pinero, were soon comfortably established. His father, John, was past middle age when Pinero was born, and his law practice was declining. When Pinero was ten, he was taken away from school, and put to work in his father's offices in South Square, Gray's Inn, and in Prince Street (now called Bedford Square). It was assumed that he would follow the family tradition and become a lawyer. There was nothing that the young lad wanted to do less. He disliked the law, and wanted to become an actor. He had become stage-struck at an early age, because his parents were keen theatre-goers, and frequently took their young son with them. The Pineros' local theatre was Sadler's Wells, then flourishing under the actor–manager Samuel Phelps. As he grew older, Pinero was frequently given the price of a seat to attend performances there. After Phelps retired from Sadler's Wells in 1862, the young Pinero transferred his allegiance to the little Prince of Wales Theatre ('the Dust-Hole') in Tottenham Street, just off Tottenham Court Road, under the management of Marie Wilton (later Mrs Bancroft), where T. W. Robertson's plays were first played. Pinero was to say, in later life, that Robertson had been a major influence on him as a dramatist.

In 1870 John Pinero gave up his legal practice and retired to the country near Greenwich, leaving young Arthur, now aged fifteen, to find work. After working for a while in the Circulating Library in Wigmore Street, he took a place as a solicitor's clerk in a firm in Lincoln's Inn Fields, where he stayed for nearly four years. His starting salary was £1 a week, but he eventually was given a rise to the princely sum of £1. 10s. Most of this was given to his impoverished parents. In all, he spent nine years in solicitors' offices, and the influence of this can be seen in many of his plays. Not only do a number of them contain legal details, particularly to do with wills and trusts, but also his attitude to life tends to be sceptical, indeed cynical. His experience of human nature, particularly in circumstances of stress, must have been wide; and he would have seen a great deal of the law's inequity to women in a male-dominated society.

To offset the aridity of his working life, he studied elocution from 1870 to 1874 at the Birkbeck Literary and Scientific Institution, now Birkbeck College in the University of London. The class staged recitals, and even took plays and recitals on tour to places such as Edinburgh and Bristol. Pinero was soon a leading light of the class, and became reader to the elocution class. He also avidly kept up his theatre-going. His letters to his aunt Mrs Eliza Schneider are full of references to plays seen and performances noted. In a speech to the Garrick Club, at a dinner given in his honour on 12 February 1928, Pinero described his commitment to the theatre rather than to the law:

> while I was in Lincoln's Inn Fields I was often guilty of suborning my companion and, behind my employer's back, composing dramas and sending them about to the various theatres. My manuscripts were always accompanied by a letter written, to impress the recipient, on my employer's note-paper, and I remember how discomfited I was on one occasion when inadvertently he opened a letter from a London manager addressed to myself, saying 'Dear Sir, Your stuff is of no earthly use to me. For God's sake, fetch it away as soon as possible.'

Pinero was undeterred, and continued to write, even when, in 1874, at the death of his father, he was able to fulfil his childhood dream: 'I threw up my berth in Lincoln's Inn Fields and, as the saying goes, went upon the stage. I obtained an engagement at the Theatre Royal, Edinburgh, to play what was known in theatrical parlance as General Utility.' The company he joined was that of R. H. Wyndham, a stock company. He was obviously very happy. His letters to Mrs Schneider are full of bustle, energy and enthusiasm. He still managed to find time to go to other theatres, and his critical responses to plays became more and more discerning as he himself became more experienced. The parts he played were not all 'walk-ons': Le Beau in *As You Like It*, Snake in *The School for Scandal* (which he played 'with a very sallow complexion, red eyebrows and very weak-looking eyes'), Ross in *Macbeth*, Catesby in *Richard III*. Sadly, the Theatre Royal burned down in February 1875, but Pinero was fortunate enough to be recommended by Wyndham to his brother-in-law, Edward Salter, at the Alexandra, Liverpool.

His life for the next year was hectic. He worked not only in Liverpool, but also in Belfast and Glasgow. He acted with some leading players, among them Mrs John Wood, E. A. Sothern, Charles Matthews, Rose Leclerq and J. L. Toole, all of whom were talented and popular comic performers. This fact may account for Pinero's astonishing ability as a dramatist to build a comic scene to a nicety, giving performers plenty of room for individual invention, but from a secure foundation of situation and dialogue. While at Liverpool, Pinero attracted some hostile notices, but seems to have been unperturbed. In November, good fortune came his way. He was playing a role in *Miss Gwilt*, Wilkie Collins's own adaptation of his novel *Armadale* (1866), at the Alexandra. The novelist himself came to see his play and, seeing Pinero in it, gave him an introduction to R. C. Carton, manager of the Globe Theatre, in London. Subsequently, Pinero was engaged to play in *Miss Gwilt* when it transferred to the Globe in April 1876. Fortune continued to smile. Henry Irving happened to drop in to the theatre one afternoon, and was taken with young Pinero's performance. When the run of *Miss Gwilt* ended, Pinero was engaged by Irving to act as Claudius in a tour of *Hamlet* (he got a very bad notice for this performance). The tour over, he was engaged in the permanent company at the Lyceum, acting a considerable variety of parts. Within two years, he had become a London actor, with a reputation for being steady, reliable and attentive to details. He specialised in 'character parts', especially old men and silly asses.[1] He stayed at the Lyceum until 1881, nearly five years. These years with Irving convinced him of the necessity for a disciplined company, and thoroughness and hard work in the theatre. His liking and respect for Irving were considerable.

Basically, he was learning how to write at the same time as he was learning what could be done on stage. Once he had left the turmoil of the provincial theatre, with its continuously changing repertoire and constant rehearsals, and had settled to the less feverish pace of life in the London theatre, he found time to write. His first play to be staged was a one-actor called *£200 a Year*, performed at the benefit performance for F. H. Macklin at the Globe Theatre on 6 October 1877. Irving encouraged him in his writing, and not only staged some of Pinero's early one-act plays himself, but also introduced his young protégé to his friends – most notably J. L. Toole, the great comic actor–manager, who also staged some of Pinero's early work. During the production of *Daisy's Escape*, staged by Irving in 1879–80, Pinero met and fell in love with a young actress, Myra Holme. They were not married until 1883, as Pinero wanted Myra to give up the stage and she wished to continue her career. She was a widow, with two small children. Pinero was to have no children of his own, but was devoted to his step-children, particularly little Myra, his step-daughter.

In November 1881, Pinero joined the Bancrofts at the Haymarket. There he encountered a completely different atmosphere. Irving was always 'the star', and his productions were built round him, disguising his weaknesses, heightening his talents. Marie and Squire Bancroft believed in ensemble work, and frequently took minor roles in a production if they felt it was necessary for the overall balance. Their discipline and attention to detail was as great as that of Irving, but their style was different, striving towards intimacy and naturalistic effect, eschewing the melodramatic and spectacular. They and Pinero became fast friends. He continued to write while a member of their company, and it was during this period that the influential critic William Archer, in his book *English Dramatists of Today* (1882), wrote of Pinero as 'a thoughtful and conscientious writer with artistic aims, if not yet in command of his artistic means . . . [showing] sufficient promise to warrant a hope that we have in this author a playwright of genuine talent, whose more mature work will take a prominent and honourable place upon the stage in coming years'.

On 19 July 1884, he gave his last performance as an actor with the Bancrofts, as Sir Anthony Absolute in *The Rivals*, and by 1885 his long apprenticeship in the theatre was over. Asked by an American journalist whether he had found his work as a playwright influenced, helped or hampered by his experience as an actor, he replied,

> That is a big question, and certain things have to be explained before it can be answered. On the one hand I should say that the dramatist who has been an actor is better able than others to overcome the difficulties of the craft; on the other, too intimate an acquaintance with the theatre and its associations is apt to narrow a man's view of life – to beget mere theatricalism. On the whole, however, practical experience of the actual theatre is of advantage to the playwright. It shows him, if he has eyes to see, that anything can be done on the stage by the man who knows how to do it.[2]

He played one more role (Dolly Spanker in *London Assurance*), at the Bancrofts' farewell night, but otherwise gave himself over entirely to writing. He followed a rigid routine which must have been a little hard on his wife:

> He began work at tea time and was not disturbed until the following morning, after he had partaken of breakfast in bed. That is, he did not have dinner with his family or take his work out in the evening. He was working with monotonous regularity. In the morning he was a human being. And guests who were invited to see him came for luncheon and to spend the early afternoon with him. But by tea time he was restless and quite unhesitating about leaving and setting to work. This rigid schedule he followed throughout his life.[3]

There is little readily available information about Pinero's life after he ceased to act. He shunned publicity, and kept information about himself and his family to a minimum. From his letters one surmises that, between the production of one play and the beginning of work on the next, he travelled abroad. He was a friend of Sir Thomas Sutherland, chairman of P. & O. Liners, and, when a new ship was fitted out, he usually went as Sir Thomas's guest on the maiden voyage. He appears to have been particularly fond of France, and quite frequently comments on some play he has seen in Paris. In 1887 he achieved the fulfilment of a dream: he was elected to the Garrick Club. He was proposed by John Hare and seconded by Squire Bancroft. The next year, an event of utmost importance to him occurred: he made the acquaintance of William Archer, who became a life long friend. He became a founder member of the Independent Theatre in 1890. This private society was primarily founded to avoid the censor, and was able to stage plays which were forbidden on the public stage. J. T. Grein, its energetic Dutch organiser, was of great assistance to Pinero in getting his plays put on in Belgium and Holland. It is, therefore, a mistake to think that Pinero was a reactionary, not interested in developments in the theatre. Anything to do with the theatre was of the greatest importance to him. In his letters to Archer there are many interesting and illuminating remarks about Ibsen's plays, although he denied categorically that Ibsen had had any influence over him when he wrote *The Profligate* or at any other time.

By the time he had written the 'court' farces and *Sweet Lavender*, Pinero was the most popular dramatist in London, and honours began to come his way. Birkbeck, the training-ground of his youth, elected him a vice-president of the college council and appointed him an honorary examiner in elocution. Established as England's leading dramatist by *The Second Mrs Tanqueray*, he presented the address to Irving on his knighthood. This was a new departure for him, because he avoided public appearances of any kind.

By 1896, Pinero's confidence in his theatrical judgement had grown to such an extent that he was able to write to Irving suggesting some alterations in his movements in *Cymbeline* which he felt would enhance Irving's performance, and also a slight change in the lighting which he felt would make the discovery of Imogen's birthmark more plausible. Irving thanked him for his suggestions, 'which I have put into practice greatly'. In 1898, in *Trelawny of the 'Wells'*, Pinero paid tribute to the happy hours of his childhood spent at Sadler's Wells Theatre, and to Tom Robertson. In the same year, he ventured into romantic opera, at the Savoy. The work in question was *The Beauty Stone*, and the libretto was written in conjunction with

J. Comyns Carr; the music was by Arthur Sullivan. In 1903, he gave a public lecture on 'Robert Louis Stevenson as a Dramatist' to the Philosophical Institution, Edinburgh. This is one of the few public statements on the drama that Pinero made. Otherwise, with the exception of a lecture on Browning, his ideas and opinions have to be dug out of letters, or the occasional articles he wrote.

Pinero became more and more concerned with the 'politics' of the theatre. He became deeply involved in schemes for a national theatre, about which he made a speech at the Lyceum on 19 May 1908. He was one of a party, including Gilbert Murray, J. M. Barrie and W. S. Gilbert, that went to see the Home Secretary, Gladstone, about theatre censorship, and he gave evidence to the parliamentary committee on the subject. He was chairman of the executive committee for the Ellen Terry Jubilee celebrations. He was chairman of the Dramatic Sub-Committee of the Society of Authors; he was the first president of the Dramatists' Club. His letters to Shaw of this period are most amusing. He always seems to be trying to restrain Shaw from being tactless, or precipitate, in his dealings with officials or fellow dramatists. In 1909, he was knighted.

In 1910, Pinero was made a Fellow of the Royal Society of Literature. This was a great honour, showing the high regard in which his plays were generally held. The younger generation of critics, however, were beginning to criticise him. Max Beerbohm in particular was severe in his criticisms. Pinero himself said that he had never been able to understand the rancour with which Beerbohm pursued him. Archer continued to praise and to scold him. In 1913, Pinero was made a member of the Council of the Royal Society of Literature. Then came the First World War. The conflict had a profound effect on Pinero. He found it difficult to work:

> it is as if an iron door had suddenly banged and shut out the operations of one's brain before the war. . . . Various volunteer corps are being formed in this country for Home Defence. One of them is called the United Arts Force and I am its Chairman. This interests me more for the moment than playwriting.[4]

He was shattered by the sinking of the *Lusitania*, and wrote an impassioned letter to *The Times* calling upon all Germans who had become British citizens to protest at 'the policy of barbarism pursued by the German powers'. More than 400 naturalised Germans responded.

During 1916, he received the great honour of being elected to the Athenaeum, but his depression over the war was exacerbated by the long illness of his wife. She had had a weak heart for some time, was seriously ill in 1917, and in December 1918

> was terribly frightened . . . by an aeroplane which came down in a meadow adjoining my garden in Godalming, Surrey. After nearly removing my chimney pots, it hovered over her and the dogs for some time, and she thought she would never escape from it. She has been seriously ill ever since, as a consequence of this upset. . . .[5]

Six months later she was dead. Pinero grieved inconsolably. His step-daughter, Myra, came to his house regularly to be with him. He forced himself to work, hoping that 'something will come of the effort. But the theatres are in a parlous state here, and most of the managers people one would not touch with the end of a twenty-foot scaffold pole.'[6]

In January 1921, he was sufficiently restored to become

chairman of the general committee organising Warriors' Day (31 March 1921), the aim of which was to raise money for Lord Haig's Fund. The effort raised £115,140. When Pinero retired, Squire Bancroft took over as chairman. In 1922, his most popular post-war play, *The Enchanted Cottage*, was produced; but he no longer had his old confidence. With rehearsals approaching, he wrote of this play as 'a fanciful thing which may amuse or (more likely) fail miserably. . . . But oh, the altered feeling with which one enters a theatre nowadays! With rare exceptions, nothing but commercialism of the vulgarest kind.'[7] However, in another letter he said, 'if one didn't work one would go cranky'.[8]

In 1926, Pinero's dear friends Squire Bancroft and William Archer died; in 1929, so did Henry Arthur Jones. Back in 1911, hearing that Jones was ill, Pinero had written to him, 'We have been fellow-workers, side by side, as it were, . . . any mishap to you comes to me as with a sense of shock.'[9] With Archer and Jones dead, Pinero must have felt that he was beached on the shores of time – old and alone. He wrote to John Drinkwater and his wife in 1929 to thank them for their kindness in remembering his 'withered old birthday'.[10] He was now seventy-four; but little sign of his age appears in his work of the time, which shows no diminution in vigour, technical skill or invention. He died on 23 November 1934. He had been ill for some months. He was rushed from his home in Harley Street to the Marylebone Street Nursing Home for an emergency operation which was not successful.

The Memorial Service was held in St Marylebone Parish Church on the following Wednesday morning. His money (£63,310, 16s. 10d.) he left to his step-daughter Myra. At her death, the residue of the estate, his copyrights and royalties, went to the Garrick Club, the Royal Literary

Fund – and the Middlesex Hospital.

The Plays

During a life as a working dramatist which spanned fifty-seven years, Pinero wrote fifty-four plays: a prodigious output from the man who became acknowledged as the leading English playwright of the late nineteenth and early twentieth century. Even at the end of his long career, a Pinero first night was a theatrical occasion. But the aftermath of the First World War, and the rising tide of socialism, bringing with it new dramatists, critics and audiences, saw the aging Pinero becoming 'old-fashioned'. Because he was not propagating new ideals, his cynical depictions of society, with its increased materialism, were not popular. He posed problems; he did not provide facile, or idealistic, solutions. Nor did he write the brittle comedies required by the majority of West End audiences. So, he fell between two stools. He did not please the intellectuals, headed vociferously by Bernard Shaw; nor did he please the commercial audiences of the West End. Nevertheless, he never lacked an audience, and in the last years of his life he turned to experiments in theatre, far ahead of any other English dramatist of the time. He had few out-and-out failures. Many of his plays were outstanding successes. He revolutionised and galvanised an almost moribund English drama. Working at first alongside Henry Arthur Jones, his example and success in bringing serious, and hitherto censored, issues onto the stage showed other dramatists how the English theatre might be used as a vehicle for social comment and criticism, and for the propagation of ideas, yet still remain within the bounds of what the censor would pass and the audience accept. English drama and theatre owe him a great deal – a debt which is not, as yet, acknowledged.

Pinero's first six plays,[11] four of them one-acters, were written between 1877 and 1879. They are of interest in that they present in embryonic form ideas which the playwright was to develop throughout his writing career: the 'strong woman'; inheritance and its legal vagaries; compatibility within marriage; the plight of the woman who is seen as beyond the pale of 'respectable' society; the rigidity of moral standards and ideas of propriety; 'purity' as a (frequently hypocritical) ideal of femininity; youth and age; the inexorability of the past.

The turning-point of Pinero's career came with *The Money Spinner*, produced at the St James's Theatre in January 1881, after a try-out in Manchester. The play is concerned with secret marriage and its consequences. It was his first big hit and financial success. A two-act comedy of dubious morals, about gambling on both horses and cards, with a heroine who had been a professional card-sharp, it probably owed its popularity to technical facility and to the fact that the principal parts were played by the accomplished comedy performers John Hare and William and Madge Kendal. *The Money Spinner* was closely followed by another comedy, *Imprudence*, produced at the Folly Theatre in July 1881, shortly before Pinero joined the Bancrofts at the Haymarket. Clement Scott, one of the leading theatre critics of the day, lamented the cynical view of human nature that this play presented, but, again, Pinero scored a hit. The play is set in 'Lazenby's High Class Boarding Establishment' and lampoons the absurd occupants in a farcical manner. The characters are middle-class, as are those of some of Pinero's most successful later plays, and the plot structure is quite complex, balancing and interweaving three strands at the same time. In this play, it is possible to see the bones of the comic genius which led Pinero to write those plays which are commonly known as the Court farces, and it is probable that *Imprudence* would revive well.

Suddenly, when it seemed that he was set on a career of comedy-writing, *The Squire* was produced in December 1881, at the St James's Theatre. In this play Pinero did an abrupt *volte-face* and returned to an idea that he had touched on in *Hester's Mystery*: a woman farmer, and a girl who is forced to have a baby in secret – only in *The Squire* the girl is secretly and *bigamously* married. In his script for this play, Pinero initiated a practice followed later by J. M. Barrie and Shaw, who wrote their playscripts as fully as possible, in their case for a reading public. Pinero did this because he conceived his plays as *whole* theatrical entities: words, setting and performance together. He was ruthlessly perfectionist in achieving the results he wanted. Thus, the way in which Pinero describes the set for Act I of *The Squire* is of great interest and importance.

Not only does he give the overall features of the set; he also describes in detail how it is to be built. The door opening to the tower is '*five feet from the ground*'. The stone terrace has to run off into the wings, stage right. The steps, leading right centre from the terrace are '*broken and irregular*'. The iron gates are '*broken*' and '*leaning*' against the walls of the archway. The ground is '*flagged with broken stones, which are much overgrown with moss and weed*'. This is no stereotyped rural set. It is carefully thought out to the last detail, and other minute details give the age of the mansion and indicate that the owners can no longer afford to keep it up properly. The social status of the occupants of the house is suggested by the fact that it is necessary to climb up to the front door. The ground plan of the set shows other details. In front of the backcloth of farmlands there is a '*set piece with hedge and stile*' and a bank. Through the archway, stage right, there is a cart with straw. The flagstone effect is to be created with a stage-cloth. This is the work of someone who knows exactly what effect he wants and, what is more, knows precisely how to achieve it.

Significant, too, are descriptions of pieces of stage business. For example, the play opens with Christiana, a half-gypsy maid servant, actually scrubbing out a wooden pail. She then throws the scrubbing-brush, to drive a dog away from her brother. The play is full of such instructions using practicable props. A minor character, Gunnion, is described as '*a very old man, a dirty specimen of the agriculturist, with straggling grey hair, and an unshaven chin. He wears a battered hat, worsted stockings and huge boots. He speaks a broad country dialect in a wavering treble key*.' All characters are treated with similar specificity to point up their salient characteristics, physical or psychological. In his insistence on bright lighting Pinero foreshadows Brecht. He is a pioneer in his careful specification of a *combination* of things: sets; lighting; properties and stage-dressings, which had to be practicable; and the significant physical and psychological details of characters. He was one of the first playwrights to demand that actors and actresses should *look* completely right for the part, although in casting his plays he was known to change his views when confronted by a determined performer who insisted that Pinero's idea was not the only one and that he, the actor, could perfectly well play the part. In his insistence on verisimilitude in properties, scenery and costume, Pinero was following the practice of the Bancrofts; in his insistence on appropriate lighting, that of Irving (although Irving rejected electricity, and would still use limelight if he wanted brilliant light).

From 1879 to 1884,[12] Pinero occupied himself in learning his craft and trying out different ideas and types of play, as well as writing 'pot-boilers' to keep himself and his wife. He can be seen feeling his way towards characters of greater psychological depth – a hallmark of his later work. Apart from the early farces, the most interesting of Pinero's apprentice works is *Lords and Commons* (1883), which he wrote for the Bancrofts' final season at the Haymarket. Its significance lies in the fact that it deals with misalliance, a theme to which he returned in later plays.

From 1884 onwards, Pinero's work divides into four clearly defined genres: comedy-farce; 'dramas of ideas' or, as they came to be known, 'problem plays'; social comedy; and sentimental comedy. He achieved mastery in each.

Farces

When Pinero began to write farce, which he wrote all his working life, it was at a low ebb in England: mostly either a pale imitation of French 'bedroom' farce, which at the censor's demand had to be 'cleaned up' for British audiences, or crude rough-and-tumble, more akin to harlequinade than comedy; nevertheless, farcical comedy was popular, and Pinero set out 'to raise farce a little'. He had

> openly expressed his opinion that farce must gradually become the modern equivalent of comedy, since the present age being an age of sentiment rather than of manners, the comic playwright must of necessity seek his humour in the exaggeration of sentiment. Thus, *Mr Pinero holds that farce should treat of probable people placed in possible circumstances, but regarded from a*

> *point of view which exaggerates their sentiments and magnifies their foibles*. [Author's italics.] In this light it is permitted to this class of play, not only to deal with ridiculous incongruities of incident and character, but to satirize society, and to wring laughter from those possible distresses of life which might trace their origin to fallacies of feeling and extravagances of motive.[13]

Pinero also believed that a farce should be as well-structured as any other play. Ben Travers (who based his work on Pinero's) once said, 'Why do we say, "It degenerated into farce"?'

In *The Rocket* (1883), Pinero could be seen learning to structure a farce. The precision of its movement is as exact as a clock is; but the solidity, the 'probability' of characterisation and the serious satirical purpose can only faintly be descried. In his next farce, *In Chancery* (1884), which he wrote for the comic actor Edward Terry, the same applies. The structure is far more complex; the characters are exaggerated, some almost to the point of caricature. In fact, it has been said that the whole play is so 'over-the-top' that Pinero is parodying the conventional farce form.

However, it was when he began to write for the Court Theatre that he really came into his own as a writer of farce. His earlier experiments had taught him about structure and characterisation. He now put what he had learnt to good effect. His first Court farces all took specifically social targets: the law (*The Magistrate*, 1885), the Church (*Dandy Dick*, 1886), politics (*The Cabinet Minister*, 1890), education (*The Schoolmistress*, 1886) and marriage (*The Amazons*, 1893).

The two farces for which Pinero is best known, *The Magistrate* (see Chapter 6) and *Dandy Dick*, have much in common. Both take as their central figure a representative of authority, respectively a magistrate and a dean. Both men, Poskett and the Dean, are pompous, timid, gullible, hypocritical, although essentially affectionate and kindly. Both are led astray to disaster; both are manipulated by the younger generation; and, as each fresh mishap occurs, the audience waits for the next misfortune with anticipatory glee. Both endure brushes with the police involving humiliation and escape, and physical dishevelment. Both have their hypocrisy revealed and their pomposity thoroughly deflated. Both have to learn the lessons of humility and tolerance, and that they are fallible.

Of the two, *The Magistrate* works the better, because it has no weak points; *Dandy Dick* loses tension in scenes with the Dean's daughters and their irritating suitors, who would probably have been more amusing in their time than they are now. The success of these two farces probably lies in the absurd spectacle of one clearly defined figure of authority being reduced to an object of fun. Both Poskett and the Revd Augustus Jedd are probable characters placed in possible circumstances which, because of their own sentiments and foibles, gradually become more and more involved and ridiculous. All their misfortunes spring from their characters and, as such, the plays are not only funny but also satisfying. Following the success of *Dandy Dick*, Pinero, the debunker of the Establishment, was elected to that place of his dreams – the Garrick Club.

None of the other farces has this defined central character: all are concerned with groups of people, with one or two characters emerging as more important from time to time. They also lack, apart from a few isolated moments, the inspired lunacy of *The Magistrate* and *Dandy Dick*.

In *The Schoolmistress*, the eponymous Miss Dyott does not dominate the action, with the exception of a spectacular shock entrance at the end of Act II, which is incredibly funny. Miss Dyott, the typical, respectable headmistress, rides up from Piccadilly on a fire-engine, and, climbing the firemen's ladder, suddenly appears at the window. She is in the gorgeous dress of the bouffe queen, with a flaxen wig, much disarranged, and a crown on one side. Her husband gasps, 'Caroline!' She enters the room, drags him to the window by his collar – and the curtain falls.

The play focuses much more on Vere Queckett, her worthless, snobbish husband, and the girls of the school. Although much of the action revolves round the effects of what Miss Dyott does, the true centre of the play is the girls, and their attitudes to men and marriage. Underneath the absurdity of many of the situations in this play, Pinero has some serious observations to make on marriage, as indeed he also has in *The Amazons*. Pinero described *The Amazons* as a whimsical play. Nevertheless, the whimsy carries a sting. The three girls at the centre of the action are brought up as boys, because their father was disgusted that they were girls ('Damn it, Miriam,' he observes to their mother after yet another female birth, 'you've lost a whole season's hunting for nothing.') The audience is presented, albeit in comic form, with the dilemma which faces young women who, educated like men and behaving with the independence and freedom of men, find the position difficult, indeed impossible, to maintain in the face of love and possible marriage. Light-hearted and comic though the play may be, Pinero presents issues which even today are of vital importance to women struggling to survive in a male-dominated world, faced with a seeming choice between a successful career, and marriage and children.

The Cabinet Minister is quite different. The success of Pinero's first serious play, *The Profligate*, in the previous year and an awareness that the public would take stronger meat may account for the change of tone. The play, puzzling critics and audience alike, had a half-hearted reception on the first night. They found themselves laughing at seemingly serious situations which they felt should provoke tears; feeling sympathetically interested in passages of sentiment at one moment, only to see them mocked the next; in fact, experiencing constant perplexity as to their emotional duties. Dealing as it does with a grasping money-lender, a society blackmailer, stolen Cabinet papers, and idealised thoughts of life in the country, away from 'society', *The Cabinet Minister* is diffuse, lacking in in-depth characterisation, and melodramatic. It is an amazingly 'busy' play, creating a satirical picture of society life, its values, its preoccupation with behaviour, money, marriage and politics, and the people who batten onto such a society, using their wits unscrupulously to climb through its ranks. It has much in common with the comedy of manners of an earlier age, for it is more concerned with satirising a stratum of society than with presenting a close study of a respectable member of society caught in the trammels of ludicrous circumstances and brought about by a fatal decision of his own.

In *A Wife without a Smile* (1904), the subject matter is explicitly sexual, although, once again, the main focus of the play is on marriage – in this case, a remarkably unhappy, unsuccessful one. Pinero calls the play 'a comedy in disguise', but the techniques of confrontation, reversals of situation and exaggerated characters all belong to farce, albeit of a satiric nature. Unlike his earlier farces, there is no affection for the people whom he depicts. It is as if Pinero's increasing disillusion, cynicism and disgust at the society he saw around him permeated the play. It is fast-moving and well-structured, but it lacks the gaiety and sparkle of the earlier farces. There is not one character with whom it is possible to sympathise: all the characters are foolish, small-minded, hypocritical and downright materialistic. They represent some of the least attractive features of the middle-class. The press loathed the play, and condemned it for prurience and indecency.

The picture of middle-class narrowness and hypocrisy in *Preserving Mr Panmure* is similarly unattractive. The play centres round religious hypocrisy and the blight which that can cast over marriage in the home where the smallest gesture of impulsive affection is seen as symptomatic of sexual misbehaviour. It is frequently assumed, quite wrongly, that Pinero subscribed to the values of his society. This farce, if nothing else, demonstrates the depth of his dislike for the hypocritical standards imposed in the name of religion on so many households.

Playgoers (1912) stands entirely on its own, both in subject matter and technique. Once again, it is fairly acid social satire, aimed in this instance at the increasingly unstable relationship between the middle classes and their servants, a theme tackled earlier (in 1902) with disguised cynicism and irony by J. M. Barrie in *The Admirable Crichton*, and by Henry Arthur Jones in *The Lackey's Carnival* (1900). The very oddity of Pinero's play merits consideration. The playwright is working on the premise that servants dominate the household in which they are employed, and that it is impossible to find any who are completely satisfactory. J. P. Wearing considers this play to have in it elements of the Theatre of the Absurd, and sees it as initiating the series of experimental plays which mark Pinero's last phase.

As we have seen, *The Magistrate* and *Dandy Dick* are closely linked in both technique and theme. Of the other farces, only *The Schoolmistress* and *The Amazons* are similarly related, though to a much smaller degree. The rest are quite different from each other, in their cast of characters and the way these are manipulated, and also in structure.

All the farces, however, contain final 'twist' dénouements, frequently unanticipated and, therefore, all the funnier. They all contain the stock-in-trade of farce: incremental chaos building all through the play; abrupt reversals of situation; a rapid pace of action; different story-lines skilfully interwoven. Pinero frequently arouses expectation of some dénouement, only to interrupt the revelation, and delay it, thus maintaining the anticipation and heightening the subsequent laugh. Above all, the circumstances in a Pinero farce arise from choices which the characters themselves make; they are not mere puppets dancing on the strings of an imposed plot.

The humour in Pinero farces lies not only in the situations, but also in the language, which in the earlier farces sparkles from joke to joke. In the later farces, the jokes are there, but they lack the gaiety, the abandoned lunacy, of some of the earlier plays. The dialogue is full of puns and double meanings. Characters all speak their individual 'language' and often talk at cross-purposes. The dialogue also moves at great speed, and at a first hearing it is not always easy to catch all the jokes, many of which may have a common theme; for example, in *The Magistrate* there are many jokes about horses, and food.

Pinero was praised after *The Magistrate* for his style. The critic of the *Daily Telegraph* wrote, 'It is a thoroughly amusing play because it is funny without being vulgar, and ludicrous without a trace of that deplorable buffoonery which too often passes for wit.'[14] *The Magistrate* was a smash hit at home and abroad, and has been regularly revived ever since. There have been several film and television versions. *The Schoolmistress* was a hit in Britain, Australia and North America, while *Dandy Dick* was yet another runaway success. None of the other farces attained the popularity of these three.

From the very beginning, the critics praised Pinero for creating a new, entirely English variety of comedy – farce, centred on character. All subsequent English practitioners of farce have followed this model, though unfortunately the genre itself has fallen in critical esteem. It is, on the whole, thought to be trivial, and not worthy of serious consideration by intelligent people. For this reason, Pinero's brilliance and his pioneering-role have been either overlooked or patronisingly dismissed; or, even worse, he has been decried as a *mere* writer of farce whose other works cannot be taken seriously.

Plays of Ideas

Pinero's own generation none the less took some of his plays extremely seriously, and, when in 1889 he had a play called *The Profligate* produced at the Garrick Theatre, critics were loud in their acclaim, and hailed it as a breakthrough in English drama.

This play had actually been completed in 1887, but the author had to wait for two years for a production, until John Hare summoned up the courage to present it. Those people who like to attribute all Pinero's virtues to a slavish imitation of Ibsen's stage practice are here shown to be somewhat misguided in their judgement. Up to 1889, there had been only three private performances of Ibsen's work in London: *The Pillars of Society* (1880); a version of *A Doll's House* entitled *Breaking a Butterfly* (1884); and *A Doll's House*, at a charity performance (1985). Pinero himself wrote in a letter, 'When I wrote *The Profligate* I had no knowledge of Ibsen, nor have I, I believe, been influenced in the smallest degree by his works. But it is the critical fashion here to ascribe any new movement in English art, no matter of what kind, to foreign influence.[15] Pinero had sensed, nevertheless, that there was a climate receptive to serious ideas, in the theatre as well as in novel-writing, and so he experimented. Although *The Profligate* owes a debt to melodrama in its heavy use of coincidence and in the use (albeit skilful) of aside and soliloquy, and a debt to the 'well-made play' for the character of the *raisonneur*, the plot is unified and contains no comic characters or humorous interludes. The tension and moral earnestness are unremitting. The theme had been explored before by Pinero (but not in tragic form) in *The Squire* and *The Rector*: the past will always rise up to defeat the good intentions of the present and to destroy the future. *The Profligate* also contains the theme of the healing-power of 'purity' (touched on in *La Comète*). Where the play broke new ground thematically, and made its impact, was in tackling head-on the important social issue of the 'double standard' of sexual morality. It must therefore be seen in the context of the battle for the repeal of the Contagious Diseases Acts. This raged from 1864 to 1886, and it says something for the power of the campaign that the Lord Chamberlain's Office did not deem it necessary to censor the play. It is a parable, rather than a study in realism. Pinero's main protagonists are Lesley Brudenell – innocent, pure and sternly moral – and Dunstan Renshaw, the Profligate, who is debauched, dissolute, deceitful, cynical and immoral.

When Lesley discovers the truth about Renshaw, her idyllic world of innocence and illusion and his hope of salvation disintegrate. His past has reared up to confront and destroy them both. The root of the tragedy lies in the very rigidity of Lesley's morality, which, untried and immature, makes her unable to face the shock of disillusion and despair. She has not yet learnt compassion. She flees from him. There was considerable controversy over the last act. In the original version, Renshaw, thinking himself unforgiven and, therefore, lost, poisons himself, and dies just at the moment when Lesley comes to say that she will return to him. The curtain comes down as she cradles his dead body in her arms.

John Hare considered that too extreme an ending, so, for the only time in his writing life, Pinero altered a script at the request of an actor, though 'very willingly'. The alternative ending showed Renshaw deciding not to add suicide to his other mortal sins, and being reunited with Lesley before the final curtain. She says, 'We will start life anew – always seeking for the best we can do, always trying to repair the worst that we have done. . . . I will be your wife, not your judge.' Pinero printed the original ending. Both it and the one that was staged have equal virtue; but they teach different moral lessons. The first is deeply pessimistic: the destructive power of the past is infinite and, combined with rigid morality, allows no way out for a transgressor except despair and death. The second is tentatively optimistic: although illusions can never, once shattered, be rebuilt, with compassion, trust and work the damage from the past can be repaired, and there can be a future.

Although, a century later, it is possible to sneer at *The Profligate* as stagy and impossible, in its own time it had enormous impact and was regarded as a play of great significance.

Pinero's next four serious plays – *The Second Mrs Tanqueray* (1893), *The Notorious Mrs Ebbsmith* (1894), *Iris*

(1901) and *Mid-Channel* (1909) – all centre round women. The playwright has been blamed by his detractors for not writing about great social issues, but he was neither a political polemicist nor an 'intellectual'. He was an intelligent man of the theatre who wrote about the social issues which were of burning interest to the majority of his contemporaries, and did so in a form which they found acceptable and interesting and which the censor would pass; furthermore, the dominant issues during most of his working life were those connected with women and their role in, and in relation to, society. His observation of women is acute, and his delineation of them perceptive and compassionate. He always shows them trapped in relation to some man, and is particularly interested in the whole issue of the relationship between women and men, both in the home and in society. He shows what the current attitudes of society were, and his indignation is evident.

None of the women in these four plays has children: Paula Tanqueray is a *demi-mondaine* who seeks happiness and salvation in marriage; Mrs Ebbsmith is a widow living, when the play opens, with a weak, attractive man in a platonic, intellectual relationship; Iris is a widow – weak, capricious, comfort-loving, generous, but basically self-centred; Zoë Blundell (in *Mid-Channel*) is a middle-aged, cultured woman unhappy in her marriage to a philistine husband. They are all quite different. The plays are psychological studies of these women, rather than deliberate debates on themes of social importance. Through the eyes of each woman, Paula, Agnes, Iris and Zoë, an audience, or reader, learns what it is for a woman to be trapped by society if she does not possess the resources within herself, or have external help, to free herself. Pinero shows the agony of ostracism, the ruthless exploitation and manipulation of women by men – the cynical operation of the 'double standard'. He explores ideas about marriage and love. In these plays, it is not possible to extricate idea from happening, for what happens, different in each play, arises from the individual character of each woman, and each, in turn, merits serious attention. A detailed analysis of Paula Tanqueray appears in Chapter 6.

Agnes Ebbsmith (originally played by Mrs Patrick Campbell) is an extraordinary portrait of a woman who betrays what she believes in for the sake of a worthless man. Her previous life with a harsh, dogmatic father and a sensual, brutal husband has led her to the paths of women's rights; of a life where women are equal to men, where subjugation in marriage is not considered a viable way of life for a woman, and where sex is unimportant in a relationship between man and woman.

Afraid to lose Lucas Cleeve back to his wife and his career in Parliament, and realising that he is a man who craves adulation and is a sensual egotist, she fights for him with the only weapon that she realises she has: her body. Drab Agnes dons a superb evening-gown and does her hair differently. She has to make him acknowledge her as a woman in order to keep him. When he responds as she knew he would, with passion, she – despising herself – tells him she loves him. Ecstatically, he accepts this 'new' Agnes (an Agnes she knew all too well from the first year of her marriage). Sick at heart, she listens to his plans for the future, where she will no longer be an equal but – just a woman. She says, 'I believe to be a woman is to be mad', and Lucas replies, 'No, to be a woman trying not to be a woman – *that* is to be mad.' These lines give the crux of the play, as relevant now as then. What is the role of woman? To be subservient to a man's sensual need, a creature 'in a harem' as Agnes had been in her marriage? To try to live on an equal footing with a man in a platonic friendship, as Agnes had done, eschewing marriage and sex? Is it necessary for women to use the weapon of sexual attraction as a means to 'hold' men or are there other ways? Why is it necessary to 'hold' men anyway? Does the fact of being regarded by a man with sexual desire automatically make a woman an inferior, debased being? Agnes herself feels unclean and debased. She has betrayed her ideal of herself; but perhaps she has not properly understood her own nature. All her assumptions about herself are destroyed.

Shaw hated this play. He condemned it because Agnes did not have the courage of her convictions and behave as a 'New Woman' ought; also because there were slight indications that, in defeat, she might turn back to religion, which had comforted her in her desolate adolescence. But Agnes had built her beliefs on hate, despair and denial of part of herself; she could not be strong in the face of the crisis of possibly losing Lucas, because these foundations were too weak. To behave as Shaw desired, she would have had to be a completely different woman, a victor not a victim, in the face of society. It is a sad play.

Iris is another victim, in whom Pinero demonstrates all too clearly the fate of the weak. Agnes, by comparison, is not a weak woman: she has plenty of character and intelligence, but also a fatal Achilles' heel in her love for the vain, selfish Lucas. Iris *is* weak, wholly exploited and manipulated by the men in her life.

Cosseted and spoilt by her father, she makes a loveless marriage to a wealthy man much older than herself. When she is left a widow, her husband continues to govern her life after his death: if she remarries, she loses all the money he has left her in trust. This provision of his will purports to be a protection against fortune-hunters, but in reality (like Casaubon's will in *Middlemarch*) it is an attempt by the husband to control and limit his wife's actions, implying from the grave that she is not fit to take care of herself, or make her own decisions. In many ways this is true: she has never been educated, or trained, never taught to handle money. She has only ever been expected to be decorative, amusing, submissive. She has had every decision made for her. Were it not for this will, there would be no tragedy, as it prevents her from marrying the young man she loves – Laurence Trenwith.

Laurence, besotted with her, does not possess the strength of character to resist her and, ignoring the social disgrace which is brings, lives with her in a villa on the shores of Lake Como; when he wants to lead his own life, he leaves her.

The lawyer Kane (note the biblical overtones of the name) absconds with her money, leaving Iris, who is used to luxury and comfort, to live on £150 a year. This betrayal and disaster bring about one of the main dramatic ironies of the play. Now poor, Iris refuses to marry Laurence and go to British Columbia with him, because she says that she must learn to live without luxury 'patiently, uncomplainingly' first. Also she must show him that there are 'better and deeper qualities in my nature than you have suspected; and I, myself, have suspected.' When she has done this, she will join him. Laurence is too weak, or too selfish, to insist that she should go with him.

Iris is play-acting, fantasising, seeing herself in a role which is flattering to her ego, but which she is unlikely to sustain. A reformed Iris is an impossible dream, and she acts on the disastrous impulse which that dream dictates. When Laurence leaves, she is alone, ostracised, a 'fallen woman' with no friend to help her.

Poor Iris – she does not realise how puny is her strength or how powerless she is against the malevolence which lies in wait for her and which finally destroys her. She is coveted by a millionaire, Frederick Maldonado ('Maldo'), who sees her as a beautiful possession 'to be as much mine as the Velasquez, the Raphael on my walls – mine, at least, to gaze at, mine to keep from others'. Iris's original impulsiveness in accepting Maldo, and then rebuffing him by running away with Laurence to Lake Como, arouses his deep and implacable anger. When Laurence leaves, and she is alone, Maldo stalks her, and manipulates her. Once again, an impulse – the use of a cheque-book he has given her (in case she should be in need) in order to help a friend – begins the long, slow process of attrition.

When, finally, she realises that she is heavily in debt to Maldo, she flees him and his money, and descends into poverty, near-starvation and despair. But he is waiting. For the sake of a roof, food, and release from the threat of death by starvation or the inevitable final degradation as a prostitute, she becomes his mistress.

Gentle, sunny, impetuous Iris becomes apathetic, cold, bitter, and disgusted with herself and with the life she leads as a beautiful ornament. Her last and fatal impulse is to send for Laurence when she hears that he has returned to England. Pinero here shows us the double standard ruthlessly in operation. Laurence, despite the fact that he was primarily responsible for her social disgrace and friendlessness, despite hearing her pitiable and squalid story, rejects her. Although she had been *his* mistress, he is utterly unwilling to tolerate her having been the mistress of another man. He cannot accept such an affront to his 'honour'. 'I'm sorry', he says, and leaves her.

Iris ends with a scene of great power. Maldo has overheard Laurence and Iris. His jealousy and rage boil over. Originally, Pinero had intended him to kill her, but decided against this. Instead, Maldo almost murders her, but then controls himself. He turns her, penniless, out into the night, and then systematically smashes everything in the room. It would have been better had he killed her, for, although she is alive, she has nowhere to go.

The play is far more distressing than *Mrs Ebbsmith*, because the destruction of Iris is so ruthless and inevitable. Agnes has the will and strength of purpose to rebuild her life. Only prostitution and final annihilation await Iris. Pinero is unsparing in his picture of a young woman, unprotected by money or reputation, who is incapable of surviving in a hostile and uncaring world. When she was the widow of a rich man, society fawned on her; when she was penniless and alone, society, cruelly and hypocritically, looked the other way.

In *Mid-Channel*, Pinero presents a quite different problem: the break-up of a marriage, with its consequent disastrous effects on the woman. Zoë Blundell is approaching middle age, and is conscious that her life is pointless and unhappy, with no hope of becoming any better. Pinero centres sympathy on Zoë by making her husband, Theodore, unattractive and unpleasant.

He brilliantly captures her sense that life has passed her by, apart from the first, hectic years of marriage, when her husband 'in those climbing days' was making money, and they were 'greedily, feverishly happy'. She has no children; they agreed that they would never 'be encumbered in our career with any brats of children ... if there had been "brats of children" at home, it would have made a different woman of me – and – a different man of you: but no, everything in the early years was sacrificed to coining money – to shoving our way through the crowd – to "getting on"'.

Theodore has grown to be 'so stodgy, pompous and flat-footed'. Pinero here gives a scathing portrait of a self-made man who, in turn, finds Zoë embarrassing and absurd: her 'little jokes and pranks that used to amuse him so – they annoy him now, scandalise him'.

Pinero shows Zoë's craving for love, for gaiety, for her lost and wasted youth, dissipated over fourteen years of sterile, materialistic marriage. As many women in a similar situation do, she surrounds herself with young people interested in the arts – in particular, with a coterie of young men, her 'tame-robins'. With them, she can momentarily forget that she is thirty-seven, married to a boorish philistine who has 'elderly ways' and is interested only in money.

Mid-Channel is an analysis of a marriage founded on the wrong values: on the belief that money is the be-all and end-all of life. The issue of whether children are necessary to make a happy marriage is very much alive today. Zoë is probably right in feeling that for a woman such as she, with no career of her own, the marriage without children lacks a centre to maintain it as the partners enter middle age. Now that divorce is so much easier, partners in a broken marriage can make a new start, not necessarily held by the children. In Pinero's time, many a marriage was held together and cemented by the children, who gave both man and wife a central interest and focus of care. Without children, a wife was left, like Zoë, to her own devices, to fill the gap in the relationship, and there were few options open to her, untrained and lacking money.

Always quarrelling, Zoë and Theodore inevitably part, and here Pinero unsparingly demonstrates the hypocrisy of the time. Theodore can take a mistress, and then pay her off, and consider reconciliation with Zoë. She, meanwhile, is willing to ignore his infidelity, confesses an affair during the very same period with one of her 'robins',

Leonard Ferris, and is repudiated. Theodore refuses to be reconciled: 'I couldn't stoop to that. The cases are as far apart as the poles.' He is unwilling or unable to recognise that his culpability is as great (or as little) as hers. The double standard once again, with a vengeance.

Zoë's suicide is a final gesture of despair. Rejected by her husband, socially disgraced, she sees no other course of action open to her. Her desperate unhappiness is shown earlier in the play; from that point her death is inevitable.

Although the language creates some difficulty, in that the conversational style of a century ago sounds stiff and strange to modern ears, the situation and the characters still have relevance, particularly in the materialistic world of the late twentieth century. Shaw said that audiences reacted unfavourably to *Mid-Channel* because

> They are the very people you are getting at in the play. . . . The women do not want to be told that they are not wives in any real sense, but only kept women. The husbands who have brought their wives to the theatre because they are afraid of quarrelling if they stay at home, do not want to have the quarrel thrown in their faces across the footlights.[16]

The last of Pinero's 'serious' plays, *Dr Harmer's Holidays*, written in 1924 (but not performed until 1931 in New York) is one of the strangest pieces he ever wrote. In 1892, he had witnessed a trial at the Old Bailey in which three men were charged with the murder of a young doctor who, up to the events which led to his death, had possessed an irreproachable character. The young man, drunk, dirty and dishevelled, had been found by the three thugs in a public house in the Borough. They had led him away from the pub into an alleyway, where they had beaten him up and robbed him. In his struggles, the young doctor was throttled. The events were seen by a witness, and the men were caught and brought to justice. In his Foreword to the play, Pinero wrote that

> What interested me at the moment, and continued to interest me thirty years later, was the problem of the respectable young doctor – the trusted assistant of an older practitioner in the City – apparently living a sober, honest and cleanly life, who met his end in such an ignoble fashion; and I set myself to the task of forging a chain of circumstances, intensifying rather than diminishing the tragedy of his death, which would, granting the premises, account naturally for that desperate, and final, fight for breath, in those lone and noisome surroundings.[17]

The solution the playwright comes up with is a man with a dual personality; but, unlike Dr Jekyll and Mr Hyde, the two halves of Dr Harmer are completely aware of each other. The play does not present a thesis, but, rather, an unremitting picture of despair, degradation and squalor. It is immensely powerful, but in it Pinero does nothing more than offer an explanation of the story the play is based on. Perhaps he wished to shock the playgoers of 1924 and make them think about the underside of society.

Dr Harmer, for a few weeks each year, feels an obsessional craving for self-degradation and squalor. The possible reasons for this, Pinero does not tell us; but it is a known psychological phenomenon. When Harmer feels this craving coming on him, he takes his holiday, and disappears into the anonymous slums of the East End. There, he lives with a prostitute, in a room of indescribable sordidity, and addles his system and brains with bad food and drink. The play ends with the dead body of the doctor lying alone in the prostitute's room, which has been wrecked in his struggles to resist the three thugs. The play is in nine 'episodes' – an experimental structure, and one which is ideally suited to the grim story. The scenes with the prostitute, and Harmer's tragic end, are shown with stark naturalism. The world of the slums and poverty is evoked with far greater effect and truth than in Shaw's *Major Barbara*, for instance. *Dr Harmer's Holidays* is a powerful and strange play, in technique and conception far in advance of other English plays of the time. The episodic structure is similar to that employed by Brecht and Piscator. Such grim naturalism was not again achieved in the English theatre until the 1960s.

Social Comedies

Unlike his dramas, Pinero's social comedies do not centre on one character; rather, he presents a group of people interacting round a central situation. Thus, *The Hobby Horse* (1886) revolves round the disastrous consequences of misdirected philanthropy; *The Weaker Sex* (1888) is concerned with feminism, and the conflict aroused by women's conditioned reflexes towards marriage and their desire for emancipation. This play contains a situation slightly altered and repeated to better dramatic effect in *The Second Mrs Tanqueray*: that of the young girl who falls in love with a man who has, in the past, loved her mother. *The Times* (1891) presents an unlovely picture of a self-made vulgarian attempting to buy a way into society for himself and his family, with the assistance of a sycophantic, *déclassé* aristocrat; this has themes in common with *The Cabinet Minister* and *Mid-Channel*.

Three much more important comedies, *The Benefit of the Doubt* (1895), *The Gay Lord Quex* (1898) and *His House in Order* (1906), all explore marriage and attitudes to marriage, within an increasingly disillusioned and cynical framework. They depict a society which Pinero has obviously come to dislike for its hypocrisy, intolerance and lack of morals.

The Benefit of the Doubt, written in the same year as *The Notorious Mrs Ebbsmith*, is one of Pinero's best comedies. Not only is it funny, with clever dialogue and ingenious, indeed ludicrous, situations, but the view of contemporary life and marriage it takes is sardonic in the extreme. The central character, Theophila Fraser, is involved in a suit for judicial separation brought by Olive, the jealous wife of John Allingham, whom Theo foolishly (but innocently) has been entertaining rather late at night while her husband, Alexander, is away.

Although Theo is shown to be silly and impulsive, and her family self-seeking and absurd, it is clear that her husband is selfish, arrogant, without humour, priggish, untrusting and unloving. She, on the other hand, although not very intelligent, is affectionate, full of fun, laughter and kindness. Her pride at the end is nearly as stiff-necked as her husband's. In *The Benefit of the Doubt*, Pinero deals satirically with the muddle a woman can make of her life; both Theo's impulsiveness and Olive's jealousy lead them to the brink of disaster.

Olive's jealousy is so monstrous that she becomes funny, in the uncomfortable way that one of Ben Jonson's 'humours' characters is funny. Theo's behaviour is not comic, nor is that of John Allingham, but, involved as they are with comic characters and situations, they act as the 'straight men' and offset the comedy round them. The sardonic ending, where Theo's aunt, the Bishop's wife, takes Theo under her wing in order to re-establish her reputation, rounds the play off well as the final hypocrisy.

The Gay Lord Quex is a beautifully constructed play, but not a particularly attractive one. It presents a world which is hypocritical, cynical and amoral. Of all Pinero's comedies, this is the one which most recalls the type of society depicted on the Restoration stage. A young girl, pressured by her family, is to marry a middle-aged roué for social position; a discarded mistress tries to reseduce her lost lover; women hide risqué books in their bedrooms; men forgather in a manicurist's parlour to gossip as they might have done in a coffee house; the manicurist's parlour is also used as a place of assignation; young men and old alike are shown as promiscuous; female virtue is cynically regarded.

In the ten years since *The Profligate*, Pinero's stage world has changed in relation to the society outside. Sophy (the manicurist) successfully earns her living; the Duchess can hope to commit adultery unscathed; the roué (Lord Quex) reforms and marries the young girl of his choice, and lives down his past with little difficulty. The characters are not idealistic; rather, they are materialistic, shallow and self-seeking – with the possible exception of Sophy, who is good-hearted, and who learns some kind of sense of right behaviour through her experiences in the play. There is a fine scene where Sophy (the only likable character in the entire piece) confronts Lord Quex, prepared to sacrifice her own reputation in order to save her foster-sister, Muriel.

One of the interests of the play lies in the contrast it draws between the casual, indeed dubious, morals of the 'upper-class' characters and the respectability of Sophy, Frank Pollitt (her fiancé) and her work girls – the representatives of what were then firmly referred to as the 'lower classes'. Sophy may behave with vulgarity and a lack of propriety but she is far more moral at heart than Muriel, who, engaged to one man, is not above clandestinely meeting another. Pinero himself says that

> The comedy does not belong to that school of composition which labels each of its characters 'wolf' or 'lamb'; that it seeks to depict men and women as they are – not wholly virtuous nor wholly evil – I am prepared to admit. But . . . the accepted dictum [is] that a man should be judged by the good that is in him; and by this standard the Marquis of Quex is not, I submit, an unamiable personage.[18]

The play is cynical, operating within society's own standards. It is not difficult to surmise that Pinero disliked the *fin de siècle* decadence which he saw around him, and so sought to satirise it in this play.

His House in Order (1906) was universally acclaimed. It contains some of Pinero's most acerbic stage portraits, and is a blistering attack on snobbery, hypocrisy and 'noble' self-sacrifice. The play castigates those things that are done and said in the name of righteousness and propriety, and lampoons hypocrisy in many forms. It has the intensity of a Ben Jonson satire and, in the same way, holds up a mirror to the times. The image it portrays is not attractive.

Although this was Pinero's greatest financial success, making him more than £50,000, there is, however, a fundamental weakness in the play, in that the dénouement relies heavily on coincidence; the circumstance that, at a crucial moment, the letters revealing the adultery of the seemingly perfect first wife, Annabel Jesson, fall into the hands of the rebellious second wife, Nina. Also hard to believe is that Nina, having the means, through the letters, of repaying all the slights and humiliations heaped on her by Annabel's appalling family, should be persuaded not to use them.

Admittedly, she is a clergyman's daughter, but such saintly self-restraint seems rather beyond the capabilities of human nature. However, this is satire, and Pinero uses this unlikely happening to attack the whole concept of noble self-sacrifice. Another character, her brother-in-law, Hilary, releases Nina from her misery at the hands of her tormentors. Nina's pompous, selfish husband, Filmer, is made to send the family packing. Whether he will ever manage to be a reasonable husband is another matter.

With the exception of Nina, Hilary and a horrid little boy, most of the characters are more satiric caricatures than naturalistic portrayals. Hence the likeness to some of Ben Jonson's plays. Savage though *His House in Order* may be, it is, nevertheless, funny and splendidly constructed, with lively dialogue, and it aims at many of the same targets as *The Benefit of the Doubt* and *The Gay Lord Quex*. In the same biting satirical vein, but set in a middle-class milieu, *The Thunderbolt* (see Chapter 6) appeared in 1908.

Three other comedies written towards the end of Pinero's career are satirical: *The Big Drum* (1915), *The Freaks* (1918), and *Child Man*, which was published in 1930, but never performed. The targets here have changed. Pinero is no longer attacking the status of women, and marriage. The 1914–18 war brought many changes, and he saw other aspects of society which impelled him to satire. *The Big Drum* and *Child Man* centre on publicity and the effect it can have, and *Child Man* also satirises 'modern' education. *The Freaks* is an extraordinary experimental play, taking as its central characters a troupe of circus freaks.

Pinero found *The Big Drum* difficult to write. He had started work on it just before war broke out on 4 August 1914, and wrote to George Alexander, who was to play the lead, Philip Mackworth, that 'the stroke of circumstance has thrown the piece thoroughly out of touch and tone with the times' and that he might just as well 'fling the manuscript into a drawer and endeavour to forget its existence and all the thought and labour it has given me; . . . I must antedate the play and describe its period as 1913.'[19] The play is, in some ways, the most 'personal' of Pinero's plays, for it revolves round the themes of self-seeking, self-enhancing publicity, and artistic integrity. Pinero was the most private of persons and had a horror of 'beating the drum' himself. To 'beat the big drum' was to seek publicity, even notoriety. Philip, the hero, like Pinero, has a horror of such self-advertisement. He says,

> I have no dislike for publicity – for fame. By George, sir, I covet it, if I can win it honestly and decently . . . and I humble myself before the men and women of my craft – and they are many – who succeed in winning it in that fashion, or who are content to remain obscure. But for the rest – the hustlers of the pen, the seekers after more blatant applause, the pickers-up of cheap popularity – I've a profound contempt for them and their method . . . no amount of ability, of genius if you will, absolves the follower of any art from the obligation of conducting himself as a modest gentleman.

Philip also talks about capturing the great public, and this need to capture 'the great public' was one of Pinero's own criteria. Writing of the young school of modern dramatists 'knocking on the door', he said that he would like to see them writing for the 'regular' theatre, not for the 'side-shows', for 'the only victory worth gaining in the theatre is victory, by high aim and artistic means, over the great public'.[20]

The Big Drum is the last major play that Pinero wrote. Many of the pieces that follow are of great interest, but lack the substance of *The Big Drum*, which has the power and intensity of great comedy. His wife's increasing ill-health, as well as the anxieties of the war, disturbed his concentration, and with *The Freaks* he began the ceaseless experimentation which characterised his work for the rest of his life.

Although it has moments of pathos, *The Freaks* exhibits strongly satirical overtones and, like *The Big Drum*, has no facile, 'happy' ending. The play concerns a troupe of freaks (an eight-foot giant, two midgets, a contortionist, and a 'human skeleton') who, under the terms of her late brother's will, have been left to the care of Mrs Herrick, a wealthy widow. Shortly before the play opens, she has been landed with her sister and brother-in-law, Sir Norton and Lady Ball-Jennings, who have lost all their money. They have descended on her, taken over the house, which they treat as their own, and made the family's life a total misery. They are a type frequently depicted by Pinero, but with rather more savagery in this play. They are utterly selfish; very similar, in fact, to the family in *His House in Order*, parasitical, pompous, priggish, unkind, arrogant, domineering. They have no good points whatsoever. They are freaks of a materialistic society, and much of the play deals with the question of what is really meant by 'a freak'. Tilney, the human skeleton, states the main thesis:

> Besides, here is something for you to think over! (*With a wry smile.*) Who is a Freak and who is normal in this world? Who shall decide?. . .Are there no freaks in your

> list of acquaintances? Are all the women you like, and all the men you rub palms with, beautiful specimens of the normal – the Christian type? I declare to you, Miss Herrick, that looking into the faces in front of me at our shows, my hardest task has been to refrain from crying out that we ought to change places – *to change places* – the so-called Freaks upon the rickety platform and the damned sniggering spectators on the tan floor.

It is a funny (and sad) play. Pinero himself said of it, 'The little piece is simple in subject and treatment, and has no higher aim than to amuse – which I take to be the function of the theatre at the present moment.'[21] This satiric lesson of man's inhumanity to man suffered the effects of two air-raids in its opening days and, despite full houses and an enthusiastic welcome, closed.

Child Man is a savage satire on modern ideas about bringing up children and on family life; on morals; on artistic integrity and family life as they are affected by publicity. It is as relevant now as it was in 1930, and, though it has never been performed, would stage well.

The rest of Pinero's comedies have little affinity to each other in either technique or theme. *Letty* (1903) has much in common with *Iris*, in that Letty is a drifter: she nearly marries her wealthy employer, for security and riches; she breaks the engagement to become entangled with Letchmore, a decadent young wastrel. Pinero, however, did not intend him to be entirely worthless: 'I have attempted to draw, not the mere gross "man-about-town", but a creature of refinement and some culture – a man who, as you put it, is superior mentally to his conduct.' Through him Pinero states, once again, the determinism which so characterises his work. Letty realises that he has a too-easy acceptance of his 'rottenness', and leaves him.

Then, using a device followed by Shaw ten years later in *St Joan*, Pinero provides an epilogue which takes place two-and-a-half years later. Letty marries someone else, a photographer (who has appeared in the second act). She has recovered her health and happiness, and works with her husband in the studio. By coincidence, Letchmore, now a sick man, and Florence, his sister, come to be photographed, thereby contrasting the situations of Letty and Letchmore.

It is possible to draw almost any conclusion from this ending with its ironic twist, and it may be that Pinero, sardonic as ever, thought he would allow people to supply their own. Feasible interpretations might be that those who make decisions, and work hard at the life that ensues, thrive; that upper-class drifting and decadence lead to misery; that heredity will out. It is typical of Pinero, in his continual quest for theatrical growth, that at the end of what appears to be a 'conventional' satirical comedy, he should provide a technical surprise before the final curtain.

The 'Mind the Paint' Girl (1912) can be paired with *Trelawny of the 'Wells'*. It is another 'back-stage' play, also centring on marriage between a stage performer (this time a chorus girl) and a member of the aristocracy. It was a thinly disguised (and most unpopular) satire on the famous Gaiety Girls. George Edwardes, proprietor of the Gaiety Theatre, was highly indignant that they should receive such treatment, and sent in 'bullies' to break up the performance. They gave Marie Lohr, as Lily Paradell, a very bad time. Pinero was accused of libelling the stage. This was the time of the famous aristocratic 'stage-door Johnnies', who waited for the girls at the stage-door; who took them out to supper, supposedly drank champagne from their slippers and, in some famous cases, married them. The play explores the latter possibility.

It is also interesting that the leading girl at the Pandora Theatre (the play's equivalent of the Gaiety) is called Lily: perhaps a reminder of Lily Langtry, a not very good actress who was a mistress of the Prince of Wales; or of the famous Gaiety Girl, Lily Elsie. Pinero shows that, contrary to romantic notion, such marriages are often doomed to failure. Two of his girls, Enid and Gabrielle, are out-and-out gold-diggers; a third girl, now Mrs Stiddulph, is bored and discontented, and her husband miserable. To 'mind the paint' in the slang of the time meant to lead a man on as far as possible without actually being compromised. Lily Paradell is unlike her fellows: she is generous, good-hearted, and affectionate underneath her tough flippancy. She has earned her nickname from her rendering of the song *Mind the Paint* from *The Duchess of Brixton*, the show at the Pandora Theatre. There are frequent reprises of the number throughout the play.

Although three acts of the play follow in a conventionally structured manner the fortunes of Lily, and her attempts to choose between one ardent suitor and another, the second act is technically outstanding. Pinero here handles the difficult problem of numbers of parallel dialogues with astonishing skill. It does not further the plot much, but is an excuse to show off the Pandora girls in their beautiful costumes, and to provide a slice of back-stage atmosphere with the girls seen in their true colours.

In later life, Pinero was to say that he considered *The 'Mind the Paint' Girl* to be his best play. Despite its accurate rendering of an aspect of Edwardian life which fascinated the general public, and its humour, it would be difficult to find anyone to agree with him.

A Cold June (1932) is closer to his early farces than any of his comedies, and shows him to be very much in touch with the times. In its sophistication, cynicism and wit, it has a great deal in common with plays of the same period by Noël Coward, Somerset Maugham and Frederick Lonsdale, and is light-hearted and beautifully structured; the comic situations are some of the best Pinero had written since the Court farces.

In the first act we are introduced to the basic situation: at the age of eighteen June Callross finds herself confronted with two possible 'fathers' (her mother had been a dazzling lady of easy virtue). Faced in the third act by a third 'father', June's glacial sophistication cracks; she throws an immense tantrum and, at the first opportunity, flies to Lord Linthrop, a married admirer, and his yacht – telling her 'fathers' in a letter (with which the play ends) that she knows they will take her back when the affair ends. The dialogue is brisk and the action moves fast; the characterisation is excellent. The structure is nicely balanced; and the introduction of the third 'father' in the last act is a splendid piece of comic plot-building, leading naturally to the final dénouement. *A Cold June* was the last of Pinero's plays to receive its premiere during his lifetime.

What is fascinating is that it presents the same deterministic beliefs as most of Pinero's other plays: much of life is governed by chance; the past inexorably pursues the present and the future. Pinero's moral viewpoint shifts, but his beliefs remain unaltered. The 'fathers' Hugo Faulkner and Major Twinn are as much confronted by their past, in the form of June (who represents retribution for their relationship with her mother), as are Dunstan Renshawe in *The Profligate* and Paula Tanqueray.

The difference in *A Cold June* lies in the moral standpoint and the nature of the punishment. June is also the victim of her past, driven by the well-meaning but unacceptable protection of her 'fathers' into the kind of life her mother led. In 1895, Theophila Fraser has to be given the 'benefit of the doubt' for her innocent liaison with a married man, estranged from his wife; in 1932, June, unscathed, runs away with a married man, safe in the knowledge of being received back by her 'fathers'. Pinero faithfully reflects the moral values of his age.

Completely different from all the other social comedies – indeed, more related to sentimental comedy – is *The Princess and the Butterfly*. But it really stands completely on its own, fitting no category, and, despite having themes in common with other plays, such as *Mid-Channel* (in its exploration of middle age) and *Bygones* (in dealing with age and youth), it is a deliberately romantic fantasy portraying the fears, despairs and weaknesses of middle age. This it does with understanding and compassion, but also with underlying irony. The Princess (Laura) and Sir George Lamorant (the Butterfly) are both adjusting with difficulty to the slow, remorseless toll of the passing years. The structure of the play is interesting and effective. Act I deals with Laura and her women friends, all middle-aged and feeling that their lives have been wasted; all frightened of the future and meeting it in different ways; all realising that there are fewer years ahead than lie behind; 'always turned in the direction of the sunset', as Laura puts it.

Sir George provides the masculine equivalent of Laura. Act II centres round him and his middle-aged friends, and their ways of keeping the years at bay.

Acts III and IV show both Laura and Sir George deeply in love with people younger than themselves, and afraid. Pinero has stacked the cards in their favour, though, because Edward, whom Laura loves, adores her and is a grave young man, old beyond his years. Fay Zuliana, whom Sir George loves, is street-wise and worldly, and it is she who states the apparent theme of the play: 'Love, real love, cannot see age.' Act III centres on Laura;

Act IV on Sir George.

The last act takes place in the equivalent of a magic wood: an orchard near Fontenay-sous-Bois. There, in true fairy-tale style (which accords with the play's title), all is made right, but Lady Ringstead, the female *raisonneur* of the piece, and Laura's aunt, says, 'Are you sane, all of you – any of you? To me you appear like dream people – fantastic creatures.' So, wryly, Pinero comments on his own fairy-tale. The lovers do not necessarily live 'happily ever after'. In time, Edward would probably bore Laura to distraction, and Fay be unfaithful to Sir George; but, within the magic wood, in which this beautifully constructed play ends, anything is possible.

Sentimental Comedies

Despite Pinero's skill and variety as a writer of social comedy, many people think of him as a writer only of farce, or of sentimental comedy. It is difficult to define exactly what is meant by 'sentimental comedy'. Probably the nearest definition is: a play in which wit and satiric content are mingled with pathos and material aimed at arousing emotion of some kind (frequently by means of a tangled love story). Usually, plays of this kind have a 'happy' ending, so that, although tears may have been aroused, all comes right at last. Pinero wrote few examples of this genre, because his clear-eyed, satiric view of human nature did not naturally lead him that way. Nevertheless, in 1888, realising that the public had a taste for such entertainment, he wrote a play which was to become one of the most popular pieces of the late nineteenth century: *Sweet Lavender*.

The original production ran for 684 performances; the

play was performed throughout the English-speaking world, and was translated into Italian and German. Pinero was a confessed disciple of Robertson, and *Sweet Lavender* is closely modelled on Robertson's practice. In particular, it has affinities with *Caste*, in its exploration of the barriers to 'true love' set up by social class. It does not set out to be anything other than entertainment, although it is possible to discern an underlying wry tone. The central character, Dick Phenyl, is a drunken, impoverished lawyer, and, throughout all the gyrations of the plot, he stands out as kindly and affectionate, trying to reform his drunken ways and helping everyone to the best of his inefficient ability. Drunk or sober, he has many funny lines. His drunkenness gave rise to some adverse criticism of Pinero for making his most important character (though the term had not then been coined) an alcoholic. In the original production he was played by Edward Terry, a popular comic actor, who successfully revived the play several times. Pinero himself, in later life, wrote to Henry Arthur Jones that 'They may adapt *Sweet Lavender* until it is sage and onions for all I care . . . .'[22] Normally he was adamant that plays should be translated properly, not adapted. The comment seems a little ungrateful, since *Sweet Lavender* made him a rich man, and thus gave him the freedom to experiment – a freedom which led to his revolutionary play, *The Profligate*.

Pinero's next play in this genre, *Lady Bountiful* (1891) was more serious. Once again, the theme of misalliance is present, but other ideas predominate: the right use of wealth; the necessity of work; the destructiveness of poverty. The work has a wider, more novel-like scope in its action, with four different locations, and spreading over seven years. The Lady Bountiful of the title is a rich woman, Camilla Brent, who, although he does not know it, financially supports (and loves) her idle cousin, Dennis Heron, and his reprehensible, parasitical, dishonest father, Roderick Heron (whom Pinero describes as belonging to the family of Skimpole in Dickens's *Bleak House*).

The play ends on a question-mark. In a rhyme appended to the cast list in the programme, Pinero refers to 'a simple tale', containing 'no war, no lust, not a Commandment broke'. The simplicity of the story, however, is offset by the characterisation. There is a close affinity to Dickens, not only in the insufferable Roderick Heron, who is so unscrupulous and appalling that he is comic in a 'black' way, but also in the depiction of the good-hearted, kindly Veales, who gives Dennis work in the riding-school. Such comedy as there is arises from character, not situation. The death of Margaret, the wife of Dennis, also brings the world of Dickens close; but the scene is handled with the minimum fuss (no dying speech) and maximum dramatic effect. *Lady Bountiful* did not succeed as a play. Possibly the diffuse nature of the story, the genuine pathos, allied to the difficult character of the heroine, and the semi-serious handling of the themes made it too much of a hybrid for audiences to feel comfortable with it. Too much reality obtruded too often.

Pinero's next sentimental comedy, *Trelawny of the 'Wells'* (1898), was his best. This work (discussed at length in Chapter 6) is one of the few Pinero plays to have remained in the theatrical repertory since the time it was written. It is a satisfying play, full of wit and charm, and lovingly re-creates the theatre of the days of Tom Robertson. This, the period costume, the ironic undertone and the fascination that the lives of stage-folk hold for audiences all help to explain its continued appeal.

After *Trelawny of the 'Wells'*, Pinero wrote no more full-length sentimental comedies. A one-acter, *A Private*

Room, written and performed towards the end of his life (1928) has been classified as a sentimental comedy, but it is too ironic and sad a play to fit comfortably into the genre.

As in middle age Pinero had written a threnody to lost youth (*The Princess and the Butterfly*), so in his old age he wrote an elegy for wasted lives, for lost opportunity, for the might-have-been. The protagonists of *A Private Room* are General Darenth and Lady Chinnery. He is eighty, she is seventy-four. Every year for fifty years, whenever it has been possible, they have met on the same date in the same restaurant for dinner. They had been engaged, but her parents had stepped in and stopped the engagement. She had married; he had married; but, all through the years, secretly meeting on this one annual occasion, they had kept alive the belief that they would have been so much happier together, and yearned for the might-have-been.

It is a sad, sad play – such wasted lives, such false illusions. It calls into question the whole idealistic concept of romantic love, showing it to be destructive, bringing unhappiness and bitterness in its wake; making it impossible to settle for what is, because of the enticing illusions of the might-have-been. And it demonstrates the damage inflicted on men and women caught in a stifling social code.

Pinero wrote two other love stories which might be called sentimental comedy, except that he escapes from the naturalistic mode into fantasy, employing the devices of the supernatural and the dream, and experimenting with Expressionistic techniques. The first of these plays, *The Widow of Wansdale Head* (1912), is a one-acter set in the late eighteenth century.

It deals with the love of Edward Fane, a poet, for the widow Jesmond, whose husband has been dead for two years. She is the proprietress of an inn, and owner of an estate. Edward grows increasingly jealous when he hears her talking to a man in her room at night. It transpires that she talks to the ghost of her husband. The shutters of the inn, made of scrim, and back-lit, grew transparent as the ghost faded away, and his various entrances and exits employed techniques associated with Expressionist rather than naturalistic drama.

Far more wholeheartedly Expressionistic is a full-length play, *The Enchanted Cottage* (1922). This presents dream, nightmare and symbolism on stage: children appear from out of the walls; evil goblins and witches gambol round the house; thunder rumbles and lightning crackles. The play tackles the problem of a young man, Oliver Bashforth, who, horribly maimed and shell-shocked in the war, cannot come to terms with his injuries and is bitterly resentful of any kind of pity or interference. He is helped to acceptance of his life by a blind friend, and a very plain girl whom he marries.

The play strongly suggests that it is the basic things in life – affection, home and children, continuity, and honesty – which provide the path out of the morass of despair, self-pity and disillusion into which it is so easy to fall when life seems cruelly broken asunder. The idea is straightforward, but the play is moving in its simple sincerity. It has been successfully filmed twice: once in 1924 and again in 1945.

Pinero wrote one other fantasy, in 1917, and this was a propaganda play for the War Savings Committee, *Mr Livermore's Dream*. He was, in this, years ahead of his time, because it reads like a straight television commercial. Mr Livermore is impossible: stupid, greedy, selfish, self-satisfied, unpatriotic, at odds with his family over his refusal to curtail his way of life. Mr Appleton, his friend, gives him a strong lecture, which he resents and ignores. After an immense lunch of liver and bacon, and currant roll, accompanied by stout and Kümmel, he retires for his afternoon nap. He then dreams of himself reconciled to his friend, and regenerated and healthy, through practising economy; his weight reduced by a stone and a half through doing his own gardening. He wakes, and comes downstairs to realise his dream: to give up the car, and smoking; eat less, and – most important – lend the Government his savings! Critics bewailed the play's lack of 'delicacy and grace', and condemned it as being 'repulsively prosaic', but it is unashamed propaganda and, as such, the 'commercial' is amusing, direct, and effective.

Pinero's last play, *Late of Mockford's*, was written in 1934. He died before it could be performed. In the fifty-seven years of his career, he had written the best farces in English, creating a distinctive farce of character; he had launched the serious English 'play of ideas' quite independent of the influence of the Ibsen 'movement'; and he had written the best social comedies of his period. In the craft of writing for the theatre he had no equal; in his old age, when he might have been expected to turn out 'more of the same', he had experimented ceaselessly with form and technique. He raised the standards of theatre production and stagecraft; he set an example by publishing his plays at the same time as they opened on stage, so that the public could read them and pass judgement. Quite early in his career he complained to Joseph Hatton,

> I am sadly conscious that I disappoint you and many good friends. You speak of the tastes or traditions which influence me and I feel the censure which is here implied. Yet when some years ago I started my attempt to purge the popular comic play of something worse than mere

> vulgarity I had little tradition to guide me, while my tastes in this connection at any rate, though they may have been simple hardly deserve to be more severely described. I thought the work would be really serviceable to the theatre and I set out upon it with some, very likely misdirected, enthusiasm. As far as I can gather my reward is only this – blame for not having done something else.[23]

Although the comment was written three days before the opening of *The Second Mrs Tanqueray*, which received great critical acclaim, nevertheless it was not long before some critics, led by Shaw, were attacking Pinero for not having done it all differently.

All through his long career, Pinero was blamed for not being something else, for not doing something else. However, Pinero's ear was finely attuned to the public. Until after the 1914–18 war, he was closely in touch with currents of general thought.

A new Pinero play was an 'event'. With the death of his wife in 1919, and the worry and anxiety generated by the war, he wrote less. But what he did write was experimental, in touch with the development of the theatre. *A Cold June* is as much a play of the 1930s as any play by Noël Coward. *An Enchanted Cottage* catches the despair of returned, wounded ex-servicemen, and provides simple, homely and sincere advice. Its great popularity as a film after the Second World War is a testament to its lasting appeal.

Pinero's reputation has suffered an undeserved eclipse. The leading English dramatist of the late nineteenth and early twentieth century is remembered by only a handful of plays. It is time that the body of his work was again seen on stage. The National Theatre, which is committed to reviving forgotten English plays, and which owes its existence to those, such as Pinero, who campaigned so hard for its foundation, is the ideal institution to make a start.

6
Four Plays by Arthur Wing Pinero: 'The Magistrate', 'Trelawny of the "Wells"', 'The Thunderbolt', 'The Second Mrs Tanqueray'

Pinero's outstanding characteristics as a playwright are his versatility, his brilliant stagecraft, the depth of his psychological understanding, particularly of women, and his deterministic philosophy and ironic view of life. His versatility is amply illustrated by the different genres to which the plays discussed in this chapter belong: comedy–farce (*The Magistrate*), sentimental comedy (*Trelawny of the 'Wells'*), satiric social comedy (*The Thunderbolt*) and tragic drama (*The Second Mrs Tanqueray*). Only in social comedy did any other English dramatist of his time come near him in achievement; and that was Henry Arthur Jones. Oscar Wilde's plays are wittier in language, but, with the exception of *The Importance of Being Earnest*, weak in structure and derivative in plot.

All four plays clearly illustrate Pinero's stagecraft: entrances and exits, moves, the placing of furniture, the structure of acts, the positioning of climaxes, the use of sub-plot are all carefully calculated. The plots themselves are subservient. Things happen in these plays because the characters are the *people* they are, with their particular thoughts and emotions. Their lives are affected because of what they are, and what they have been. Paula Tanqueray says, 'the future is only the past again, entered through another gate'; and this belief is present to some degree or other in all Pinero's mature work, even in his most hilarious farce, *The Magistrate*.

The Magistrate was first presented at the Court Theatre on 23 March 1885, The management, John Clayton and Arthur Cecil, had applied to Pinero for a new play to help raise the theatre out of the doldrums. Although normally the Court put on serious plays, it was willing to risk Pinero's new comic play, thinking that perhaps a change of direction might alter the luck of the house. The play was a smash hit and hailed as a new type of English comedy. It ran for over a year, even over the summer holiday. So successful was it that three companies took it on tour round the provinces, and in September 1885 Pinero took his only trip to the United States, to direct the New York production, at Daly's Theatre. Productions quickly followed in Australia, India and South Africa. The play was translated into German, and played, under the title *Der blaue Grotte*, all over Germany and Austria. It became a great favourite in Prague. A French adaptation was suggested: but Pinero would not permit adaptations – only translations. *The Magistrate* was revived at Terry's Theatre seven years later, and has been frequently revived since – one of the most celebrated of modern productions being the 1969 revival, with Alistair Sim as Mr Posket. John Mills starred in an adaptation called *Little Lies* in 1983. There have been several film versions, and the play has been shown on television.

One of the reasons for its great popularity lies in the central character, the Magistrate, Aeneas Posket, and the absurd situations in which he finds himself, because he is too good-natured and weak to resist the blandishments of his stepson, Cis, and the bossiness of his clerk of the court, Wormington. Pinero's belief that farce should 'treat of probable people in possible circumstances, but regarded from a point of view which exaggerates their sentiments and magnifies their foibles' is well-illustrated. Mr Posket is, indeed, a 'probable' person. Despite his pomposity and hypocrisy, he is kindly, good-natured, philanthropic, naïve, trusting and easily led. His position as the magistrate of Mulberry Street Court has given him unique opportunities for his philanthropic ideas; and his clerk, Wormington, sees to it that he gives the right sentences. (Because he tends to pay a number of prisoners' fines himself, he doesn't always fine severely enough.)

On a holiday, drinking the waters at Spa, he meets an attractive widow, Agatha Farringdon, whom he shortly afterwards marries; here is where his troubles begin. For Agatha, vain, and anxious not to lose this chance of a secure second marriage, takes five years from her age, announcing herself to be thirty-one instead of thirty-six. This in itself is harmless enough, but Agatha has a son, Cis, who is nineteen years old. Recklessly Agatha puts Cis into an Eton collar, and announces that he is fourteen. Cis himself has always been kept in ignorance of his age and, in a parody of Victorian adolescent behaviour, believes what his mother tells him. Before he descends on the Posket household, he has been living the life of a young man-about-town, deceiving his mother, who has convinced herself that he is the innocent fourteen-year-old that she declares him to be. The play centres on the interplay of Posket and Cis, complicated by Agatha's desperate attempts to prevent Posket from finding out the lie she has told him, because if he finds out 'I should have to take such a back seat for the rest of my married life.' A sub-plot is framed round Agatha's sister, Charlotte, and her broken romance.

Act I is concerned with presenting the central characters, Agatha, Cis and Posket, and with setting the main lines of the plot. The first section of the act concentrates on the effect that Cis has on those around him. Early in the action, Cis's real age is revealed to the audience, and much amusement is derived from his behaviour, which certainly is not that of a lad of fourteen. Agatha, his mother, confesses her lie to the audience: 'Fourteen! Oh what an idiot I have been to conceal my child's real age!' She does not disclose his true age, or her reasons for hiding it. The information is imparted in an aside – a device which Pinero eventually did much to banish from the stage, but which, for the purposes of farce, is useful and often comical. It is later in the scene, in a conversation with Charlotte, that the whole truth is told.

Cis has a disturbing effect. He flirts with his young music-teacher, Beatie (a protégée of Posket's); the romance-reading parlour maid, Popham, is madly in love with him; Cook has never been the same, we are told, since he arrived. He smokes and drinks. He has bribed Wyke the butler, one of Posket's reformed criminals, to obtain drink for him. Wyke says of him, 'What a young gentleman it is! and only fourteen! Fourteen – he behaves like forty!' He calls his stepfather 'the mildest, meekest of men' who wouldn't say 'Boo to a goose'; enticing him and Bullamy, his fellow magistrate, to gamble at cards, he fleeces them both. Bullamy is an incessant sucker of jujubes (fruit gums) and it is a sign of his humiliation at Cis's hands that he has no jujubes left at the end of the game. Mr Bullamy's eating or offering of jujubes and the cracking underfoot of nuts scattered earlier by Beatie, who was illicitly eating them, are running gags in this scene, extraneous to the action but comic in themselves. The comic business and the dialogue, which is frequently at cross-purposes, lend a somewhat lunatic air to the proceedings.

Each character has some individual quirk which gives rise to laughter: Agatha's vanity and fear of her lie being found out; Charlotte's attitude to her broken romance and her desire for food; Bullamy's pomposity and his continual sucking of jujubes; Beatie's and Popham's infatuation with Cis, and their rivalry; Posket's inability to stand up to Cis's blandishments. Posket's good heart, his weakness of will, his timorousness, and his desire for respectability are the traits in his character which enable Cis to enmesh him; but also there is obviously within Posket a repressed desire to kick over the traces and enjoy himself. When he has to give a bribe to Wyke, he is so shocked at himself, and so nervous, that he makes a mess of it and hands the outraged Wyke only twopence, a mistake which comes home to roost later in the play.

The structural centre of the first act lies in the formalised letter-reading, which gives the plot its main impetus. Two of the characters, Cis and Agatha, are given a reason to go to the Hôtel des Princes. Cis involves Posket, and Agatha, Charlotte. Posket's letter from his old friend Colonel Lukyn panics Agatha, for Lukyn is Cis's godfather and can reveal the truth about her own and Cis's ages; Cis's letter is from Achille Blond, the proprietor of the Hôtel des Princes, demanding that Cis settle his account. Charlotte's letter from her fiancé, Captain Vale, breaking off their engagement, and Agatha's letter from Lady Jenkin are not central to the main plot, but both are intertwined with it and used to comic effect.

The act ends in a rush. Agatha and Charlotte, unbeknown to Posket, dash away to find Lukyn, but ostensibly to sit with Lady Jenkins, who is unwell. A few moments later, a reluctant Posket is dragged off by Cis to pay his bill at the Hôtel des Princes and, as the audience realises, to inevitable disaster.

By the end of this act, Posket has been established as a gullible, but likable man, who is as putty in Cis's unscrupulous hands. Only calamity can befall him. He is a 'probable person', but his circumstances, manipulated by Cis, are becoming increasingly less 'possible'. He has many foibles: not only his kindness, timidity and pliability, but also pomposity and hypocrisy. Once he sets event in train through any one of these, circumstances will remorselessly entrap him. Agatha's vanity has been the mainspring of the action; but it is Posket who will trigger further developments.

The momentum generated at the end of Act I is carried over in to Act II. Cis and Posket are the first to arrive at the Hôtel des Princes, and Posket is initiated into more villainy by Cis. When Lukyn and Vale arrive, the device of putting Cis and Posket into the next room is ingenious. The audience is conscious of their presence, and of Posket's increasingly uninhibited enjoyment, as laughter and song sound through the wall. Also, a showdown with Agatha seems inevitable, and the audience anticipates this. It also awaits the inevitable meeting between Charlotte and Vale, her ex-fiancé.

All through the conversation carried on at cross-purposes between Agatha and Colonel Lukyn, expectations are aroused that Vale, out on the unsafe balcony in the pouring rain, will go crashing though. He is brought back into the room because he is hungry, as is Charlotte. Much of the 'business' concerning the meal verges on slapstick, and needs most careful timing. The use of properties, all connected with food, is important. Charlotte's determined munching of any food she can get, and her insistence on staying for a meal, is the cause of her own and Agatha's downfall.

The act gathers speed, culminating in the police raid. The immediate thought in the audience's mind is 'What will happen to Mr Posket?' When he and Cis dash into the darkened room, and he flings himself under the table (unsuspectingly apologising to Agatha, who is already there); it is only the entrance of the police which prevents the anticipated dénouement – yet another use of delayed revelation, a technique Pinero uses to such effect a number of times in the play. One of the chief reasons for laughter in this scene is that, apart from Cis, all the people down on their hands and knees, hiding from the police, are so respectable; and, worst of all, Posket, that pillar of the law, incorruptibility itself, is breaking the law. His exposure is awaited with glee; but Cis, that hardened embryo reprobate, grabs him from under the table and whisks him onto the balcony. Then the misfortune anticipated by Lukyn, and the audience, for Vale occurs: the balcony collapses – another instance of the interrupted pay-off. The collapse occurs to great effect, with many cries and crashes of broken glass. Off speed Cis and Posket, with some of the police in hot pursuit. Again Pinero arouses the audience's anticipation: whatever will happen to Mr Posket now? In the meantime, the lights go up on stage. The four unfortunates are arrested. The women veil themselves, and give false names. They are taken away, to appear in the magistrate's court in the morning. The audience waits, expectant. This time its hopes are fulfilled. They are to appear in front of Mr Posket.

The act builds from the entrance of Charlotte and Agatha until the curtain. The dexterity of movement and speed of timing required to keep the momentum are considerable, and, although the action slows down after Cis and Posket escape through the window, the final lines of the act are a fitting climax:

INSPECTOR MESSITER. Very sorry, gentlemen, but you and your party are in my custody.

LUKYN.
VALE. } What!

AGATHA.
CHARLOTTE. } Oh!

MESSITER. For assaulting this man in the execution of his duty.

LUKYN. You'll dare to lock me up all night?

MESSITER. It's one o'clock now, Colonel–you'll come on first thing in the morning.

LUKYN. Come on. At what?

MESSITER. Mulberry Street.

AGATHA. (*with a scream*). Ah! The Magistrate?

MESSITER. Mr Posket, mum.

AGATHA *sinks into chair,* CHARLOTTE *at her feet.* LUKYN, *overcome, falls on* VALE'*s shoulders*.

CURTAIN

Act III is divided into two scenes: the first takes place in the Magistrate's Room at Mulberry Street, and the second in Mr Posket's drawing-room, the setting for Act I. Scene i has fewer characters than any other scene, and is quite static compared with the frenetic activity of the previous act. Two questions dominate the opening of scene i: what has happened to Mr Posket, and what will he do when confronted with his wife in court? The first question is quickly answered. It is not until the very end of the scene that the audience know the answer to the second. Pinero provides many humorous situations in between. At the beginning, Posket's ragged and dishevelled appearance provides the main comic focus of the action. He obtains a bright red tie, which makes his appearance still less sober, and gives an account of his escape, narrated in a brilliantly handled soliloquy. He shows no concern when Wyke announces that Agatha has not been home all night. Wyke behaves insolently and returns the twopenny bribe. The next 'set piece' is the interview with Lukyn and the lead up to it, where Wormington is trying to stiffen Posket's resolve. Posket wriggles and squirms, trying to avoid imposing any severe sentence, but Wormington is probity itself. Mr Posket represents the law and there must be no backsliding. Bolstered by Wormington, and as much to impress him as to impress Lukyn, Posket lectures a fuming Lukyn on morality. His pomposity and hypocrisy are outrageous. This is Posket at his worst, a Posket who so far has only been hinted at. The function of this interview is twofold: first, to reveal Posket's less amiable characteristics, and through him to cast a satirical eye on social hypocrisy; second, to build up the audience's expectations of his reaction when he finds himself confronted by his wife.

Agatha's lies to him about Lady Jenkins' illness now play a part. Wyke comes rushing in to tell him that Agatha has never been to Lady Jenkins – she is missing. Posket is frantic, but he has to go in to court to sentence the rest of the malefactors from the Hôtel des Princes. He staggers towards Nemesis on Wormington's arm.

As in a Greek tragedy, the action now takes place offstage, although Police Sergeant Lugg and Wyke remain on stage, discussing Posket's vagaries. This is a good piece of stagecraft, because it gives Mr Posket time to get into court, and presumably, for Agatha and Charlotte to remove their veils. The audience waits. Shrieks are heard. Still the result is unknown. What is happening? More shrieks; then at last Mr Posket staggers on, supported by Wormington. It is not until the last line of the scene that the suspense is broken. He has sentenced Agatha and Charlotte to 'seven days, without the option of a fine'.

As the curtain goes up on the last scene, the question is, how is it all going to be sorted out? The scene opens with Cis and his two young ladies. His condition is as deplorable as Posket's, but his spirits are much better. The scene starts slowly, but, as more and more characters enter, it gains tempo. The action centres on two revelations: Agatha's deception and Cis's true age, and Posket's guilt and hypocrisy.

The scene begins to build incrementally with the arrival home of the shattered Posket; then Bullamy, using his powers as a magistrate, returns Agatha and Charlotte safely. He is once again sucking jujubes, the symbol of his self-esteem. Charlotte, seeing Cis's breakfast, brought him by a loving Popham, shrieks 'Food!' and falls upon it. As the inevitable showdown between Agatha and Posket begins, Charlotte picks up the tray and tiptoes from the room, thus completing the running gag about her hunger. The food gag is then taken up by Agatha, who crams her mouth full of teacake, thus putting her at a severe disadvantage in her quarrel with Posket. As their row becomes increasingly acrimonious, Cis saunters on, in clean clothes and full of the joys of spring. Once more, he comes to Posket's rescue and takes the blame for Posket's behaviour. Overcome, Agatha confesses her deception over her own and Cis's ages. Thus, she has to eat humble pie for her conceit and vanity.

But Posket is not to go unpunished. His guilt, deceit and hypocrisy are all revealed. As he cowers before the collected wrath of Lukyn, Vale and Agatha, Cis again delivers him by creating a diversion. He announces that he is going to marry Beatie, as he is old enough to do so. Joyfully Posket consents: 'on the day you marry and start for Canada, I will give you a thousand pounds. . . . I am his legal guardian, gentlemen, bear witness. I solemnly consent to that little wretch's marriage.' With Cis out of the way, Posket hopes to return to the even tenor of his ways, but a humbler and a wiser man.

The review in the *Daily Telegraph* on 23 March 1885 says, 'the pivot of the play lies in a grave, solemn and respectable personage. . . . It is a delightfully farcical idea to watch the misguided magistrate struggling with his sense of duty and yet seeing afar a vision of youthful delight.' All the critics praised Pinero for creating a new kind of entirely English comedy–farce, free of French sexual innuendo, and 'faithful to English notions of the humorous'.

The humour lies not only in the situations, but in the language as well, which sparkles from joke to joke. The dialogue is full of puns and double meanings. The characters all have their individual language, and frequently talk at cross-purposes. Jokes about food and horses are frequent. Because of the speed at which most of the play moves, it is not always easy, at a first hearing, to catch all the jokes – a characteristic also of Pinero's latter-day successor, Tom Stoppard. It was Pinero's style that made the play so successful, in the eyes of the *Telegraph* critic. He ended his criticism, 'It is a thoroughly amusing play, because it is funny without being vulgar, and ludicrous without a trace of that deplorable buffoonery which too often passes for wit. It is the work of an extremely able man'.

Not as popular as *The Magistrate* on its first production

was *Trelawny of the 'Wells'*, although to Pinero's surprise it gained in popularity, and by 1928 had been filmed twice and revived on stage a number of times. Following a production by the National Theatre in 1965, there have been many more revivals, including a musical version in the West End. To a late-twentieth-century audience, the play's period charm, comedy, strong characterisation and portrayal of theatrical life prove a delightful mixture. Pinero's contemporaries praised individual performances, particularly those of Dion Boucicault (the younger) as Sir William, and his wife, Irene Vanbrugh, as Rose Trelawny, but found some of the elements too strong to take. In fact, *The Times* called the play 'sordidly disagreeable, too destitute of romance or story'. In particular, the play was attacked for its realism: the lack of refinement in the behaviour of the company of Bagnigge Wells was felt to reveal stage people in too harsh a light (a similar criticism was later levelled at *The 'Mind the Paint' Girl*). The hideousness of the costumes also attracted universal comment. Indeed, the use of 'period' costume and setting was found so remarkable that several newspapers gave detailed accounts of the clothes in each act. To a modern audience the clothes of the 1860s and the 1880s have equal charm; but to Pinero's generation the clothes of their grandparents were hideous, and they had no scruple in saying so. However, Pinero had been adamant that no concessions should be made. In a direction to the stage-manager he wrote,

> The costumes and scenic decoration of this little play should follow, to the closest detail, the mode of the early Sixties – the period, in dress, of crinoline and the peg-top trouser; in furniture, of horsehair and mahogany, and the abominable 'walnut-and-rep'. No attempt should be made to modify such fashions in illustration, to render

them less strange, even less grotesque, to the modern eye.

The critic of the *Daily Telegraph* (21 Jan 1898) referred to their 'encumbering rotundity' of the costumes, but he understood very well what Pinero was setting out to do in *Trelawny of the 'Wells'*:

> we are only apt to think that humanity itself has disappeared and that heroines are no longer heroines, because they are absurdly and tastelessly dressed. . . . Every now and then we had to rouse ourself to the remembrance that, however fantastic the dressing, it was absolutely necessary for the particular purpose which the author had in hand.

Now that the period setting is no longer a barrier, it is easy to see what Pinero was setting out to do in the play. First, he was paying a tribute to Tom Robertson, to whom he felt he personally owed a great debt, for his contribution to English drama. It is easy to see in Tom Wrench, the struggling playwright, the character of Robertson, who, after years of hack translating of French plays, at last managed to get a play of his own (*Society*, 1865) performed, and for a time offered hope of a rebirth of English drama. Imogen Parrott is, as obviously, Marie Wilton, the extravaganza queen of London, who, finding no material suitable for her desire to become a comedy actress, and no management to back her, took a dilapidated little theatre known as the 'Dust Hole' and, turning it into an elegant little theatre renamed the Prince of Wales, engaged Robertson to be her playwright. Together, they took London by storm. The dialogue of the play *Life* (the play-within-a-play in *Trelawny*) is a pastiche of Robertson's writing – conversational, everyday and witty; the characters Dora and Peggy are typical Robertson girls; even the one-word title is an imitation. Thinly disguised as Bagnigge Wells, the theatre is obviously Sadler's Wells, which Pinero haunted when he was young; Tom Wrench's experiences as a 'General Utility' are close to those of Pinero himself.

The play is also one of contrasts: the new theatre of Tom Wrench, with its naturalistic dialogue and controlled acting, is contrasted with the exuberant school which it finally replaces. The affectionate, uninhibited, cheerful world of the old-time theatre with its rivalries, petty quarrels and generous loyalties is contrasted with the repressive world of the upper-class Arthur, who is in love with Rose. Each world must learn from the other: Sir William, Arthur's grandfather, must learn to tolerate the world of the 'gypsies' with whom Arthur has chosen to throw in his lot. Rose, through contact with Arthur's world, sees the life of the 'Wells' with different eyes, and can no longer belong there. From the compromise effected between the two worlds will emerge the new generation of actors who will raise the status of drama. Pinero is, of course, writing with hindsight, for in the 1890s actors and actresses had become for the most part 'respectable'. A further contrast lies between that naturalistic characterisation and settings, and the sentiment and pathos in elements of the story. Although much of the writing is comic, there is considerable pathos in Tom Wrench's love for Rose, never to be requited, and in his attempts to hide his poverty; also in the fading fortunes of the Bagnigge Wells company.

The comedy is of considerable variety. Much of it, as always with Pinero, springs from the inner nature of a character. Thus Colpoys is always putting on a comic act as if he's on stage and Sir William's very intransigence is intensely humorous. Much of the dialogue is comic, arising frequently from an individual character's idiosyncrasies of speech. There are situations which are humorous in them selves. This is particularly noticeable in Act II, when Rose is incarcerated at the Gowers. The incongruity of her behaviour in that particular milieu gives rise to many comic incidents.

In the opening moments of the play, Pinero skilfully establishes Rose's background. In the stage-directions, he is very specific as to the details of the room, and so gives the audience precise information on the financial and theatrical status of the characters soon to be seen. The room, in a lodging-house, is rented by Mr and Mrs Telfer. The lodging-house is *respectable*; the room, though shabby, is *clean* and *well-kept*. The grate is hidden, not by ferns and other plants as in many other Pinero plays set in middle-class homes, but by wood-shavings and paper roses. There is a cottage piano and a piano-stool, on top of which are music, wax fruit and flowers, and a wig-block, with an iron-grey ringlet wig. There is a large black theatrical trunk, bulging with *'soiled theatrical finery'*. Under the sofa are worn satin shoes; upon the sofa a yellowed white-satin bodice, a *'heap of dog-eared play-books, and some other litter of a like character'*. In the corners of the room stand an assortment of walking-sticks and swords. In faded lettering on the trunk is 'Miss Violet Sylvester, Theatre Royal, Drury Lane'. Immediately an audience realises that the people who inhabit this room are not young, that they have been 'in the business' a long time. That one 'Miss Violet Sylvester' worked at the Theatre Royal, Drury Lane, and has come down a long way in the world; that Mr Telfer plays 'costume' parts, requiring wig and sword; that they are required to sing or play the piano in their present engagement; that they are disorganised.

A large table is being laid all through the opening of

the scene by Ablett the greengrocer, who has come in to wait at table to oblige Mrs Mossop, the landlady. This 'business' sets the scene for Rose Trelawny's farewell party, and gives the opportunity for Ablett and Mrs Mossop, chatting while they lay the table, to impart essential background information about Rose's engagement to Arthur Gower: that she is giving up the stage; that she is going to live with Arthur's grandfather, Sir William Gower, and his great aunt for 'a short term' in order 'to habituate herself to the West End'.

The first main character to to be introduced is Tom Wrench, who in many ways can be seen to be the central figure. Quickly his poverty, his lack of success as an actor, his love for Rose, and his humour and charm are established. Pinero describes him as being an '*ungraceful man, with a clean-shaven face, curly hair, and eyes full of good humour*', and it is this good humour, allied to a volatile temperament and an unshakable faith in himself, which are his most striking characteristics.

The first guest to arrive is Imogen Parrot, once at the 'Wells', now the star of the Olympic. It quickly becomes obvious that she and Tom are very close, and that she takes a great interest in the plays which he writes. From his discussion with Imogen we get the first intimations of Tom's dreams for the stage:

IMOGEN. You know, the speeches were so short and had such ordinary words in them, in the plays you used to read to me – no big opportunity for the leading lady, Wrench.

TOM. Mm, yes. I strive to make my people talk and behave like live people, don't I – ?

IMOGEN (*vaguely*). I suppose you do.

TOM. To fashion heroes out of actual, dull everyday

men – the sort of men you see smoking cheroots in the club windows in St James's Street; and heroines from simple maidens in muslin frocks. Naturally, the managers won't stand that.

IMOGEN. Why, of course not.

TOM. If *they* did, the public wouldn't.

IMOGEN. Is it likely?

TOM. Is it likely? I wonder!

IMOGEN. Wonder what?

TOM. Whether they would.

IMOGEN. The public.

TOM. The public, Jenny, I wonder about it sometimes so hard that that little bedroom of mine becomes a banqueting hall, and this lodging house a castle.

These lines, delivered early in the play, are important because they state the main theme: the difficulties of presenting 'life' and 'theatre', 'reality' and 'illusion'. Rose, a creature of the theatre, has to learn the difference (as does her fiancé, Arthur) between life outside and life in the theatre. Tom Wrench tries to present 'life' in the theatre. This is why his play is called *Life*. The lines also, in their shortness and simplicity, point to the fact that Wrench's (Robertson's) reforms have now been accepted.

Act I is concerned with theatre. All the guests at Rose's 'farewell-to-the-"Wells"' dinner are theatre people, except Arthur. There are the Telfers, in whose room at the lodging-house the scene takes place. Elderly, dignified, obviously at the end of their career, they are nevertheless respected by the rest of the company. Gadd, the young male lead, is flashy, spiteful, self-important, obviously a bad actor. Colpoys, the 'low comedian' despised by the others, desperately seeks the laughs which he can no longer get on stage. Avonia, the soubrette, vulgar, cheerful, kind-hearted, is generous and impulsive and obviously fond of Rose. Rose herself, who, despite possessing sweetness, grace and charm, behaves as if all her life were a theatre, is extravagant in her speech and gestures. Arthur is like a fish out of water, coming as he does from a totally different social milieu. Tom Wrench is impecunious – a 'Utility', a company dogsbody, subsisting on the kindliness of the landlady and Rose's generosity, yet he has a vision which will change the face of theatre. Imogen, the ex-member of the company, has achieved success in the West End; but it is her affection for Rose and Tom Wrench which provides the central impetus for the plot.

There is no action in Act I. The whole act takes place round the meal table, and is concerned mainly with establishing character and creating a strong feeling of 'theatre'. The act ends with Rose, at her most dramatic, bidding farewell to the 'Wells' as she leaves to live with Arthur's family in Cavendish Square, before their marriage:

> And shall I tell you the moments which will be the happiest to me in my life, however happy I may be with Arthur? Why, whenever I find that I am recognized by people and pointed out – people in the pit of a theatre, in the street, no matter where; and when I can fancy they're saying to each other (*pointing*), 'Look! that was Miss Trelawny! You remember – Trelawny! Trelawny of the 'Wells'!'

Act II is concerned with 'life' outside the theatre, but, curiously, because of the broadly comic nature of the first half, seems less true to life than the first act. It is paradoxical that the presentation of theatre in the first and third acts seems more naturalistic than the presentation of life in Act II. Rose is seen fretting in Arthur's stuffy, repressive home. She fits in here less well than Arthur fitted in at the 'Wells'. The company tolerated him; but his elderly relatives thoroughly disapprove of Rose, whose temerity scares Arthur, and his sister and brother-in-law. To Sir William and Aunt Trafalgar she is without self-control, manners or understanding of how to behave. She must be disciplined. The first half of the act is extremely funny, as Rose chaffs at the demands made on her and the other young people. Rose has been brought up in the extended family of the theatre; she knows little about the rigid and frequently unreasonable demands of filial obedience and self-effacement made by elders in 'life'. She resents the lessons. The act is divided by the device of a thunderstorm, which occurs after Sir William and Trafalgar have gone to bed and Arthur has been banished to his sister's, as he is each night. Rose, left alone and mutinous, is delighted to receive a surprise visit from some of the 'Wells' company, who have come to seek her out. As they enter, drunk and dripping wet from the rain, 'theatre' surges onto the stage, into the surroundings in which Rose's 'education' is taking place. Although, in the first act, their behaviour seems absolutely right, here in Cavendish Square they are out of place, and seem stagy. Tom Wrench, however, turns the visit to good account. He notes the design of the room, and plans for the future:

> This is the kind of chamber I want for the first act of my comedy. ... I won't have doors stuck here, there and everywhere; no, nor windows in all sorts of impossible places! ... Windows on one side, doors on the other – just where they should be architecturally. And locks on the doors, *real* locks, to work; and handles –

Thus Pinero, through Tom Wrench's plans, shows how

Robertson's reforms achieved at the Prince of Wales in 1865 were commonplace on the stage of 1898.

As the noise mounts, despite Rose and Tom's efforts to quell it, the audience waits for the inevitable: the arrival of Sir William. Finally he erupts on stage, wrath personified. With his entrance, the act once again changes key, passing into high theatricality, as Rose, reverting to a heroine of melodrama, sweeps out, renouncing Arthur for ever. Tom Wrench, the proponent of naturalism, undercuts the effect, by instructing Arthur to come and see him in the morning. Tom has different ideas on the matter.

The act shows great variety, and like Act I ends on a note of high emotion generated by Rose, with her penchant for playing dramatic scenes as if they were real life. She has not yet learnt that life and theatre are different.

Act III takes us back to the theatrical lodgings, this time to Rose's room, smaller than the Telfers' but neat and tidy. Her theatrical dress basket, unlike theirs, is closed; the bed, which can be concealed by a curtain, is neatly made; everything is hung up tidily; there are some books on hanging shelves, writing-paper and envelopes on the table – obvious indications that the inhabitant of the room has some smattering of education and refinement. We learn that the company are largely out of work, and that Rose, whose sojourn in Cavendish Square has inhibited her, can no longer throw herself convincingly into her old roles. She is now halfway between 'life' and 'theatre' and seems to belong in neither. Salvation perhaps lies through Imogen, who is trying to raise money to put on Tom Wrench's play, which would provide Rose with a part more suited to her new, controlled style of performance. Sir William bludgeons his way in to see Rose, seeking Arthur. Rose does not know where he is either, although the audience does. Through the help of Tom Wrench, he has become an actor in Bristol. Sir William is confronted by a changed Rose, who treats him with courtesy and dignity; and also by the theatre of his youth, in the form of Rose's souvenirs of Kean – the sword and the order and chain that Kean wore as Richard III. They both affect the old man powerfully. Wearing them, he limps round the stage, lost once more in the wonder of theatre and the dreams of his youth. From that moment he is changed. He is most upset when he hears that Rose has lost her job, and blames himself. He wants in some way to help her. He finally comes to realise that he can best do this through backing Tom Wrench's play. From this point in the play, Sir William and Rose run parallel courses towards a point where 'theatre' and 'life' are reconcilable. Although Sir William's irascible exterior remains the same, it is his change of heart from the moment that theatre reached out to him from the past that eventually reconciles Arthur and Rose, and 'life' and 'theatre'.

Tom Wrench's play achieves it all. Sir William demands to hear the play, and the curtain falls on Tom reading '*Life, a Comedy*, by Tom Wrench'. The title is, of course, symbolic. Not only is it an imitation of Robertson's single-word titles, but it is also indicates that *real* life is to be portrayed in the theatre, in the comedy. No more fustian, but real, ordinary people, doing ordinary things, speaking ordinary words.

Whereas Act II, and Cavendish Square, represent life *outside* the theatre, Act *IV* presents life *inside* the theatre. This was emphasised by the original set, which put the proscenium arch up-stage, with an empty auditorium behind it, obviously painted on a backcloth. The prompt-table was up-stage centre, in front of some footlights. In this way, the illusion of being part of the theatre was complete. In modern copies of the play the set of the 1925 revival is described. This had the proscenium arch of the Pantheon theatre down-stage, coinciding with the proscenium arch of the real theatre. In this way, one is looking into a theatre, not *out from* it, and Pinero's original conception of 'life' and 'theatre' is lost.

The act begins with the old order that is fading from the theatre. Imogen has found employment for the Telfers in her theatre; but Telfer is relegated to a small part that can accommodate his old-fashioned style. He is to play '*an old stagey, out-of-date actor*'; Mrs Telfer is to be the wardrobe mistress. Telfer is humiliated. 'Let us both go home', he says.

> MRS TELFER (*restraining him*). No, let us remain. We've been idle six months, and I can't bear to see you without your watch and all your comforts about you. [He has obviously had to pawn his watch.]
>
> TELFER (*pointing towards the Green room*). And so this new-fangled stuff, and these dandified people, are to push us, and such as us, from our stools!
>
> MRS TELFER. Yes, James, just as some other new fashion will, in course of time, push *them* from their stools.

Another vestige of the 'old' theatre remains in the character of O'Dwyer, the stage-manager. Before the rise of the director in the theatre, the stage-manager was responsible for taking rehearsals, blocking moves, checking lines, coaching the actors (with, of course, the exception of the great stage performers, who were a law unto themselves.) Strict rules for conduct were put up in the theatre, and it was the stage-manager who enforced them. It was playwrights who were largely responsible for changing the custom, insisting on taking their own rehearsals. Dion Boucicault, the great writer of melodrama, was the first to do this. Pinero himself took all his own rehearsals, and was a hard taskmaster.

In O'Dwyer, Pinero is making affectionate mockery of this all-powerful figure, showing the transition from stage-manger to author-directed rehearsals, and the chaos that a stage-manager could cause. Through Tom's endeavours to get O'Dwyer to address the performers more respectfully, and with less familiarity, Pinero also tries to demonstrate the need to grant actors and actresses higher status, no matter how small a part they are playing.

The rehearsal of *Life* slowly gets under way. Then the unexpected occurs. Sir William turns up to see the rehearsal; the play has disturbed him with its likeness to actual events. In Tom's play, life is impinging on theatre, and it has unnerved Sir William: 'That comedy of yours – it buzzes continually in my head, sir.'

> TOM. It was written with such an intention, Sir William – to buzz in people's heads.
>
> SIR WILLIAM. Ah, I'll take care ye don't read me another, Mr Wicks [he never get's Tom's name right]; at any rate, another which contains a character resembling a member of my family – a late member of my family. I don't relish being reminded of late members of my family in this way, and being kept awake at night, thinking – turning over in my mind. . . . When I saw Kean, as Richard, he reminded me of no member of my family. Shakespeare knew better than that, Mr Wicks.

So, Sir William is escorted into a stage box, where he can see the rehearsal without being seen.

The 'young man from Bath' who is to play Gerald arrives just on cue; it is, of course, Arthur. Tom Wrench has deliberately written the part of Gerald closely to resemble Arthur (which is why Sir William has been so disturbed) and has engaged him to play himself. It is Tom's way of effecting a reunion between Rose and Arthur, without either knowing it. At this point in the play, Tom deliberately makes life and theatre the same, so that make-believe is indistinguishable from fact – and yet, as in Pirandello's *Six Characters in Search of an Author*, it is all, after all, only make-believe.

Somehow, a reunion must be brought about with stubborn, proud, irascible Sir William. Arthur is trying to be what Rose is – a gypsy. On the new ground created by Tom Wrench they can be together. He also has gained in assurance and independence, and can face his grandfather now with courage; he has learnt about life away from Cavendish Square.

ARTHUR. Then, if Aunt Trafalgar will receive me, sir, do you think I may be allowed to – to bring Miss Trelawny with me – ?

SIR WILLIAM. What! ha, I perceive you have already acquired the impudence of your vagabond class, sir; the brazen effrontery of a set of –

But the memory of Kean, operating more strongly in the old man in a theatre, wins the day for Arthur and Rose.

ROSE (*rising and facing him*). Forgive him! Forgive him! Oh, Sir William, why may not Arthur become, some day, a *splendid* gypsy?

SIR WILLIAM. Eh?

ROSE. Like –

SIR WILLIAM (*peering into her face*). Like – ?

ROSE. Like –

Tom interposes, 'Yes, sir, a gypsy, though of a different order from the old order which is departing – a gypsy of the new school.'

The old man, exhausted but won over, crustily goes back to his box until the end of the rehearsal, when he, Arthur and Rose will go back to Cavendish Square together. It is ironic that Pinero brings about the reconciliations on a stage. In life, such things rarely happen.

The play ends movingly and fittingly, with Tom bringing them all back from life, where he has finally lost Rose, to the theatre, where he has gained her:

> Go on with the rehearsal. Mr Gordon and Miss Rose Trelawny! Miss Trelawny! (*Rose goes to him.*) Trelawny – late of the 'Wells'! Let us – let – (*gripping Arthur's hand tightly, he bows his head upon Rose's shoulder*). Oh my dears – ! let us – get on with the rehearsal.

In 1908, ten years after *Trelawny of the 'Wells'* was presented, *The Thunderbolt* was produced at the St James's Theatre, with George Alexander playing the lead. Pinero had moved with the times, and this play is an acid view of provincial, middle-class life in general and the hypocrisy, malice and greed of one family in particular. The strength of the satire is so great that the play has much in common with *Volpone*, whose theme, greed, it shares. Of all Pinero's comedies, *The Thunderbolt* has the most universality, and the most power.

The tone of the play is set as the curtain rises. The Venetian blinds are down, and the room is in semi-darkness, although broad sunlight can be seen through the slats of the blinds. Pinero says that the only light in the room comes from this sunlight. It is possible to see in the dim light that the room is a library, with massive furniture and decorations which, though rich, do not exhibit '*any special refinement of taste*'. Dressed in mourning, which adds to the atmosphere of gloom, are the Mortimore brothers, James, Stephen and Thaddeus, with their wives, Ann, Louisa and Phyllis, their sister Rose and her husband, Colonel Ponting. The first thing to be established through the dialogue is the heat in the room, which adds to the general sense of claustrophobia. Then, immediately, the importance of convention to this group of people is underlined. This is a house of mourning, and it is not correct to open windows on such an occasion. As quickly, Pinero establishes the characters of some of the group: Ann, the arbiter of convention: Rose, affected and self-oriented; James, the leader, emphasised by his sitting centre-stage at the writing-desk; Ponting, coarse, bombastic and aggressive; and Thaddeus, the dogsbody of the family, meek, and thoughtful for other people.

We still do not know who has died, or why they are all assembled in this way. Apart from realising they are all one family, it is possible even in the first few moments to gather a great deal about their origins and present social status. The fact that James calls Ann 'Mother' is for the times a social give-away, putting the family firmly in the middle of the middle class, a cut above small tradesfolk: people of substance, but probably not of much education or culture. The clothes of James, Stephen, Ann and Louisa bear this out. Rose, on the other hand, is dressed fashionably, and by her affected behaviour and her marriage to the Colonel can obviously be considered to have 'made it' to the fringe of the upper classes and the borders of 'society'. Thaddeus ('Tad') and his wife are different again: he is '*meek and care-worn*', she is '*white-faced and faded*'. They are shabby and lack the prosperous confidence of the rest of the family, but, as it transpires later in the action, possess a refinement and sensitivity which the rest of the family lack. Together, the family form a symbolic microcosm of the middle class, and Pinero ruthlessly reveals the characteristics of each section as the play progresses. The 'upper' section are shown to be extravagant and money-grabbing, selfish, pleasure-seeking, ruthless and hypocritical. The solid 'middle' are revealed as ambitious, mercenary and greedy, concerned more with keeping up appearances than with anything else. Though actively malevolent in attacking anything they do not understand, they can, at their best, be honest, kindly and hard-working, but only when their instincts of greed and self-seeking can be subdued. Nevertheless, these two groups often appear to be working as one, and frequently in the play Pinero shows them acting as a whole, almost as one character.

The artistic, cultured and intellectual are shown to be at a disadvantage. The forces of philistinism are stacked against them. Money can assist them in their battle to survive, but that can frequently only be obtained by loss of integrity, and it is usually integrity, pride and hard work which form the basis of their lives. Involved also in the world of the middle classes are the law and the Church. In this play, the characters of Elkin, Vallance, the lawyers, and the Revd Trist are quite sympathetic. The lawyers, acting as a chorus, stand apart from the greedy struggle taking place around them, although they are accused of self-interest. The Revd Trist is affected on a personal level. Money formed an important element in the life of the Church at the time, when many livings were so poor it was virtually impossible for some clergy to subsist; it was often necessary for them to get up to deceitful strategies to obtain enough to live on. In the symbolism of the play, Pinero envisages a possible alliance of the moral strengths of the Church and some of the more prosperous elements of 'Bohemian' culture and education, as a means of ensuring the survival of both. The play is a powerful indictment of the middle classes, and one is aware of Pinero's dislike for them very soon after the play opens.

The interaction of the family members is the fabric of the play. There is no real 'action' – merely the circling of the characters round the dead brother's money, claws outstretched like vultures. Even Tad and Phyllis, with whom it is possible to feel sympathy, are not immune to this greed. It is Phyllis's initial destruction of Edward Mortimore's will that sets the whole action in motion; and even Tad, when he thinks that money is coming his way, is not above planning and scheming.

The structure of the play is interesting. The contrast in mood, light and shade, and pace are all skilfully handled; the way the characters are arranged around the stage is masterly. There are times when the two lawyers appear to be acting as a chorus; times when Stephen, James, Ponting, Anne, Rose and Louisa seem to fulfil this function. There is little movement, and what there is is for some purpose. Much of the dialogue is conducted with the characters seated.

The first act, as already noted, opens in semi-darkness. When the set is revealed, it is shown that the furniture is grandiose and tasteless. Sparring for position and superiority within the family is indicated by careful placing on stage. For instance, when we first see Tad and Phyllis they are sitting well away from the centre. James, the dominant member of the family, usually occupies centre stage. The second act, in Tad and Phyllis's drawing-room is by contrast light and cheerful; the ornaments and general presentation of the room speak of '*good taste and refinement*'. The activities on stage as the scene opens present clearly the kind of life which the occupants follow: Tad is playing the piano for the Revd Trist, the lodger, who is singing; Helen, the dead Edward's daughter, is sketching the children; Phyllis is sewing. The audience, however, is aware of some unease, as Phyllis looks thoroughly miserable. It is ironical that Helen should be so at home there when Phyllis had originally not wanted to meet her. It is obvious from the way they talk to each other that Helen and the children have struck up a friendship. This is important for later developments in the play. The tranquil scene is shattered by the arrival of James and Stephen, who come bustling in and take over. Their lack of consideration and discourtesy are marked, particularly in relation to the good manners shown by the others, particularly the children. Following James's brusque 'Now then, children; be off with you! I want to talk to your father and mother', Joyce says to Helen, 'Will you excuse us?' and Cyril adds, 'Awfully sorry, Helen.' This little exchange, almost more than anything, shows the gulf that lies between the values of James, who doesn't even realise that Helen might mind her project being interrupted in this fashion, and the children, whose sensitivity and good manners make them aware of James's boorish behaviour.

There is obviously some resentment that Helen, while waiting for the results of the advertisement for the will, has chosen to stay with the unpretentious Tads rather than with either James or Stephen; but she obviously recognises in them kindred spirits who have struggled with pride and integrity to maintain their own standards in the face of much opposition and contumely. Phyllis is not without her own brand of arrogance.

James and Stephen have come to tell Tad that Elkin has the results of the advertisement and that there is to be a meeting at four o'clock. Tad's protests are overridden rudely: 'It's your holiday time: what have *you* got to do?' says James.

When Phyllis and Helen are left alone together on stage, considerable tension builds while Phyllis unsuccessfully tries to persuade Helen to accept an allowance. Phyllis's distraught and odd manner strikes an audience forcibly. What is wrong with her? By now it is obvious that she must know something about a will – but what?

The emotional tension is broken by the following scene, between Helen and Joyce. This scene has comic overtones and is important because it clearly indicates the affection and trust which have built up between the Tads' two children and Helen. The mood changes once again in next scene, between Helen and Trist. This time a completely different Helen is seen, one who more obviously belongs to the Mortimore family than has so far been apparent.

It has already been demonstrated that Helen and Trist are at ease with each other, both absorbed into the Tads' family circle. Now he is seen in much closer focus, and performs an important function. Because he is a parson and is, what is more, a kindly, humorous man who is not involved with the Mortimore money in any way, she is honest with him, and the audience learns her true feelings. Up till now, she has been a gracious, elegant enigma. To Trist, she pours out her real feelings:

> I've the makings in me of a most accomplished liar and hypocrite. . . . There's to be a meeting of the Mortimore family . . . to arrange with the lawyers to administer my father's estate without any more delay. And I was double-faced enough to receive the news smilingly and agreeably, and all the time I could have struck them – I could have seen them drop dead in this room without a pang of regret. . . . I can't *bear* that father should have

forgotten me. I can't bear it; I can't resign myself to it. . . . I've been praying daily, hourly that something – anything – might be found to prove that father had remembered me. And I loathe these people who step over me and stand between me and the being I loved best on earth; I loathe them. I detest the whole posse of them, except the Thaddeuses; and I wish this money may bring them, and those belonging to them, every ill that's conceivable.

It is important that she should so reveal herself to an audience, because up till now she has been almost too good to be true. Although her dignity and self-control are an essential part of her character, it is necessary that she should be known to have strength of feeling as well.

Again the mood switches to the comic, as Helen determinedly fends off Trist's declaration of love.

The climax of Act II comes as Phyllis is finally left alone with Tad. She breaks down and confesses that there *had* been a will and she has destroyed it. Under the most painful cross-examination Tad drags the facts from her. Barely has he had time to take in the full enormity of what she has done, when he is summoned to go to the family meeting. This is a real 'cliff-hanger' of an act-ending. What will Tad do now? The confession strengthens the irony of the fact that Helen likes the Tads and is staying with them. What will she do when she finds out?

Act III, set in James's ugly and pretentious dining-room, provides an atmospheric contrast with the previous scene. The large dining-table, in a skilful piece of stagecraft, provides a good focal point, and the changing positions of the characters round the table during the early part of the act are cleverly managed to clear the chair centre back for Tad when he makes his entrance. Pinero's moves and placings of characters on stage are always carefully thought out to give maximum significance to his text. A modern director and cast ignore them at their peril.

The beginning of the act, satiric and comic in tone, overlaps in time with Phyllis's confession to Tad, thus making the family's indecent gloating deeply ironic. From his dominant position, centre-stage back, Tad drops his bombshell at the moment when they are rejoicing in their certain acquisition of wealth. 'There was a will', he declares, and then proceeds to try to take Phyllis's guilt on his own shoulders. The family, lost to all sense of decency and propriety, are after him like a pack of wolves, howling imprecations at him, screaming questions. Finally, they trip him up, and realise that it is the hated and despised Phyllis who has really destroyed the will; he is only trying to protect her. The end of the act gathers great momentum. The family, savage in their frustrated hopes and carried on like a spinning top, turn on each other in a hysterical screaming row of incriminations and insults. They even come to fisticuffs, and so their realisation that Tad and the lawyers have gone is delayed. Thus the act ends, as it began, in savage, satiric comedy – an exposition of greed and spite. It is immensely effective. Tad's chivalry and courage in trying to protect his wife from his enraged family arouse the greatest admiration and pity. Of all the members of the family, including Helen, who has revealed her own hypocrisy, he is at this point the only one for whom it is possible to have any real respect or sympathy.

At the beginning of Act IV, set once again in Tad's drawing-room, it is impossible to know how the play will end. The balance of power has now shifted from the brothers to Helen, and Pinero, with immaculate staging, has made this particularly clear by seating Helen in a commanding position down-stage left, sitting at a table with Elkin.

Ponting is up-stage right, in one of the window embrasures, well out of the action, as is Rose, down-stage right. Phyllis is seated on a settee, with her back to Helen, with Tad standing beside her, holding her hand. Ann, Louisa and Stephen are all well out of the way, stage right, round the fire-place. James, however, is nearly dead centre, seated on an ottoman. He, who is normally the leader, does not speak until well on in the act. Nor does Helen.

Unfortunately, Phyllis cannot remember the names of the witnesses on the will, so a legal stalemate exists. Nor will Helen allow Phyllis to suffer the consequences of her action. 'We must all unite in sparing her and her husband and children.' This statement shows the importance of the relationship that Helen has developed with the children, particularly Cyril, earlier in the play. It provides good reasons for Helen's subsequent behaviour.

Elkin explains that there is a deadlock. Nobody can claim the money, because nobody can swear that the deceased died intestate. Everyone knows that it was Edward Mortimore's will that Phyllis destroyed. Helen says,

> Yes, of course I know it. I know he didn't forget me; I know I was all to him that I imagined myself to be. And it's because I've come to know this at last – through her – that I can afford to be a little generous to her ... Mrs Thaddeus did a cruel thing when she destroyed that will. It's no excuse for her to say that she wasn't aware of my existence. She was defrauding *some* woman; and as it happens – I own it now! – defrauding that woman, not only of money, but of what is more valuable than money – of peace of mind, of contentment, belief in one who could never speak, never explain, never defend himself. However, she has made the best

reparation it is in her power to make – and she has gone through a bad time – and I forgive her.

As Elkin protests at the impossible situation that she has created, Helen suggests that James should administer the estate as had been intended and then she should decide the disposition of the estate. It is now that James, at last, comes in to his own. He advances centre-stage to meet her, and speaks to her with sincerity and honesty, showing that the flashes of a kindly, decent man that have been evident throughout the play have some foundation. He hushes Stephen and Ponting, and speaks:

> Miss Thornhill, we're poor, we Mortimores. I won't say anything about Rose – it wouldn't be polite to the Colonel; nor Tad – you see what he's come to. But Stephen and me – take our case. (*To* ELKIN and VALLANCE) Mr Vallance – Mr Elkin, this is sacred. (*To* HELEN) My dear, we're prominent men in the town, both of us; we're looked up to as being fairly warm and comfortable; but in reality we're not much better off than the others. My trade's being cut into on all sides; Stephen's business has run to seed; we've no capital; we've never had any capital. What we might have saved has been spent on educating our children, and keeping up appearances; and when the time comes for us to be knocked out, there'll be precious little bar a stroke of luck – precious little for us to end our days on. So this is a terrible disappointment – an awful disappointment. Aye, the money's yours – it's yours – but – (*opening his hands*) what are you going to do for the family?

The tables turned indeed.

Helen, speaking to James, says, 'Well, since you put it

this way – I'll tell you what I'll do. I'll share with you all.' However, she insists that the estate be divided into six, the sixth share being given to a hospital in Linchpool, as a memorial to her father. Stephen and Ponting, joined by Ann, Louisa and Rose as might be expected, protest in the most mean-minded and petty way. They have no thought for her magnanimity – only for their own gain. But James quells them. Whereupon they rush to paper and pencil to calculate their share. James stands aloof. Then Pinero's refusal to take the easy, sentimental way asserts itself.

Suddenly Tad and Phyllis stand. For them there is no easy way – no happy ending. Their sense of guilt and shame is too strong. They will not profit from Helen's magnanimity. They refuse their share, knowing that that means no escape ever from Singlehampton; no escape from their poverty, and the spite of their in-laws; no end to struggle for themselves and their children. Delighted, Stephen and Ponting fall to their sums again. Ann is bewildered: she obviously cannot understand how anyone can give up so much money willingly. However, Helen has the last word. She insists that the sixth share be settled upon Joyce and Cyril, of whom she has become so fond. She tells Tad and Phyllis that they have no right to stand in their children's light. There is silence, and then Phyllis, tottering forward, kneels in front of Helen, bowing her head in her lap, weeping.

Helen calmly disengages herself–and, rising for the first time in the act, walks away. There is no comfort on a personal level for Phyllis. Helen may have forgiven her, but it is no sentimental forgiveness, ending in reconciliation. She clearly indicates that she does not want to have anything to do with Phyllis. Tad lifts the weeping Phyllis from the ground, and leads her away, upstage, to the window.

Thus the wheel comes full circle, and the money is finally

disposed much as Phyllis had suggested in the beginning, but through Helen's generosity. An ironic contrast lies between her attitude and that of the family. They get less than they had calculated was theirs, but they are lucky to get anything at all.

The ending, however, is typically downbeat. At present, Helen does not want to see or talk to Phyllis. She forgives her, but that is all. Perhaps she'll feel differently in the future. She enlists James's aid to make the Tads' life easier.

> HELEN. She's done a wrong thing, but recollect – you all profit by it. You don't disdain, any of you, to profit by it. (*He looks at her queerly, but straight in the eyes.*) Try to make their lives a little easier for them.
>
> JAMES. Easier?
>
> HELEN. Happier. You can influence the others if you will. (*A pause.*) Will you?

As he goes, he calls to Tad and Phyllis, saying he'll see them both in the morning. He nods to Phyllis. 'Goodbye, old girl', he says.

Opinion of James has been so changed during the last scene that it is possible to feel that he will really try to help them. He has appreciated Helen's generous spirit, and through her has acquired a little of the sensitivity so lacking in the others. Helen has shown him he has a debt to pay Phyllis, and James is a man who honours his debts. His influence over Stephen and Ann is so great that he may be able to help the Tads.

Helen is left alone with the Tads. Knowing that Helen does not want to see her, Phyllis goes upstairs. Helen decides that she will leave to go to London that night; but, despite the unsentimental ending, Pinero does not end the play without a hint of some possible rapprochement in the future between herself and Phyllis. Helen suggests to Tad that, after six months of complete silence, Phyllis should write and send her another invitation. 'By that time, we shall, all of us, have forgotten a great deal – shan't we?' Her generosity in this instance is most moving. Her magnanimity to the family had been a kind of justice, in answer to James's appeal; holding out a hope of possible reconciliation to Phyllis betokens a compassionate heart, and an unmercenary nature, for it is through Phyllis that she has been deprived of the bulk of her fortune. Tad is given a fine exit. Overcome with emotion and gratitude he breaks in to a final apologia for Phyllis. His life has been ruined by marriage to her. He has to persuade others, and himself, that it has all been worthwhile.

> Miss Thornhill – my wife – my wife – you've seen her at a disadvantage – a terrible disadvantage. Few – few pass through life without being seen – once – or oftener at a disadvantage. She's – she's a splendid woman – a splendid woman – a splendid wife and mother. (*Moving to the door*) They haven't appreciated her – the family haven't appreciated her. They've treated her abominably; for sixteen years she's been treated abominably. (*At the door*) But I've never regretted my marriage – (*defiantly*) I've never regretted it – never, for a single moment – never regretted it – never – never regretted it – (*He disappears.*)

Poor Tad.

Tad's impassioned defence of Phyllis does not bring down the curtain, as might be expected. The curtain finally falls quietly and undramatically on Helen packing up her sketching things, telling Trist that she is going to London. 'Don't let this make any difference between us', she says, and the curtain falls.

The Thunderbolt is a fascinating play, full of ironies, changes of mood, and brilliant observation of people. The satire on the middle classes was strong enough to rouse outraged comments at the time of the first performance, but the general feeling seemed to be that it was a very good play. The *Times* critic wrote, 'Mr Pinero's play deals with humanity, fundamental and eternal, and in essence is unrelated to time or space . . . the theme of *The Thunderbolt* is quintessentially a 'classic' theme.'[1]

If, in *The Thunderbolt*, Pinero deals with 'humanity, fundamental and eternal', fifteen years earlier, in 1893, he had written another play on this theme, *The Second Mrs Tanqueray*. It was a play that shook the English theatre to its roots, and finally changed the course of English drama.

The Second Mrs Tanqueray was hailed by the *Daily Telegraph* after the first night as 'one of the must serious, the most valuable, the most 'considerable' studies which an English author has for years put before a metropolitan audience'.[2] The *Daily Graphic* commented that 'Mr Pinero's piece, the depth and sorrowfulness are almost beyond expression', and a French writer stated a widely held opinion when he wrote, 'C'est, de l'avis des meilleurs critiques, l'oeuvre la plus remarquable de l'histoire du Théâtre Anglais pendant la deuxième partie du XIXe siècle.'[3]

Like *The Profligate* before it, the play must be seen not only in relation to the social values of the day, but also against the background of the rising tide of demands for women's rights, both legal and social, and the Suffragette movement. However, although it is usually referred to as a play about the 'double standard' of sexual morality current at the time, it has other themes as important.

Because it is an *early* 'serious' play, it has faults of technique and character delineation which are not to be found in Pinero's later plays. It is written as a 'star' vehicle for the actress who plays Paula Tanqueray, and this creates an imbalance. Whereas in *The Notorious Mrs Ebbsmith, Iris* and *Mid-Channel* all central characters are fully drawn, and the heroines, therefore, have relationships with understandable people, in *The Second Mrs Tanqueray* the central characters of Ellean and Aubrey Tanqueray are ill-defined. Ellean, like Lesley Brudenell before her in *The Profligate*, is more a symbol than a person; Aubrey is not clearly enough drawn to make his relationship with Paula or his motivation sufficiently obvious. Pinero wrote the play with either John Hare or George Alexander in mind. Either of these actors would have brought a particular 'atmosphere' to the part of Aubrey: John Hare, sophisticated, humorous, slightly cynical; George Alexander, also sophisticated, but a little more earnest and less worldly than Hare. In the event, it was Alexander that played the part, and illustrations show him to have portrayed Aubrey as long-suffering, sincere, 'a good fellow'. It is possible, writing for an actor–manager of the competence of either man, that Pinero did not completely 'think through' the character.

The play is also one in which stage setting and movement do not play an important part: partly because, after the first act, most of the action takes place in duologue, and therefore positioning on stage is not vital as it is in *The Thunderbolt* for instance; and partly because dialogue predominates over action for nearly the whole course of the play.

The most remarkable feature of the play is the depth of psychological understanding with which Pinero portrays the unfortunate Paula. She is a victim not only of the events of her past, but also of her nature, and Pinero shows how inseparable the two are. However, it is not only her own past which destroys her: it is Aubrey Tanqueray's as well. The first Mrs Tanqueray haunts the play as much as Annabel Jesson dominates *His House in Order*, and Aubrey allows the spirit of the first wife to estrange him from the second. Although, on the surface, Aubrey's character does not seem particularly well-developed, there are clues as to his nature, and to his share of responsibility for the final disaster.

The first act takes place before Aubrey marries Paula. He is giving a 'goodbye' dinner to his closest friends, because he is going to get married the next day and retire to the country. It is obvious from the way that he speaks that he does not expect to see them after his marriage. Significantly he says, 'Well, your wives may not – like – the lady I'm going to marry.' (In Victorian society, wives were often more censorious than their husbands.) Aubrey then continues, 'When my wife and I settle down at Willowmere it's possible that we shall all come together. But if this isn't to be, for Heaven's sake let us recognize that it is simply because it *can't* be, and not wear hypocritical faces and suffer and be wretched.' One immediately wonders what sort of man this is that is prepared to marry some woman, obviously an 'unsuitable' one, take her down to the country, and accept that none of his old friends will continue to know him.

Aubrey then goes to a writing-desk at the other end of the room, clearing the ground for Misquith and Jayne, the two friends who have already arrived, to talk over his news. While they are gloomily doing this, Cayley Drummle bustles on. He is a debonair bachelor, neat and brisk – a man whose role in life is to be the life and soul of every party, full of wisecracks and conventional wisdom, though he is also kindly and well-intentioned. He makes a splendid entrance. He is full of news. He is late, because he has been consoling Lady Orreyed on a misalliance contracted by her son George. He gives a brilliant and malicious portrait of the young lady in question, one Mabel Harvey, an actress. In describing the misalliance between George and Mabel, he is indicating the type of marriage that Aubrey is about to embark on. He also suggests the importance that Aubrey's dead wife had in his life, and the influence that she is likely to assume over his future, through her daughter. He describes the first Mrs Tanqueray vividly:

> She was a lovely creature – by Jove she was; by religion a Roman Catholic. She was one of your cold sort, you know – all marble arms and black velvet. I remember her with painful distinctness as the only woman who ever made me nervous. . . . He loved her – to distraction as they say. Jupiter, how fervently that poor devil courted her! But I don't believe she allowed him even to squeeze her fingers. She *was* an iceberg. As for kissing, the mere contact would have given him chapped lips. . . . He had reckoned, poor wretch, that in the early days of marriage she would thaw. I used to picture him closing his doors and making up the fire in the hope of seeing her features relax. Bless her, the thaw never set in! I believe she kept a thermometer in her stays and always registered ten degrees below zero.

Allowing for Cayley Drummle's customary exaggeration, it is obvious that the first Mrs Tanqueray was a cold, sexless woman who gave Aubrey little affection, and certainly no passion.

However, she did her wifely duty, and a daughter was born. Having failed to stir up 'some sympathetic religious belief' in Aubrey,

> she determined upon strong measures with regard to the child. He opposed her for a miserable year or so, but she wore him down, and the insensible little brat was placed in a convent, first in France, then in Ireland. . . . Miss Tanqueray – a young woman of nineteen now – is in the Loretto Convent at Armagh. She professes to have found her true vocation in a religious life, and within a month or two will take final vows. . . . absolutely at the end there was reconciliation between husband and wife, and she won his promise that the child should complete her conventional education. He reaped his reward. When he attempted to gain his girl's confidence and affection he was too late, he found he was dealing with the spirit of the mother.

Drummle also emphasises Aubrey's loneliness.

The information imparted here by Drummle is crucial to an understanding of the rest of the play. The fact that Ellean, at nineteen, has never been out of a convent, and is on the verge of taking her final vows, must have a great effect on the way she thinks and reacts to the world and people she finds about her when, out of duty, she comes to her father. She has been greatly influenced by her mother all her life. Drummle leaves no room for doubt as to Miss Tanqueray's nature.

When Misquith and Jayne leave, Drummle remains behind, and after some shilly-shallying Aubrey at last informs him whom it is he is to marry. It is a Mrs Jarman.

Drummle's reaction is unexpected: 'Are you serious?' he says. Quickly, through a cut-and-thrust account of Mrs Jarman's history, of which Drummle knows a great deal, the audience gathers that she is a high-class prostitute, moving with some rapidity from one man to another. Her real name is Paula Ray. A query surfaces at this point.

Where did Aubrey meet her? Was he consoling himself after his repudiation by his daughter? Or after the death of his wife? Or before?

He feels strongly about the plight of Paula, because, at an implied comparison with Mabel Harvey, he flashes out, 'To you, Cayley, all women who have been roughly treated, and who dare to survive by borrowing a little of our philosophy are alike. You see in the crowd of the ill-used only one pattern; you can't detect the shades of goodness, intelligence, even nobility there.'

This implies that he can see these things in Paula, and that he can become angry and protective on her behalf. However, when he continues, 'I know what I'm doing, and I do it deliberately, defiantly. I injure no living soul by the step I'm going to take', and talks about being 'drawn to' Miss Ray, and having 'a temperate, honourable affection for Mrs Jarman', some doubt begins to creep in about whether he really knows what he is doing. He continues in this vein: 'She has never met a man who has treated her well – I intend to treat her well. That's all. And in a few years, Cayley, if you've not quite forsaken me, I'll prove to you that it is possible to rear a life of happiness, of good repute, on a – miserable foundation.'

In view of the ideas expressed by Cayley and other representatives of 'respectable' society, this would seem to be highly optimistic – and oddly complacent. To talk about the foundations of the marriage as 'miserable' does not seem to augur well for that marriage; also it does not seem to credit Paula with any good qualities.

What her qualities are, the audience shortly sees. Morse, his servant, comes to tell Aubrey that Paula has arrived to see him. He has shown her into Aubrey's bedroom. Immediately this says something about Paula. In coming so late (at a quarter to eleven) and unchaperoned to a man's rooms, she shows herself to have no sense of propriety; and Morse immediately places her for what she is. Drummle, meanwhile, has put himself out of earshot, and then takes himself off, saying that he at least will remain Aubrey's friend.

As Aubrey shows him out, Morse returns with the late post, which he props up on the mantelpiece. Waiting for Aubrey, he asks if he should go to bed – another indication of his opinion of Paula. Aubrey says, 'certainly not'. The whole incident of Morse's behaviour is fascinating, because it shows that such an instruction would not be unusual from a man such as Aubrey. Aubrey, by telling Morse not to go to bed, is denying the implication that Paula will be staying the night.

When she comes in, young, beautiful and superbly dressed, she immediately displays one of her most self-destructive characteristics: jealousy. Who has he had to dine? She is flippant one moment, dreaming the next. She recounts a daydream of a dinner party five years hence, when she will be an accepted hostess in society: then, with another swing of mood, she tells him she has scribbled a letter. He is continually seeking physical contact with her, which is made plain in the stage-directions. He calls her 'dear baby' (a term reminiscent of some of Torvald's endearments to Nora in *A Doll's House*). It is made obvious pretty quickly that he is besotted with her sexually, for all his high talk.

Then, with a gesture of great courage and generosity, she hands him the letter, saying it contains a list of all her *amours* since the beginning, which she would like him to read. If he would like to change his mind about marrying her when he has read it, she'll 'take the blow'. 'It's because I know you're such a dear, good fellow that I want to save you from the chance of ever feeling sorry you married me. I really love you so much, Aubrey, that to save you that I'd rather you treated me as – as the others have done.' However, Aubrey does not have Paula's clear sight or honesty. 'I can't bear to hear you always talking about – what's done with. I tell you I'll never remember it.' He never realises the effort it has cost her; the sacrifice she was prepared to make. Immersed in his own self-image, he burns the letter unread.

Paula, predictably, reacts strongly: 'Well, I think you might have said 'You're very generous, Paula' or at least 'Thank you dear', when I offered to set you free.' Aubrey's answer, equally predictable, is to catch her in his arms. When she then says, 'I do so want to be married', that, combined with her castles-in-the-air about the dinner party, shows an innate yearning for respectability and security quite at variance with some of her behaviour.

The unread letter plays a crucial part in the dénouement of the play, for it contained Paula's past, and her past brings about the final crisis. He asks her what she would have done had they parted, and she replies completely matter-of-factly, 'Why, killed myself . . . . It's true. Do you know I feel certain I should make away with myself if anything serious happened to me.'

Paula also says that she never takes anything seriously, 'not since a long while ago. I made up my mind then to have done with taking things seriously. If I hadn't, I –', and a few lines further on she says, 'I know I couldn't swallow a second big dose of misery. I know that if ever I felt wretched again – truly wretched – I should take a leaf out of Connie Tirlemont's book.' (Some years later Pinero was to use the same technique in *Mid-Channel*, in the first scene of which Zoë Blundell talks about killing herself.) One other important thing Paula says in his scene is 'Only, Aubrey, mind you keep me always happy.' Paula has a great need for love, affection and attention. She is like a child in this, and needs to feel she is loved.

When she runs off to get her cloak to go home, Aubrey takes his letter from the mantelpiece. It is from Ellean, his daughter:

> My dear father – A great change has come over me. I believe my mother in Heaven has spoken to me, and counselled me to turn to you in your loneliness. At any rate, your words have reached my heart, and I no longer feel fitted for the solemn life. I am ready to take my place by you. Dear father, will you receive me?

The voice from the grave indeed.

Paula returns to find him staring into space. He is in an impossible situation. How can he rebuff his daughter, whom he had implored to come home? How can he reject Paula now, after the things she has said to him in the last few minutes? But however can the nun-like girl and the Magdalene live together?

The curtain falls on Paula's words 'I'm so happy!' They are cruelly ironic.

All the themes to be developed in the course of the play are set in the first act. The central theme is social ostracism of the 'fallen woman', and the near-impossibility of her acceptance into society. (At the time the play was written there was considerable controversy in the press and in Parliament about whether a prostitute could ever be redeemed; whether the sexually 'fallen' could ever become 'good', and fit to mix with 'decent' women.) The other major themes are related to this: the double standard of morality, with one standard applicable to men, and another, much stricter one reserved for women; the necessity for tolerance, compassion and mercy; the need for honesty in human relationships; and the destructiveness of jealousy, insecurity and uncontrolled anger.

Aubrey obviously does not understand Paula, and is essentially passive in his acceptance of society's decrees. He sees his marriage to Paula as a great favour to her: he does not see or understand her need to be a *wife*, a married woman, not just a sexual ornament. Paula is shown to be lacking in propriety or self-control, jealous and insecure, but generous and courageous, child-like in her need for love, and pathetic in her need for approval and security. She is obviously deeply in love with Aubrey, and desperately wants to be a real wife to him, to sit proudly at the head of his dinner table; to be accepted as a 'good woman'. Her daydreams are so at variance with the truth of the situation as Aubrey has already discussed it with Cayley Drummle that already, by the end of the first act, we know that only tragedy lies ahead, because Aubrey has little to give her–only his name and a home. Her suicide is clearly indicated from the first curtain.

Ellean's nature has been revealed to us, both by her letter and by Drummle's description of her. Obviously disaster lies ahead. Much of the power of the play lies in the tragic inevitability of the end; in the desperate battle that Paula, so ill-equipped, puts up for her happiness and ultimately for her life. Even good-natured, bustling Drummle cannot help her; in fact, most of his efforts serve to precipitate yet another crisis. The past – symbolised by Paula's letter, which Aubrey so lightly burns, and by the first Mrs Tanqueray, as presented to us by Drummle – rises up to defeat not only Paula, but Aubrey as well.

Act II is set in a morning-room in Highercoombe, Aubrey's country home. Since he shared it with his first wife, presumably all the ornaments and furnishings were chosen by her. Paula is, as it were, a tenant in somebody else's house. She fits easily enough into the gracious surroundings. It transpires that she plays the piano well; and, although her behaviour lacks propriety, her accent does not betray any origins other than middle-class. It is to be assumed that her birth is perfectly respectable; but, if the hints she has dropped in the first act are followed to their logical conclusions, she presumably allowed herself to be seduced, was deserted by the man in question, and thereafter led a life of dissipation and gaiety.

Several things are established in the first few lines of the dialogue: she is bored; she feels herself neglected and unloved; and she is jealous of her step-daughter. The family have been at Highercoombe about two months, and no one has called on them – not even Mrs Cortelyon, who is their closest neighbour and an old friend of Aubrey's. At this point another thought about Aubrey strikes: if she has been a close friend, why hasn't he quietly visited her and asked her to help them? Aubrey's masochistic passivity in the face of the situation he has brought upon himself is extraordinary; and it transpires, furthermore, that he is being actively cruel to Paula.

There is a struggle taking place inside him between his craving for sexual satisfaction, frivolity and gaiety, which Paula can satisfy, and the demands of his first wife upon him, re-enacted in her nun-like daughter: chastity and self-control. The battle is carried out on the first Mrs Tanqueray's home ground, so what chance has Paula? Because he does not wish his daughter to think less of him, he dare not risk her discovering Paula's antecedents. Therefore, all three of them remain at Highercoombe, seeing no one, going nowhere. Paula says she is bored, but that is only another word for 'unhappy'. If she had been alone with Aubrey, life would have been unadulterated happiness. Ellean has destroyed all chance of that. Aubrey's past life rises up, remorsely to confront Paula wherever she turns – and, what is worse, he is forsaking her for Ellean, for his past.

During the quarrel between them which takes place at the beginning of this act, Paula's clear-eyed, remorseless vision of the life he has apparently condemned her to at last breaks through his egoism. At her words, 'It's true I did want, dearly, dearly, to be a married woman, but where's the pride in being a married woman among married women who are – married! If – ' Then she sees that Aubrey is weeping. In a rush of tenderness and concern she goes to him; but, before there can be any rapprochement, any reconciliation between them, Ellean enters, and the moment is gone. This is a technique which Pinero uses all the way through the play, which is basically structured on a line of 'interrupted cadences'. No situation is ever fully played out; someone always comes in to interrupt it. Pinero describes Ellean '*as a low-voiced, grave girl of about nineteen, with a face somewhat resembling a Madonna*', and he adds, '*Towards* PAULA, *her manner is somewhat distant and cold*.'

Paula, typically, makes a gesture of affection: she kisses her; Ellean rejects her. Paula's desperate need for Ellean's affection is repulsed several times in the play. In symbolic terms, worldliness and heedless promiscuity can never regain lost innocence. Strict, puritanical, religious belief cannot come to terms with lack of moderation, gaiety, even affection. It is not necessary to labour the symbolic core of the play, but, as in so many Pinero plays, it is firmly entrenched at the heart of the action. In psychological terms, also, Ellean is interesting. Apparently as cold and reserved as her mother, she is jealous of this woman who has taken her mother's place. She will make no concessions to her. Paula interestingly says, 'She is marble', picking up Drummle's image of her mother ('marble arms and black velvet') in Act I, and Aubrey says that she resembles her mother. There is no way in which he can escape from his past now; and it is engulfing Paula as well.

In the first confrontation between Paula and Ellean, sympathy lies with Paula, who shows all her best qualities: humility, honesty, courage and an affectionate heart. Ellean is cold, unresponsive, ungenerous. She represents not only the worst elements of rigid religious belief, but also the social standards applied by 'virtuous' women, married and single, who, like the wives of Misquith and Jayne, would not receive women such as Paula into their homes.

Pinero, with deft theatre-craft, interrupts the scene at a crucial moment by the brisk entrance of Drummle. This not only serves to leave the situation hopelessly unresolved, but changes the tempo and the mood completely. Left with Drummle, who, as he revealed in Act I, knows Paula very well, she tells him of her jealousy of Ellean, her unhappiness, her boredom. She refers to her life as 'a dog's life'. 'I'm sleek, well-kept, well-fed, never without a bone to gnaw and fresh straw to lie upon.' He's amazed when she suddenly begins to talk about the good times they had on Peter Jarman's yacht. She is horrified at herself also – but, before she can say any more, Aubrey comes in, delighted to see Drummle. The interruption prevents her from explaining herself, and Drummle, whose well-meant interfering provides the impetus for the play's catastrophe, does not understand her true feelings until it is too late.

Aubrey, left with Drummle, quickly unburdens himself. He refers to Paula's feverish, jealous attachment' to Ellean. showing how little he understands the nature of Paula's need, which manifests itself in jealousy because she feels so insecure, so unloved, so excluded. When Drummle says soothingly, 'These are early days, Ellean will warm towards your wife by and by', Aubrey reveals how completely his past has defeated Paula. 'I ask myself, am I doing right in exposing her [Ellean] to the influence of poor Paula's light, careless nature.' In saying this he shows that he has never appreciated anything other than the surface of Paula. He has already shown in Act I that he is not aware of her generosity or courage, or of the depth of feeling banked down under the frivolous exterior. Her surges of temper distress him, and her need for Ellean's love he does not really understand. He himself, obviously, is able to respond to her warmth and affection: but he feels that it is unreasonable of her to expect affection from his pure daughter ('I don't believe a purer creature exists out of heaven'). He admits that he neither can, nor tries to, break down the barriers between Ellean and Paula, and then out tumbles his judgement of Paula, seen now against the background of his life with his first wife:

> Cayley, there's hardly a subject you can broach on which poor Paula hasn't some strange out-of-the-way thought to give utterance to; some curious, warped notion. They are not mere worldly thoughts – unless good God! they belong to the hellish world which our blackguardism has created; no, her ideas have too little calculation in them to be called worldly. But it makes it the more dreadful that such thoughts should be ready, spontaneous; that expressing them has become a perfectly natural process; that her words, acts even, have almost lost their proper significance for her, and seem beyond control. Ah, the pain of listening to it all from the woman one loves, the woman one hoped to make happy and contented, who is really and truly a good woman, as it were maimed. Well, this is my burden, and I shouldn't speak to you of it but for my anxiety about Ellean – Ellean! What

> is to be her future? It is in my hands; what am I to do? Cayley, when I remember how Ellean comes to me, from another world I always think, when I realize the change that's laid on me, I find myself wishing, in a sort of terror, that my child were safe under the ground!

Here, in one speech, is the 'double standard' laid bare. Paula has lived almost exclusively in the company of men, and women like herself, for some years. She has lived in the man's world of promiscuous sex, a world where no topic of conversation is barred, because none of the women is deemed worthy of 'respect', or of protection from the harsher realities of life. Paula, naturally, thinks and still reacts in a man's world. She doesn't understand the prudery and cosseted ignorance of 'nice' women. In referring to 'the hellish world of our blackguardism', Aubrey is condemning that male world, with it freedoms and licence. When he refers to the pain of listening to it all from the woman he loves, he is being disingenuous. He must have known she was like this before he married her. In saying that she is really 'a good woman', he is, of course, implying that, at heart, she belongs to the world of 'respectable' women; he had hoped that that under his tutelage she would learn propriety, self-control, seemliness. By 'good' he obviously means more like his first wife, or his friend Mrs Cortelyon, in outward behaviour. He imagined that Paula could change radically from her true self to someone who could join the ranks of women imprisoned by social convention and masculine rules. In condemning her for the socially enforced virtues which she does not have, he quite overlooks the very real ones she does possess.

Aubrey shows his passivity over Ellean. Instead of saying to her that Christ showed great mercy to repentant sinners, appealing to her religious training in an active way, imploring her to try to love Paula, he allows her to act as a Pharisee, pandering to her intolerance and his ideas of virtue.

No wonder Drummle somewhat briskly takes the matter in hand. Something must be *done*. Ellean must be treated like flesh and blood. She cannot be allowed to stay here thus sequestered from the world. What does it matter if she is told Paula's history? Perhaps she will learn to be tolerant and forgiving. Before he can discuss properly with Aubrey the plans he has made with Mrs Cortelyon for her to take Ellean to Paris with her, Mrs Cortelyon unexpectedly arrives – another interruption. She is, Pinero says, '*a handsome, good-humoured, spirited woman of about forty-five*'. She is accompanied by Ellean, with whom she has been talking.

The short scene that follows, in which Paula is so rude to Mrs Cortelyon, is funny but painful. It shows Paula at her worst: insolent, offensive and totally lacking in propriety or good sense. Her motives are not easy to disentangle. However, with the partial exception of Ellean, the other people in the room have all known each other for many years, so, on coming among them with her rejections by both Aubrey and Ellean still rankling, and knowing that Drummle has been staying with Mrs Cortelyon, Paula probably feels that there is some conspiracy against her. In a sense she is right; but, where normally an honest appeal such as Mrs Cortelyon's would have appealed to her own honesty and generosity, she is too much in the grip of her emotions to react rationally; and so she brings misfortune on her own head. The scene rushes to a crescendo; Ellean leaves to go to Paris with Mrs Cortelyon; and the act ends with two marvellous moments of theatre: the first where Paula tears off her outdoors hat and coat and, taking her huge hat-pin, stabs her hat again and again, uttering inarticulate cries of pent-up grief and rage; and the second where, after a blazing row with Aubrey, she slams out of the room as the curtain falls.

Pinero, writing to Mrs Patrick Campbell, the first Paula, implored her

> not to allow the shrewish side of Paula's disposition to get uppermost . . . Constant repetition may lead you into developing too fondly – for that is the side of the character more easily reproduced perhaps – the termagant aspect of poor Paula at the expense of her more sympathetic, her equally natural and more genuine, qualities.[4]

The apparent rage and jealousy which Paula exhibits are not mere temper. They have their roots in many other emotions: chiefly insecurity, and a deep-seated need for love and approval. Aubrey has been alienated from her; Ellean draws her skirts aside from her; Drummle and Mrs Cortelyon seem to be in league against her. For many years now, she has not moved in a society where restraint is a principal tenet of behaviour, although it is possible that her capacity for self-destruction has been her chief enemy most of her life. She can do no other than be true to herself under such stress.

Act III is set in the drawing-room of Highercoombe, another gracious, elegant room. It is evening, and the garden outside is flooded with moonlight. The Orreyeds are in residence. Lady Orreyed (Mabel) is exactly as Drummle described her in Act I. Sir George is 'about thirty-five, with a low forehead, a receding chin, a vacuous expression, and an ominous redness about the nose' – he drinks heavily. They provide a comic parallel to Paula and Aubrey. Mabel is too thick-skinned and mercenary to care about social ostracism. She is quite happy with her lot, and spends a great deal of time patronising Paula. They provide a welcome touch of humour in a play so far predominantly serious.

Paula is tired of them and finds them sickening. Like Rose Trelawny, she has begun to change, without realizing it, under the influence of a different life. Mabel notices this, saying, 'Oh how dreadfully changed you are, Paula.' The Orreyeds have been there about a fortnight, and Paula realises how much she would have preferred to spend the time alone with Aubrey. She hasn't spoken to him since Ellean went, except in front of the Orreyeds.

When Drummle, the well-meaning 'fixer' attempts to reconcile Aubrey and Paula, he is nearly successful. For the first time in their relationship, relieved of the incubus of Ellean's presence, they are able to talk honestly to each other, and he tells her the truth about herself, as he sees it, sparing neither himself nor her. Whether it is the truth or not is a matter for some conjecture. It is possible, but unlikely, that the girl whom Aubrey sentimentally envisages would have gone to live with some man at nineteen or twenty, although, taking Paula's reaction into consideration, perhaps Pinero intended it to be the truth. The critic William Archer made exactly this point.

> without overstepping the limits of the dramatic form, it might surely have been possible to give us a somewhat clearer view of her antecedents. I do not mean of her life as 'Mrs Jarman' or 'Mrs Dartry' (that we can take on trust), but of her parentage, her girlhood, her education, of the instincts and influences that have made her what she is. She talks now and again like a woman of intelligence, and even of culture, and she acts like a perverse child, so utterly incapable of self-restraint as to fly in the face of her own ambitions and interests at every second word. I do not say that this is inconsis-

> tent; on the contrary, I believe it to be absolutely true to nature; but I think a little retrospective analysis, so to speak, might have shown the underlying harmony of certain superficial discords.[5]

In Aubrey's analysis of Paula, 'The chapter that relates to the time when you were – like Ellean' presumably means the time of her initial seduction. It is likely that Paula was no unwilling victim; her emotions are highly charged, and her will is strong. By the time Aubrey has finally cracked the hard shell with which Paula surrounds herself and made her weep, it is possible to feel that Aubrey is as narrow and priggish as his daughter. If he felt that her behaviour was so objectionable, he should long since have tried to discuss the matter with her. His failure shows, once again, his lack of understanding of the strength of her love for him, and her genuine desire to be better. It also emphasises his essential passivity and lack of belief in her. Paula's words 'A few years ago' are significant in that they tie up with those numerous references about an incident in her past when she had some 'trouble'. The whole focus on the young Paula is also especially important, given what is to happen next. At the end of this painful scene, the audience feels that some understanding has at last been reached between the unhappy pair, and that there is some hope for the future. Perhaps Aubrey without Ellean coming constantly between them will learn to appreciate Paula's better qualities.

But, following the pattern of the play, any hope is dashed by the arrival of Mrs Cortelyon and Ellean, brought about by Paula's foolish spite in withholding their letters from Paris. Also, in a repetition of the fatal pattern of Act I, Aubrey does not bother to look at the letters when Paula gives them to him. So, when Ellean and Mrs Cortelyon sing the praises of the young soldier whom Ellean has fallen in love with, the fact that they do not name him leaves Paula totally unprepared for his appearance, like a bad dream from her past. Mrs Cortelyon's account of Hugh Ardale is glowing, but a nineteenth-century audience would have known from the way he makes his entry that he is not an entirely respectable young man.

It is evidence again of Pinero's skill that, without any sense of incongruity, he contrives to leave Ellean alone on stage. Then there is an abrupt change in the action. A rose is thrown through the window and lands at her feet. She goes to the window, and there is Hugh. Immediately an audience is made aware that Hugh may not be quite as described by Mrs Cortelyon. At that time, no entirely respectable young man would have attempted to see a young girl unchaperoned and alone, particularly when he was due to meet her parents the next day. As Pinero describes him, he is twenty-seven – the same age as Paula. He has '*a boyish face and manner*'. He tries to embrace Ellean. She is offended and shocked. He has behaved in a similar manner before, for she says, 'It's when you're like this that you make me feel utterly miserable.' He wants her to come out into the garden with him, but she adamantly refuses. He asks her to forgive him, trading on his boyish charm, and entreats her again to come out into the garden with him. At this point, it is only the fact of Ellean's rectitude which prevents her from behaving very foolishly; he selfishly is doing everything he can to lead her astray. Impressions of Hugh are by now not very favourable. In the 1990s *her* behaviour seems unreasonable. In the 1890s it is *his* behaviour which is unreasonable and dishonourable. He is the prototype for a number of caddish young men in Pinero's plays.

In the encounter between Ardale and Paula, the significance of her previous scene with Aubrey becomes apparent. Obviously, at Ellean's age the young Paula, ardent and self-willed, had allowed herself to be seduced by the young, handsome Hugh. Tiring of her, he had left her to go out to India in the army, not bothering to keep track of her or follow her 'doings' after they separated. She, heartbroken (there are various references in the text to her reactions to a past disappointment), has, in an untypical gesture, kept the key to the escritoire in their apartment. She is not deceived by the handsome, boyish soldier hero; she knows Ardale for what he is: promiscuous, faithless, deceitful. His name was on that 'account of myself, furnished with a list of my adventures' which Aubrey so lightly threw onto the fire. It is essential that he should be prevented from marrying Ellean. Paula is too honest, and has, in a strange way, too highly developed a moral sense to live out such a lie. Ardale, in Aubrey's terms, is as tainted as she. Ellean and Mrs Cortelyon adulate the military hero; Paula knows the man.

Confronted by her past, she must tell Aubrey in order to save Ellean, and so shatter her own frail hopes of happiness. When she picks up the mirror to study her haggard face, as she has done earlier in the act, she is gazing relentlessly, without hope or illusion, at her future; and later she is not afraid to tell Aubrey what she sees. The curtain falls as stonily she gazes at her reflection.

As the curtain rises on the last act, she has not moved. The dark mood is momentarily dispelled by the entrance of the Orreyeds, who provide another interlude of satiric counterpoint to the main plot. This episode serves several functions: it lightens the mood of the play; it brings Paula out of her despairing reverie; it shows the distance that she has travelled from her old friends; and it breaks the action of the play sufficiently for the preparation in a lower key for the coming climax.

The tension slowly builds, through Paula's confession to Aubrey to Aubrey's confrontation with Ellean. For the first time Aubrey has to bear the full consequences of marrying Paula. In the same way as his past has nearly destroyed her, so now her past has risen up to destroy him, and he is torn apart by the results of his own actions. His pain is increased by Ellean. She tells him that Ardale has confessed to her about his 'wild, dissolute life in London'. He has told her 'what a man's life is – what his life had been'. Aubrey is horrified. His *wife* is part of that 'wild, dissolute life'. Ardale's past has helped to corrupt Paula; now he has talked about his 'man's life', and not only besmirched Ellean but also shown the contempt he had for Paula. Ellean tells her father that 'as far as I could forgive him, I forgave him' and explains that, although Ardale has sinned, he has redeemed himself by his conduct in India. She sees her 'hero' being taken from her, and there is menace in her words 'And so, Father, if Paula has reported anything to Captain Ardale's discredit – it *must* be Paula; it can't be anybody else.'

Aubrey makes a desperate bid again to protect Paula: 'You'll – you'll please keep Paula out of the question. Finally, Ellean, understand me – I have made up my mind.'

Hard and determined, Ellean says, 'I have made up my mind also.' Aubrey, faced with this unfamiliar young woman, suddenly recognises her 'Ah! I recognize your mother in you now.' Ellean flashes back, 'You need not speak against my mother because you are angry with me.' But Aubrey is not angry: he is afraid, for himself and for Paula. He dare not think what Ellean may do. He cannot face her any more, so he leaves.

Finally, the climax is reached, as Paula confronts Ellean. Ellean is merciless in her questions; Paula is subdued, doing her best to fend them off. Suddenly the realisation dawns on Ellean: 'You – you knew Captain Ardale in London.' She turns and tries to leave the room. Paula, characteristically, brings the next disaster on her own head. Losing control, she prevents Ellean from leaving, hysterically forcing her to explain what she meant by her accusation. 'You've always hated me! You shall answer me!' Ellean cries out, 'I have always known you for what you were.' Paula lets her go, and feebly supports herself on a chair; but she still cannot let well alone. 'Who told you?' And Ellean finally says the words that destroy Paula:

> Nobody but yourself. From the first moment I saw you I knew you were altogether unlike the good women I'd left; directly I saw you I knew what my father had done. You've wondered why I turned from you. There – that's the reason. Oh, but this is a horrible way for the truth to come home to everyone.

Ellean's censoriousness applies to Paula where it does not apply to Ardale. They have shared the same 'dissolute life', but, because Ellean is in love with Ardale, she will not judge him, will forgive him, would marry him. Paula she condemns, will not forgive. Her father had done something wrong in marrying Paula; but she will not even try to understand.

Without her fragile belief that she is inherently good, Paula has no further reason for living. Forcing Ellean to her knees, Paula frantically denies her accusation, trying to make Ellean beg her pardon.

Aubrey is brought back into the room by Ellean's screams, and raises her from the ground. 'It's my fault', she says. 'Father, I – I don't wish to see Captain Ardale again', and she goes out.

Left together, Aubrey and Paula begin to talk almost at cross-purposes. Paula tells him that Ellean knows about her, and follows her own thread of thought. Ellean had merely confirmed what Aubrey had said to her earlier: 'I'm tainted through and through.' She muses about what his first marriage must have been, if Ellean resembled his first wife. 'She's a regular woman too. She could forgive *him* easily enough – but *me*! That's just a woman!' Aubrey is obsessed by what they can do – they must drive the idea out of her head – but what can they do? 'Nothing', says Paula. 'She'd have no difficulty in following up her suspicions. Suspicions! You should have seen how she looked at me.'

In the disjointed conversation that follows, Aubrey and Paula come closer to each other than at any other time. He has his eyes set on a fresh start, ever optimistic. Paula, the realist, will not let him escape the truth as she sees it: 'You'll never forget this, you know .... Tonight, and everything that led up to it. Our coming here, Ellean, our quarrels – cat and dog! – Mrs Cortelyon, the Orreyeds, this man. What an everlasting nightmare for you!' But Aubrey rejects this: 'We'll make our calculations solely for the future, talk about the future, think about the future'; and Paula says the chilling line which enshrines the philosophy of the play, which is, indeed, the deterministic philosophy of much of Pinero's work: 'I believe the future is only the past again, entered through another gate.' Aubrey, shocked, replies, 'That's an awful belief', but Paula answers, 'Tonight proves it. You must see now that, do what we will, go where we will, you'll be continually reminded of – what I was.'

He tries to comfort her, to deny it: 'The world isn't quite as small as all that', but she only replies,

> The only great distances it contains are those we carry within ourselves – the distances that separate husbands and wives, for instance. And so it'll be with us. You'll do your best – oh, I know that – you're a good fellow. But circumstances will be too strong for you in the end, mark my words.

Not only does she envisage a future where the past continually confronts them, but also a future where she will lose her only hold on him, her physical attraction.

> That horrid irresistible truth that physical repulsion forces on men and women will come to you, and you'll sicken at me . . . . You'll see me then, at last, with other people's eyes; you'll see me just as your daughter does now, as all wholesome folk see women like me. And I shall have no weapon to fight with – not one serviceable little bit of prettiness left to defend myself with . . . . Oh Aubrey, what shall I be able to say to you then? And this is the future you talk about!

He tries to comfort her; but, once again, Drummle interrupts, and unknowingly brings about the final catastrophe. They hear him singing as he comes up the lane. Paula cannot face him, so she leaves the safety of Aubrey's arms and goes out, quickly, on her own.

Drummle is all agog about Ellean and Ardale; but it is too much for Aubrey. He breaks out into an indictment of Ardale, and of all men who, like him, have had 'a man's life':

> Curse him! Curse him! Yes I do curse him – him and his class! Perhaps I curse myself too in doing it. He has only led 'a man's life' – just as I, how many of us have done! The misery he has brought on me and mine it's

likely enough we, in our time, have helped to bring on others by this leading 'a man's life'! But I do curse him for all that. My God, *I've* nothing more to fear – I've paid *my* fine! And so I can curse him in safety. Curse him! Curse him!

It is Paula he thinks of, at last, not Ellean. 'My poor wretched wife! My poor wretched wife!'

But it is too late. Paula, alone, with no shred of self-respect or illusion left, has killed herself.

The curtain falls on Ellean's words 'If I had only been merciful'; and therein lies the moral heart of the play. Ostensibly the play deals with the 'dual standard'. Indeed, Aubrey's speech had a great effect on those who heard it, and Pinero's courage in writing it was praised; but the play is also a plea for tolerance, understanding and compassion. Paula's frantic cry 'I am a good woman' is true, only no one would judge her for her virtues. She was measured by the yardstick of a censorious and hypocritical code, and found wanting. She was allowed no future – only a past.

She is the scapegoat for them all.

Appendix I
Films Made from Plays by Jones and Pinero

The research for this appendix was carried out by Lisa Swinglehurst.

Henry Arthur Jones

1914 *The Lie* (a rather free version produced by Lubin, USA)

1915 *The Middleman* (London Film Co.)

1916 *The Morals of Weybury* (based on *The Hypocrites* and produced by G. L. Tucker, UK)

1918 *Mrs Dane's Defence* (Paramount Artcraft; directed by Hugh Ford)

1918 *A Society Exile* (adapted from a play entitled *We Can't Be as Bad as All That* which was not produced in the West End; directed by George Fitzmaunce)

1920 *The Call of Youth* (from a play which was never staged; Famous Players – Lasky, directed by Hugh Ford)

1921 *Beyond* (apparently an original screenplay, though

bearing some resemblance to *The Rogue's Comedy;* directed by Desmond Taylor)

1923 *The Hypocrites* (Granger-Binger; directed by Charles Giblyn)

1928 *The Physician* (Gaumont; produced by Maurice Elvey and directed by George Jacoby)

1929 *The Silver King* (Welsh–Pearson–Elder; produced by G. & D. Pearson and directed by T. Hayes Hunter; reputed to have cost about £60,000)

1933 *Mrs Dane's Defence* (National Talkies, Paramount; produced by Harry Rowson and directed by A. V. Bramble)

Jones wrote four other scenarios, which were not produced.

Arthur Wing Pinero

1915 *Sweet Lavender* (produced by C. M. Hepworth; Henry Ainley played Dick Phenyl)

1916 *Trelawny of the 'Wells'* (produced by C. M. Hepworth)

1916 *Iris* (produced by C. M. Hepworth; Henry Ainley played Maldonaldo)

1916 *The Second Mrs Tanqueray* (Ideal; directed by Fred Paul, with George Alexander as Aubrey Tanqueray; reported to have cost £20,000)

1917 *The Amazons* (Paramount, directed by Joseph Kaufman)

1917 *The Profligate* (produced and directed by Meyrick M. Milton)

1918 *The Gay Lord Quex* (Ideal; produced and directed by Maurice Elvey, with a cast including Ben Webster, Irene Vanbrugh and Lilian Braithwaite)

1920 *A Slave of Vanity* (based on *Iris* and produced in the USA)
1920 *His House in Order* (Paramount; directed by Hugh Ford)
1920 *Sweet Lavender* (Paramount; directed by Paul Powell)
1921 *The Magistrate* (Samuelson; directed by Bannister Merwin)
1922 *La Seconda Femma* (Italian version of *The Second Mrs Tanqueray)*
1924 *The Enchanted Cottage* (USA; directed by J. S. Robertson)
1928 *The Actress* (based on *Trelawny of the 'Wells'*; (produced by Sidney Franklin and starring Norma Shearer)
1928 *His House in Order* (Ideal; produced by Meyrick M. Milton, directed by Randle Ayrton, and starring Tallulah Bankhead)
1934 *Those Were the Days* (version of *The Magistrate* made at Elstree Studios; produced by Walter Mycroft and directed by Thomas Bentley, with a cast including Will Hay, Angela Baddeley, George Graves, John Mills, Wally Patch and Jimmy Hanley)
1935 *Dandy Dick* (Elstree Studios; produced by Walter Mycroft and directed by William Beaudine, with a cast including Will Hay, Esmond Night, Wally Patch and Moore Marriott)
1945 *The Enchanted Cottage* (RKO; produced by Roger Proudlock and directed by Dallas Bower, with Dorothy McGuire, Herbert Marshall and Robert Young)
1952 *The Second Mrs Tanqueray* (Vandyke; produced by Roger Proudlock and directed by Dallas Bower,

with Pamela Brown as Paula Tanqueray, Virginia McKenna as Ellean, and Hugh Sinclair as Aubrey Tanqueray)

In 1919 Pinero was invited to join the consultative literary committee of Alliance, an ambitious new British company. Unfortunately, the company over-extended itself financially and was wound up in 1922.

Appendix II
Henry Arthur Jones versus G. B. Shaw and H. G. Wells*

Although, in his earlier years, Henry Arthur Jones had flirted with socialism, and was an ardent admirer of William Morris, he was appalled by the 'anti-British' attitude of Shaw and Wells during and after the First World War. Despite the fact that he had been a close friend of both men, particularly Shaw, he attacked them in pamphlets and in the press. He interpreted their writings as traitorous and subversive, and, indeed, considered them to be agents of Bolshevism and revolution. In 1919, he published a book entitled *Patriotism and Popular Education,* which contains a vehement and direct attack on Wells's political ideas. On 10 March he wrote to Wells, before attacking him publicly,

> In my forthcoming book, *Patriotism and Popular Education,* I have attacked what seem to me to be the most mischievous fallacies in some of your recent articles and

* The quotations in this appendix are extracted from Doris Jones, *The Life and Letters of Henry Arthur Jones* (1930) pp. 307–28.

letters. You advocate principles and schemes which, so far as they can be put into operation, tend to disintegrate and shatter not only the British Empire, but all civilised structure. Now as I wish the British Empire to be preserved and strengthened, you will not be surprised that I have used the most effective means in my power to expose what I consider to be the radical unsoundness of your political theories. I should not think myself a good citizen if I neglected to fulfil this duty to my country to the best of my ability . . . . If my arguments are wrong, I shall think you are doing me a service if you refute them . . . . I shall be sorry if this action of mine loses me an old friend, and can assure you that I shall always dwell with the kindliest remembrance on our long and pleasant associations.

Wells replied with great kindliness:

I am quite sure that nothing you can say about my opinions is likely to alter the very kindly feelings I bear you. I've no doubt you'll *go for* me with the utmost spirit and violence and fairness. I think the British Empire in its present form is a sham and a nuisance.

When the book was published, Wells published an open letter to Jones in the *Evening Standard,* but otherwise ignored it all, and left Jones to say or write what he wanted.

As a patriot, Jones felt in duty bound to try to counteract the influence of Wells and Shaw, which he considered pernicious. Jones attracted considerable support not only in Britain, but all over the Empire. Many eminent figures backed his campaign, and he received hundreds of letters encouraging him, and thanking him for his services to Britain

For twenty years he had been a close friend of Shaw's. Their correspondence is affectionate and intimate. Shaw's criticisms of Jones's plays are witty and very much to the point. Yet in 1914 Jones wrote to his daughter from New York, 'Shaw continues his crazy attacks. I never felt more angry with any man. He is trying to keep up the strife between England and Ireland. I do not think I can meet him in the future.'

His disgust with Shaw came into the open in October 1915. Shaw had been asked to refrain from attending the fortnightly lunch of the Dramatists' Club because of his attitude to the war. On behalf of 'several members', the secretary wrote to Shaw to this effect. Shaw wrote to Jones saying that he hoped Jones was not one of the 'several members', and received Jones's reply that he was. Jones went on in his letter,

> I believe that England's cause is a most righteous one. I am sure that England did not provoke this war. I am sure that Germany did. These are to me, not matters of opinion, but clearly established facts.
>
> Your writings on the War have done great harm to our cause in America and neutral countries. Germany is everywhere making use of your utterances to justify her own actions and to befoul and slander England. Whether you know it or not, and whether you care or not, you are one of our country's worst enemies. And you are an enemy within our walls. One of the leading American papers, in commenting on your pamphlet, said that if you had written in Germany on behalf of her enemies, you would have been shot.
>
> I cannot think you were so shortsighted as not to have foreseen that you were furnishing Germany with a powerful weapon to attack England, that you were

> offering evidence that our cause was unjust, that we were to blame for this War. . . . you should not be surprised that in the agony and bloody sweat of fighting for our life we have no patience with a man who tries to trip us up – and with us the mercies and humanities of European civilisation.

Shaw's answer to this is a masterpiece of witty exculpation; and he accuses Jones of lack of faith in England, 'And you think England, your mother, is on a sick-bed. She never was stronger in her life, as you will find out if you annoy her too much by your shrieks of terror at the German menace . . . .'

Three weeks after this exchange of letters, an interview with Shaw entitled '"Shoot your Officers, and Go Home," says Shaw' was published in the *San Francisco Bulletin*. The effect of this interview on the American public was bad; and, though Shaw denied having ever given such an interview, his pamphlet *Common Sense about the War* said much the same things. Shaw also made mischievous statements about Belgium's neutrality. Although Shaw was used by the Mediterranean Department to write propaganda material to dissuade the Moors in Algeria and Tunisia from entering the war, all this was a red rag to a bull as far as Jones was concerned. He did not understand the leniency of the Foreign Office towards Shaw, or why Shaw was sent to the Front in 1917 to write a series of descriptive articles for simultaneous publication in London and New York.

Having written a series of letters in the *Evening Standard* in September 1920 attacking Wells, in August 1921, Jones published *My Dear Wells: A Manual for Haters of England*. The contents had already appeared in letter form in the *Evening Standard* and The *New York Sunday Times*, and contained attacks on both Wells and Shaw. Castigating Shaw, Jones wrote, 'The Nag Sedition was your mother, and Perversity begot you; Mischief was your Midwife, and Misrule your Nurse, and Unreason brought you up at her feet – no other ancestry and rearing had you.' The indictment of Shaw was based on a careful analysis of his public acts and published works, and an article published in *Trend* by an eminent American classical scholar, Professor Paul Shorey, confirms the grounds of Jones's intemperate polemic.

After the publication of *My Dear Wells,* Jones's attacks were directed at Shaw alone. He embarked on writing a book to be called *Bernard Shaw as a Thinker,* but did not finish it; instead; in September 1921 he published in the *Morning Post* letters headed 'Bernard Shaw as a Mischief-Maker.' In 1923, six chapters of *Bernard Shaw as a Thinker* were published in the *English Review*. Despite his rapidly failing health, Jones became obsessed with his campaign. The death of his wife in 1924 must have added to his unhappiness, and he had little else to think of. His daughter Doris looked after him, and she says bitterly,

> It was never out of his mind; during these years, even at meal-times, Wells's and Shaw's misdeeds formed the major, and very often the only, topic of conversation. How often have I wished that he had confined his criticism of G. B. S.'s political activities to a remark he once made to me: 'Shaw's economics are exactly those of Jack Cade in Shakespeare.'

In 1925, more chapters on Shaw appeared as 'What is Capital?', which was published in book form. Apparently the labour press did not approve of it, although Shaw, in typically mischievous mood, praised some of its pages as sound Shavian doctrine. That same year, Shaw was invited to propose the health of Shakespeare at the annual Stratford-upon-Avon Festival. Jones was beside himself with rage. He felt that such an invitation was an insult to Shakespeare, in view of the derogatory things that Shaw had said about the poet, including

> With the single exception of Homer, there is no eminent writer, not even Sir Walter Scott, whom I can despise so utterly as I despise Shakespeare when I measure my mind against his. The intensity of my impatience with him occasionally reaches such a pitch, that it would positively be a relief to me to dig him up and throw stones at him.

Jones wrote what was to be his last attack on Shaw: *Mr Mayor of Shakespeare's Town.* He had a contract to publish the book, but the publisher, afraid of libel, withdrew it. Other publishers, when approached, also refused. Shaw was asked, without Jones's knowledge, to promise that he would take no action against publisher or printer. Shaw, typically, replied that he would do everything in his power to force Jones to return to play-writing, and stop wasting his time on useless political invective – an opinion which was shared by all Jones's friends and relatives. The printer, who had set the book and run off six copies, broke up the type. At the time Jones thought the book would be printed, and extracts from it were printed in the *Daily Mail.* This elicited a letter from a reader who accused Jones of attacking Shaw through lack of comprehension of his paradoxical, epigrammatic style, and through personal jealousy. The writer remarked,

> I must, however, question your good faith in reminding

> you that Shaw is – and is recognised as – (among other things) the greatest playwright of his generation, and that you are a playwright of his generation, whom he has perforce – certainly not by design – 'put in the shade'.

The writer implies that Jones is piqued because Shaw, not he, has been invited to speak at Stratford, and he says that he finds it 'painful' that the author of so 'beautiful' a play as *Michael and his Lost Angel,* which owed its discovery to Shaw, should make such a spectacle of himself.

Shaw is said to have commented, with great good humour, 'What! Jones jealous of me as a dramatist! Nonsense! You don't suppose he considers me a dramatist, do you? To him I am only a critic who has mistaken his profession.'

Appendix III
Chronology of Works by Jones and Pinero

Unless otherwise indicated, plays received their first performance in London theatres. Dates of plays that have not been performed are dates of composition.

Henry Arthur Jones

PLAYS

The Golden Calf, 1869, never performed
It's Only Round the Corner, produced in 1878, Theatre Royal, Exeter
Cherry Ripe, 1878, never performed
Hearts of Oak; or, A Chip off the Old Block, produced 1897, Theatre Royal, Exeter
Honour Bright, 1879, re-write of *Hearts of Oak*, never performed
Elopement, produced 1879, Theatre Royal, Oxford
A Clerical Error, produced 1879
A Drive in June, 1879, never performed

An Old Master, produced 1880, Princess's Theatre
A Garden Party, 1879–80, never performed
Lady Caprice, 1880, never performed
Humbug, 1879, never performed
Home Again, produced 1881, Theatre Royal, Oxford
His Wife, produced 1881, Sadler's Wells
A Bed of Roses, produced 1882, Globe Theatre
The Silver King (with Henry Herman), produced 1882, Princess's Theatre
The Wedding Guest, 1882, never performed
Breaking a Butterfly (with Henry Herman, from Ibsen's *A Doll's House*), produced 1884, Prince's Theatre
Chatterton (with Henry Herman), produced 1884, Princess's Theatre
Saints and Sinners, produced 1884, Vaudeville Theatre
Hoodman Blind (with Wilson Barrett), produced 1885, Princess's Theatre
The Lord Harry (with Wilson Barrett), produced 1886, Princess's Theatre
The Noble Vagabond, produced 1886, Princess's Theatre
Welcome Little Stranger, 1885–90, never performed
Hard Hit, produced 1887, Haymarket Theatre
Heart of Hearts, produced 1887, Vaudeville Theatre
The Middleman, produced 1889, Shaftesbury Theatre
Wealth, produced 1889, Haymarket Theatre
Judah, produced 1890, Shaftesbury Theatre
Sweet Will, produced 1890, Shaftesbury Theatre
The Deacon, produced 1890, Shaftesbury Theatre
The Dancing Girl, produced 1891, Haymarket Theatre
The Crusaders, produced 1891, Avenue Theatre
The Mad Cook, 1891, never performed
The Bauble Shop, produced 1893, Criterion Theatre
The Tempter, produced 1893, Haymarket Theatre
The Masqueraders, produced 1894, St James's Theatre

The Case of Rebellious Susan, produced 1894, Criterion Theatre
The Triumph of the Philistines, produced 1895, St James's Theatre
Grace Mary, 1895, never performed
Michael and his Lost Angel, produced 1896, Lyceum
The Rogue's Comedy, produced 1896, Garrick Theatre
The Physician, produced 1897, Criterion Theatre
The Liars, produced 1897, Criterion Theatre
The Manoeuvres of Jane, produced 1898, Haymarket Theatre
Carnac Sahib, produced 1899, Her Majesty's Theatre
The Lackey's Carnival, produced 1900, Duke of York's Theatre
Mrs Dane's Defence, produced 1900, Wyndham's Theatre
James the Fogey, 1902, never performed
The Princess's Nose, produced 1902, Duke of York's Theatre
Chance, the Idol, produced 1902, Wyndham's Theatre
Whitewashing Julia, produced 1903, Garrick Theatre
Joseph Entangled, produced 1904, Haymarket Theatre
The Chevaleer, produced 1904, Garrick Theatre
Chrysold, 1904, never performed
Felisa, 1904, never performed
The Sword of Gideon, 1905, never performed
The Heroic Stubbs, produced 1906, Terry's Theatre
The Hypocrites, produced 1906, Hudson Theatre, New York; 1907, Hick's Theatre, London
The Galilean's Victory, produced 1907 (as *The Evangelist*), Knickerbocker Theatre, New York
Dick, 1908, never performed
Dolly Reforming Herself, produced 1908
The Knife, produced 1909, Palace Theatre
Loo Vallance, 1909, never performed

Fall In, Rookie, produced 1910, Alhambra Theatre
We Can't Be As Bad As All That!, produced 1910, Nazimova's 39th Street Theatre, New York
The Ogre, produced 1911, St James Theatre
Lydia Gilmore, produced 1912, Lyceum
Mary Goes First, produced 1913, Playhouse Theatre
Her Tongue, 1912, never performed
The Divine Gift, 1912, never performed
The Lie, produced 1914, Harris Theatre, New York
The Goal, produced 1914, Princess's Theatre, New York
Cock o' the Walk, produced 1915, Cohan Theatre, New York
The Right Man for Sophie, 1916, never performed
The Pacifists, produced 1917, St James's Theatre
Finding Themselves, 1917, never performed
The Lifted Veil, 1919, never performed
The Woman I Loved, 1922, unfinished

OTHER WORKS

The Renascence of the English Drama: Essays, Lectures, and Fragments Relating to the Modern English Stage, 1883–94 (1895)
The Foundations of a National Drama: Lectures, Essays and Speeches, 1896–1912 (1913)
Patriotism and Popular Education (1919)
My Dear Wells. A Manual for the Haters of England (1921)
What is Capital? An Enquiry into the Meaning of the Words, 'Capital' and 'Labour' (1925)
'Mr Mayor of Shakespeare's Town', unpublished
'The Shadow of Henry Irving', unpublished

Jones wrote many letters to the press, articles, lectures and speeches. Many of these connected with the drama are included in *The Renascence of the English Drama* and *The Foundations of a National Drama*.

Appendix III

Arthur Wing Pinero

£200 a Year, produced 1877, Globe Theatre
La Comète: or, Two Hearts, produced 1880, Theatre Royal, Croydon
Two Can Play at that Game, produced 1878, Lyceum
Daisy's Escape, produced 1879, Lyceum
Hester's Mystery, produced 1880, Folly Theatre
The Money Spinner, produced 1880, Prince of Wales, Manchester, 1881, St James's Theatre, London
Bygones, produced 1880, Lyceum
Imprudence, produced 1881, Folly Theatre
The Squire, produced 1881, St James's Theatre
Girls and Boys: A Nursery Tale, produced 1882, Toole's Theatre
The Rector: The Story of Four Friends, produced 1883, Court Theatre
Lords and Commons, produced 1883, Haymarket Theatre
The Rocket, produced 1883, Prince of Wales, Manchester, and Gaiety Theatre, London
Low Water, produced 1884, Globe Theatre
The Iron Master, produced 1884, St James's Theatre
In Chancery, produced 1884, Lyceum, Edinburgh, and Gaiety Theatre, London
Mayfair (from a play by Sardou), produced 1885, St James's Theatre
The Magistrate, produced 1885, Court Theatre
The Schoolmistress, produced 1886, Court Theatre
The Hobby-Horse, produced 1886, St James's Theatre
Dandy Dick, produced 1887, Court Theatre
Sweet Lavender, produced 1888, Terry's Theatre
The Weaker Sex, produced 1888, revised version produced 1889, Theatre Royal, Manchester, and Court Theatre, London

Appendix III

The Profligate, produced 1889, Garrick Theatre
The Cabinet Minister, produced 1890, Court Theatre
Lady Bountiful: A Story of Years, produced 1891, Garrick Theatre
The Times, produced 1891, Terry's Theatre
The Amazons, produced 1893, Court Theatre
The Second Mrs Tanqueray, produced 1893, St James's Theatre
The Notorious Mrs Ebbsmith, produced 1895, Garrick Theatre
The Benefit of the Doubt, produced 1895, Comedy Theatre
The Princess and the Butterfly: or, The Fantastics, produced 1897, St James's Theatre
Trelawny of the 'Wells', produced 1898, Court Theatre
The Beauty Stone (with J. Comyns Carr, music by Arthur Sullivan), produced 1898, Savoy Theatre
The Gay Lord Quex, produced 1899, Globe Theatre
Iris, produced 1901, Garrick Theatre
Letty, produced 1903, Duke of York's Theatre
A Wife without a Smile: A Comedy in Disguise, produced 1904, Wyndhams Theatre
His House in Order, produced 1906, St James's Theatre
The Thunderbolt, produced 1908, St James's Theatre
Mid-Channel, produced 1909, St James's Theatre
Preserving Mr Panmure, produced 1911, Comedy Theatre
The 'Mind the Paint' Girl, produced 1912, Duke of York's Theatre
The Widow of Wasdale Head: A Fantasy, produced 1912, Duke of York's Theatre
Playgoers, produced 1913, St James's Theatre
The Big Drum, produced 1915, St James's Theatre
Mr Livermore's Dream, produced 1917, Coliseum
The Freaks: An Idyll of Suburbia, produced 1918, New Theatre

Monica's Blue Boy (music by Frederic Cowen), produced 1918, New Theatre
Quick Work, produced 1919, Stamford Theatre, Stamford, Connecticut
A Seat in the Park, produced 1922, Winter Garden
The Enchanted Cottage, produced 1922, Duke of York's Theatre
A Private Room, produced 1928, Little Theatre
Child Man, 1930, never performed
Dr Harmer's Holidays, produced 1931, Shubert-Belasco Theatre, Washington DC
A Cold June, produced 1932, Duchess Theatre
Late of Mockford's, 1934, never performed

OTHER WORKS

Foreword to *Two Plays* (London: Heinemann, 1930)
Introductory Note to *The Times* (London: Heinemann, 1891)
'Robert Browning as a Dramatist', *Transactions of the Royal Society of Literature*, XXXI (1912)
'Robert Louis Stevenson: The Dramatist', lecture, 1903
Robert Louis Stevenson as a Dramatist, with an introduction by Clayton Hamilton (New York, 1914)
'The Inverness Cape', *The Theatre*, II (Aug 1880)
'The Modern British Drama', *The Theatre*, XXV (June 1895)
'The Theatre in the Seventies', in *The Eighteen-Seventies*, ed. Harley Granville-Barker (New York: Macmillan, 1929)
'The Theatre in Transition', in *Fifty Years, Memories and Contrasts* (London: Thornton Butterworth, 1932)
'Theatrical Byways', *The Theatre*, II (May 1979)

Notes

1. Introduction

1. Letter dated 25 May 1892, in *The Collected Letters of Arthur Wing Pinero*, ed. J. P. Wearing (1974).

2. Henry Arthur Jones: His Life and Plays

1. Doris Jones, *The Life and Letters of Henry Arthur Jones* (1930) pp. 64–5.
2. Ibid., pp. 87–8 (letter to James Waldo Fawcett, 3 Sep 1924).
3. Ibid., p. 93.
4. Ibid., p. 96 (letter to Wilson Barrett, 17 June 1886).
5. G. B. Shaw, letter to Jones dated 11 June 1894, in Shaw, *Collected Letters,* ed. Dan. H. Laurence (1965) vol. I.
6. Doris Jones, *The Life and Letters of Henry Arthur Jones*, p. 165.
7. Ibid., pp. 176–7.
8. G. B. Shaw, in the *Saturday Review*, 18 Jan 1896.
9. G. B. Shaw, in the *Saturday Review*, 9 Oct 1897.

3. Three Plays by Henry Arthur Jones

1. *The Star*, 22 May 1890.
2. *Illustrated Sporting and Dramatic News*, 6 Nov 1897.
3. *Daily Telegraph*, 7 Oct 1897.

4. *Saturday Review*, 9 Oct 1897.
5. *Illustrated Sporting and Dramatic News*, 6 Nov 1897.
6. *Daily Telegraph*, 10 Oct 1900.

4. Henry Arthur Jones: The Prophet of the Modern Drama

Unless otherwise stated, all references in this chapter are to Jones's own writings or speeches.

1. Doris Jones, *The Life and Letters of Henry Arthur Jones*, p. 81.
2. 'The Literary Drama', *New Review*, Jan 1892.
3. Preface to *Saints and Sinners* (1891).
4. Ibid.
5. Ibid.
6. Ibid.
7. Lecture at Bradford, 'On Being Rightly Amused at the Theatre', 13 Nov 1887, in *The Renascence of the English Drama* (1895).
8. Fragment quoted ibid., p. 338.
9. 'Realism and Truth', letter to the *New York Dramatic Mirror*, 9 Apr 1890.
10. Address to the National Sunday League, '*On Playmaking*'. 15 Feb 1891, in *The Renascence of the English Drama*.
11. 'Religion and the Stage', *Nineteenth Century Review*, Jan 1885.
12. Preface to *Saints and Sinners*.
13. 'The First Night Judgment of Plays', *Nineteenth Century Review*, July 1889.
14. Ibid.
15. 'The Theatre and the Mob', *Nineteenth Century Review*, Sep 1883.
16. 'Religion and the Stage', *Nineteenth Century Review*, Jan 1885.
17. Ibid.
18. 'The First Night Judgement of Plays', *Nineteenth Century Review*, July 1889.
19. Ibid.
20. Ibid.
21. Ibid.
22. 'The Theatre and the Mob', *Nineteenth Century Review*, Sep 1883.
23. Inaugural address, Playgoers' Club, *The Dramatic Outlook*, 7 Oct 1884.
24. Lecture at Bradford, 'On Being Rightly Amused at the Theatre', 13 Nov 1887.
25. 'The Future of the English Drama', *New Review*, Aug 1895.
26. Ibid.
27. Inaugural address at the reopening of the City of London College,

'The Relations of the Drama to Education', 12 Oct 1893, in *The Renascence of the English Drama.*

28. Ibid.
29. Ibid.
30. Ibid.
31. 'Dramatic Techniques Revealed by Dramatists' is printed as an appendix to Doris Jones, *The Life and Letters of Henry Arthur Jones*.
32. Ibid., pp. 330–1.
33. Ibid., p. 408.

5. Arthur Wing Pinero: His Life and Plays

1. Walter Lazenby, *Arthur Wing Pinero* (1972) p. 14.
2. Hamilton Fyfe, *Sir Arthur Pinero's Plays and Players* (1930) p. 255.
3. Wilbur D. Dunkel, *Sir Arthur Pinero* (1941) p. 27.
4. Letter to L. E. Shipman, 6 Dec 1914, in *The Collected Letters of Arthur Wing Pinero*, ed. J. P. Wearing (1974).
5. Letter to L. E. Shipman, 24 Dec 1918, ibid.
6. Letter to L. E. Shipman, 26 Dec 1920, ibid.
7. Letter to L. E. Shipman, 29 Dec 1921, ibid.
8. Letter to Dion Boucicault the younger, 12 Nov 1923.
9. Letter to Henry Arthur Jones, 8 May 1911, ibid.
10. Letter to John Drinkwater, 24 May 1932, ibid.
11. *£200 a Year* (1877), *La Comète, or Two Hearts* (1878), *Two Can Play at that Game* (1878), *Daisy's Escape* (1879), *Bygones* (1879), *Hester's Mystery* (1880).
12. The plays of this period were *Girls and Boys* (1879), *The Rector* (1883), *The Rocket* (1883), *Lords and Commons* (1883) and *The Ironmaster* (1884).
13. M. Salaman, Introductory Note to *The Cabinet Minister* (1892).
14. *Daily Telegraph*, 23 Mar 1885.
15. Letter to H. H. Küther, 10 May 1932, in *Collected Letters of Pinero*.
16. G. B. Shaw, letter to Pinero, 29 Nov 1909, in Shaw, *Collected Letters*, vol. II.
17. Pinero, Foreword to *Dr Harmer's Holidays* (1929).
18. Letter to *The Times*, 4 Sep 1902, in *Collected Letters of Pinero*.
19. Letter to George Alexander, 9 Aug 1914, ibid.
20. Letter to *The Times*, 27 Nov 1907, ibid.
21. Letter to an unknown correspondent, 28 Jan 1918, ibid.
22. Doris Jones, *The Life and Letters of Henry Arthur Jones*, p. 108 (letter to Henry Arthur Jones, 15 Oct 1889).
23. Letter to Joseph Hatton, 24 May 1893, in *Collected Letters of Pinero*.

6. Four Plays by Arthur Wing Pinero

1. *The Times*, 11 May 1908.
2. *Daily Telegraph*, 28 May 1893.
3. *Daily Graphic*, 28 May 1893; source of the French quotation untraced.
4. Letter to Mrs Patrick Campbell, 26 June 1893, in *The Collected Letters of Arthur Wing Pinero*, ed. J. P. Wearing (1974).
5. *The World*, 31 May 1893.

Bibliography

General background

Bafch, Françoise, *Relative Creatures*, tr. Anthony Rudolph (London: Allen Lane, 1974).

Rowell, George, *The Victorian Theatre: A Survey* (London: Oxford University Press, 1956; rev. edn Cambridge: Cambridge University Press, 1979).

Thomson, Patricia, *The Victorian Heroine: A Changing Ideal* (London: Oxford University Press, 1956).

Henry Arthur Jones

Jones, Doris, *The Life and Letters of Henry Arthur Jones* (London: Victor Gollancz, 1930).

Jones, Henry Arthur, *Representative Plays of Henry Arthur Jones*, ed. Clayton Hamilton (London: Macmillan, 1926).

———, *Plays by Henry Arthur Jones*, ed. Russell Jackson (Cambridge: Cambridge University Press, 1982).

Sir Arthur Wing Pinero

Dawick, John, 'The "First" Mrs Tanqueray', *Theatre Quarterly*, 9, no. 35 (Autumn 1972).

Lazenby, Walter, *Arthur Wing Pinero* (Boston, Mass.: Twayne, 1972).

Bibliography

Pinero, Arthur Wing, *The Social Plays of Arthur Wing Pinero*, ed. Clayton Hamilton (London: Heinemann, 1917–22)

———, *The Letters of Arthur Wing Pinero*, ed. J. P. Wearing (Minneapolis: University of Minnesota Press, 1974).

———, *Three Plays*, intro. Stephen Wyatt (London: Methuen, 1985).

Wearing, J. P., 'Pinero the Actor', *Theatre Notebook*, 26, no. 4 (Summer 1972).

Index

Note. This index does not include references to Appendix III, which lists all plays by Jones and Pinero, including those not discussed in the main text. The abbreviations HAJ and AWP stand for Henry Arthur Jones and Arthur Wing Pinero.

Index

Index

Index